Songs of protest, songs of love

MANCHESTER
1824

Manchester University Press

STUDIES IN POPULAR CULTURE

General editor: Professor Jeffrey Richards

Already published

**Healthy living in the Alps:
the origins of winter tourism in Switzerland, 1860–1914**
Susan Barton

Working-class organisations and popular tourism, 1840–1970
Susan Barton

Leisure, citizenship and working-class men in Britain, 1850–1945
Brad Beaven

**The British Consumer Co-operative Movement and film,
1890s–1960s**
Alan George Burton

British railway enthusiasm
Ian Carter

Railways and culture in Britain
Ian Carter

Darts in England, 1900–39: a social history
Patrick Chaplin

Relocating Britishness
Stephen Caunce, Ewa Mazierska, Susan Sydney-Smith and John Walton (eds)

**From silent screen to multi-screen:
a history of cinema exhibition in Britain since 1896**
Stuart Hanson

Smoking in British popular culture, 1800–2000
Matthew Hilton

Juke box Britain: Americanisation and youth culture, 1945–60
Adrian Horn

**Popular culture in London, c. 1890–1918:
the transformation of entertainment**
Andrew Horrall

Horseracing and the British, 1919–39
Mike Huggins

Amateur operatics: a social and cultural history
John Lowerson

Scotland and the music hall, 1850–1914
Paul Maloney

Films and British national identity: from Dickens to Dad's Army
Jeffrey Richards

Looking North: Northern England and the national imagination
Dave Russell

**The British seaside holiday: holidays and resorts
in the twentieth century**
John K. Walton

Songs of protest, songs of love

Popular ballads in eighteenth-century Britain

ROBIN GANEV

Manchester University Press

Manchester and New York

distributed exclusively in the USA by Palgrave Macmillan

Published by Manchester University Press
Oxford Road, Manchester M13 9NR, UK
and Room 400, 175 Fifth Avenue, New York, NY 10010, USA
www.manchesteruniversitypress.co.uk

Distributed exclusively in the USA by
Palgrave Macmillan, 175 Fifth Avenue, New York,
NY 10010, USA

Distributed exclusively in Canada by
UBC Press, University of British Columbia, 2029 West Mall,
Vancouver, BC, Canada V6T 1Z2

British Library Cataloguing-in-Publication Data
A catalogue record for this book is available from the British Library

Library of Congress Cataloging-in-Publication Data applied for

ISBN 978 0 7190 7890 3 *hardback*

First published 2009

18 17 16 15 14 13 12 11 10 09   10 9 8 7 6 5 4 3 2 1

Typeset in Adobe Garamond with Gill Sans display by
Koinonia, Manchester
Printed in Great Britain
by CPI Antony Rowe, Chippenham

STUDIES IN POPULAR CULTURE

There has in recent years been an explosion of interest in culture and cultural studies. The impetus has come from two directions and out of two different traditions. On the one hand, cultural history has grown out of social history to become a distinct and identifiable school of historical investigation. On the other hand, cultural studies has grown out of English literature and has concerned itself to a large extent with contemporary issues. Nevertheless, there is a shared project, its aim, to elucidate the meanings and values implicit and explicit in the art, literature, learning, institutions and everyday behaviour within a given society. Both the cultural historian and the cultural studies scholar seek to explore the ways in which a culture is imagined, represented and received, how it interacts with social processes, how it contributes to individual and collective identities and world views, to stability and change, to social, political and economic activities and programmes. This series aims to provide an arena for the cross-fertilisation of the discipline, so that the work of the cultural historian can take advantage of the most useful and illuminating of the theoretical developments and the cultural studies scholars can extend the purely historical underpinnings of their investigations. The ultimate objective of the series is to provide a range of books which will explain in a readable and accessible way where we are now socially and culturally and how we got to where we are. This should enable people to be better informed, promote an interdisciplinary approach to cultural issues and encourage deeper thought about the issues, attitudes and institutions of popular culture.

Jeffrey Richards

Contents

List of illustrations

List of tables

General editor's foreword

This is a fascinating, vivid and valuable exploration of the popular ballad as a source of evidence for popular attitudes and values in the long eighteenth century. Claiming that the ballads are an underused source of historical evidence, Robin Ganev argues persuasively that they formed a cohesive print culture strongly linked to the oral culture transcending local identity to give voice to general issues and concerns related to the countryside and the rural population. She concedes and fully explores the complexity and the sometimes ambiguous nature of the ballad evidence. But her methodology is 'reflective', leading her throughout the book to contextualise ballad content and sympathies within the unfolding economic cycle and in relation to historical changes in rural life.

Her first chapter helpfully examines what ballads looked like, where they came from, how much they cost, who read them, how the ballad singer/ballad seller was regarded and how the ballads survived. Each of her subsequent chapters analyses the way in which ballads comment on key themes in rural history, providing a rich extra dimension to that history. In examining the ballads as social criticism, she identifies tensions between farmers and labourers and between landlords and tenants. With the ballads becoming increasingly critical during the economic downturns, they come to embody the discontents of the agricultural labourers and tradesmen more than anything else.

She explores the vivid imagery and powerful rhetoric with which the ballads denounce the enclosure movement, arguing that enclosures impoverish the peasantry and enrich the gentry. In particular she shows how the ballads stressed the social costs in terms of the loss of liberty, community and the aesthetic beauty of the unenclosed countryside.

She argues intriguingly that in celebrating the uninhibited sexuality of the rural labourer, the ballads condoned it because of prevailing fears about the depopulation of the nation, concern at the debilitating effects of urban luxury and the equation of rural sexuality with nature, fresh air, healthy exercise and rural diet as well as the regular idealisation of milkmaid and ploughboy as embodiments of robust sexuality. She suggests that as life got harder for them, the rural poor developed a new pride in their identity by positively celebrating their sexuality. The fifth chapter considers attitudes to work and finds the ballads rehearsing both the pains (physical difficulties, exhaustion, rough weather, bad masters, high prices and low wages) and pleasures (pride in skills and strength, patriotism and economic achievement) of work. The final chapter confirms the importance of the chosen themes by examining the attempts of Evangelical writer Hannah More to counteract the attitudes enshrined in the popular ballads by a series of specially written tracts designed to encourage acceptance of the social hierarchy and gratitude to the gentry. By the end of the book Ganev successfully vindicates her claim for the value of the ballads as historical evidence, thanks to her thoughtful, sensitive and carefully contextualised analysis.

Jeffrey Richards

Acknowledgements

I would like to thank Jeanette Neeson for all her advice with every aspect of this book. It would not have been possible without her. I am also deeply indebted to Ian Dyck, Kent Worcester, Doug Hay and Tom Cohen for all their ideas on how to strengthen the book. Nick Rogers provided a number of helpful suggestions. My friends Todd Webb, Jennine Hurl-Eamon and Richard Gilmour made a significant contribution to the early stages of this book. My colleagues at the University of Regina, Ken Leyton-Brown and Philip Charrier, were helpful in sharing their experience of academic publishing. I thank the *Journal of the History of Sexuality* for granting permission to reprint chapter 5, which was first published as article 'Milkmaids, Ploughmen and Sex in Eighteenth-Century Britain' by Robin Ganev, in the *Journal of the History of Sexuality* 16 (1): 40–67. Copyright © 2007 by the University of Texas Press. The Humanities Research Institute at the University of Regina generously funded the reproduction of images in the book. My research was aided by the helpful staff at the British Library and at the National Library of Scotland. Finally, I thank Jeet Heer, as well as Vladimir, Lily and John Ganev for their love and support.

Introduction

The ballad 'Resolute Dick' tells the story of a ploughman from the West Country who visits London to see the Lord Mayor and 'other fine folks'. As he stands admiring the Royal Exchange, a 'fine fellow' comes over to him and asks him to leave, calling him a 'bumpkin' and a 'country clown'. Dick refuses to comply, causing the following scene:

> With that the fine Fellow he flew in a Rage,
> And nothing but Blows would his Passion assuage,
> With that he fell into a Passion indeed,
> And thus in a Fury began to proceed,
> He made an offer to give him a kick,
> The Plowman perceiv'd him just in the Nick,
> He told him his Name it was resolute Dick,
> And he up with his whip and gave him a Lick.

This causes twenty more 'fine fellows' to run over and demand that Dick desist from beating a man of 'such worthy repute'. Dick replies that he has been insulted and that Londoners have no right to treat countrymen badly, because they depend on them for their very existence. The gentlemen are appalled, and once again ask that they be given the respect that is their due:

> Nay Plowman we'd have you to understand,
> That we have both Silver and Gold at Command,
> With silk and rich Jewels, nay Diamonds and Rings,
> With all sorts of Spices and other fine Things,
> Of many rich coffers we carry the keys,
> We have such Estates that we live at our Ease,
> We eat and we drink and we walk where we please,
> And how [at] you think by such Fellows as these.

But the ploughman is not to be intimidated:

> If we did not labour you'd never keep house,
> And your Gallants would soon be as small as a Mouse.

In the end, the gentlemen are compelled to concede that ploughmen are of vital importance to the economy and ought to be treated well:

> With that all the Londoners laughed outright,
> And in the Countryman they took Delight;
> They said it was true and did him commend,
> And then all the Quarrel was soon at an End,
> With that the Plowman began to extoll,
> He soon got the Favour of both great and small,
> And so the Debate betwixt them did fall,
> And the Plowman for wit was too hard for them all.[1]

This ballad raises a number of interesting historical questions. The first thing that strikes the reader is Dick's aggressive defence of his country origins. His identity is defined in opposition to both London and the rich gentlemen. The ballad drew on a literary trope that set the wholesome character of the country in opposition to the corruption of the city. The 'Hodge' stereotype is implicit in the gentlemen's attitude to Dick – a mere country bumpkin in their estimation, though they quickly learn their mistake. Working-class masculinity is here shown as superior to the manhood of the genteel Londoner, because Dick is easily able to force an apology out of a group of gentlemen, who do not know how to fight. The list of riches and comforts to which they have access suggests that they may have been spoiled by luxury. The ballad is sympathetic to Dick, though there is a bit of satire and the world turned upside down in the image of a rough rustic teaching a lesson to a refined London gentleman. It is also noteworthy (and I might add very frustrating) that the chapbook containing this ballad names neither date, nor town, nor printer, and as such is impossible to place. Based on other similar ballads, the early 1800s seem a plausible date, but it is hard to know for certain. These are some of the issues raised by the popular songs this book deals with.

A growing body of cultural history has connected changes in popular and elite culture at the end of the eighteenth century to changes in social conditions. This book seeks to add to these histories by examining the relationship between historical change and popular songs. It argues that popular songs can be read as an expression of a popular voice, and represent one aspect of a rural labouring identity broadly defined. This rural identity came to be more forcefully articulated as rural social relations deteriorated and as popular culture came under attack.

Representation is inherently 'reflective' – that is, it seeks to interpret reality through the medium of art. Historians who have studied artistic representations have always done so by exploring the relationship between art and literature and their social and economic contexts. In her study of landscape painting, Ann Bermingham sees paintings as representative of an elite ideology and uses the Marxian model of base and superstructure to explain the relationship between art and the social context.[2] John Barrell's classic study of representations of the rural poor in painting aims to compare ideology as revealed in art to 'the actuality of eighteenth-century life'.[3] Similarly, Christiana Payne investigates the relationship between 'a background of poverty, distress, and hard labor and class conflict and the idyllic scenes in painting'.[4]

Experts in popular songs have also related them to social change. Martha Vicinus has argued that songs, particularly broadside songs, 'reflected but seldom manipulated working-class opinion', and she believes that protest songs from the period 1780–1830 were occasioned by real hardship.[5] Alun Howkins and Ian Dyck, in their study of the song 'My Old Hat', have argued that songs reflected working-class ideas of a just society. Contesting historians' dismissal of songs about a lost rural golden age, they have shown that such songs articulated real political solutions to economic distress and had a real political explanation for its causes. 'My Old Hat' presented an accurate historical narrative of the impact of the loss of common right, poor social relations, the New Poor Law and the workhouse on the labouring poor.[6] Most recently, Vic Gammon has connected ballads to social attitudes to sex and drinking.[7]

Historians like Howkins, Dyck and Gammon are correct to point out that popular songs reflected popular attitudes. Popular attitudes were in turn shaped by social change. The popular ballad was a form of art and as such it did not have a simple relationship with empirical reality. However, it was a very flexible form consisting of many sub-genres, which could be put to different uses. Ballads could be written to commemorate an event, to spread news, to voice grievances, or simply to entertain. Because of this they could fit along a spectrum of representation, from being very close to the real world, to highly typological and very loosely connected to actual social conditions. This book includes ballads from both ends of the spectrum. Chapters 2 and 3 discuss ballads that deal with social conditions such as high grain prices, poor social relations, enclosure and the loss of customary rights. Unless they were written to protest against a specific event, such as the corn law of 1814, these ballads cannot be said to reflect social conditions directly, but they do reflect a feeling of unhappiness and a sense of injustice. Changing social conditions may account for the popularity of certain songs during certain times. Furthermore, songs' content and in some cases their language did change in the course of the eighteenth century. This change coincides with a historiographic narrative that argues for small owners' and agricultural labourers' growing economic dependence and the erosion of social relations in the countryside in the course of the eighteenth century. The songs are better understood when they are related to this historiography.

The second part of the book, comprising chapters 4 and 5, deals with ballads celebrating agricultural labour and rural sexuality. They are examples of a somewhat different representation of rural identity from that expressed by the songs in the first part, being both highly typological and conventional. They bore a more complex relation to actual rural life. While their content remained fairly static throughout the period, they went in and out of print at particular times. Their popularity, based on when they were printed, needs to be explained. The songs about sexuality need to be situated within a context of cultural attitudes towards sexuality in the eighteenth century. The songs about agricultural labour acquired a new life and popularity during the Napoleonic wars. They need to be interrogated for their possible resonance with labourers' sense of their place in society or for their connection to a discourse about labour's productivity and contribution to the war effort. Despite their differences, all of these songs, both the sad and happy ones, had a wide popular audience, and all of them represented the rural world in ways that challenged contemporary elite values.

It is important to define what we mean by 'popular voice' or a 'popular culture'. Historians have made significant progress in their understanding of popular culture. They have broadened the definition of the term. While it still retains its sense of 'a system of shared meanings, attitudes and values, and the symbolic forms (performances, artifacts) in which they are expressed or embodied', it is no longer seen as homogenous.[8] In his study of popular culture in England, Barry Reay stresses that popular culture can vary across age, gender, religion, occupation and region.[9] In addition, historians have reconsidered the relationship of the elite to popular culture. For example, Harris suggests the middling sort and the gentry might have bought ballads more than the labouring classes.[10] To what extent did popular songs belong to the elite? I think the reason why some historians have argued ballads had an elite audience is that they have looked at collectors, a very particular and unusual kind of elite consumer. When Barry Reay makes the same point about the elite's fondness for ballads he names Pepys as an example.[11] Arguably, the act of collecting suggests that these objects were seen as curiosities by the elite, rather than a part of everyday life, and may, in fact, confirm that the primary audience for them were labourers and artisans.

Some ballads do support the argument that popular culture might embody elite values. This is particularly true of songs that represented a socially harmonious rural world. Such songs could fit under John Barrell's definition of the georgic: they insisted that labourers were cheerful and industrious and did not reveal the true state of the countryside.[12] Songs complaining about a lost golden age of idyllic rural social relations overlap with the picturesque mode in elite art as defined by Ann Bermingham.[13] It is true that high and low culture should be seen as overlapping discourses, and that ballads appropriated certain elite values and attitudes. However, this book is closer to the work of Roy Palmer, Vic Gammon, Michael Pickering and Ian Dyck, who see ballads as targeting primarily the labouring population and who have emphasised the popular use of songs as a way of resisting elite culture.[14]

The work of Edward Thompson and Eric Hobsbawm on class in the eighteenth and nineteenth centuries has been criticised for its failure to consider other ways of understanding identity. Linda Colley, in *Britons*, has pointed out that the working class, the middling sort, and the elite all shared a British national identity, and so we should not always think of them as opposing one another.[15] Anna Clark, in her study of working-class gender relations, has shown that issues of gender divided the working class: artisanal culture was male, and the exclusion of unskilled female labour from the trades was at the heart of men's sense of masculinity.[16] Nevertheless, neither Colley nor Clark argues that class is not an important issue in British history. While a focus on national pride and gender allows us to see a different dimension of identity, one cannot deny that class remained central to eighteenth- and early nineteenth-century discourse. It is central to the ballad 'Resolute Dick' and, as this book will illustrate, it was central to most ballads written and sung in this period.

Aside from 'popular' the other term that requires some explanation is that of 'rural identity'. The idea of the 'rural' is central in many studies of eighteenth- and early nineteenth-century English literature. Raymond Williams has shown how, even after England was predominantly urban, literature was still emphasising rural themes.[17] John Lucas has shown how important 'the rural' was in the creation of an English national identity.[18] In popular songs the rural – symbolised by labourer, peasant and farmer characters – became an increasingly salient theme despite the fact of urbanisation. I am using 'rural' in the sense of anything connected to agriculture. Increasingly, in the eighteenth century, the British economy was driven not only by agriculture, but by various 'rural industries': trades, like textile manufacture, that flourished in small towns and villages and employed the putting-out system. I shall talk about rural industry in chapter 2 and in chapter 6, in connection with moral economy songs and in connection with Hannah More's charitable work. The moral economy and Hannah More concerned both agricultural labourers and rural industrial workers. However, the other issues the book touches on – such as the depiction of rural labouring-class sexuality, the celebration of agricultural labour and the criticism of enclosure – centre on a strong occupational identity that excluded rural industry. This question will come up again in the relevant chapters.

This book focuses on the period 1700 to 1830 because there are enough ballads from this period to make a study of rural representation worthwhile and because in this period the countryside experienced significant social, economic and, arguably, cultural change.

Relying partly on Barry Reay's definition of culture as process and his argument that 'The motion of culture, culture as change, is the particular contribution of the historian', the book seeks to describe the change in genre and content in popular songs.[19] Barrell describes a broad cultural shift in terms of representations of the poor. Depictions of the poor in painting and poetry changed at the end of the eighteenth century from the 'happy husbandmen' to 'the labouring poor'.[20] Some poetry could now depict social conflict in the countryside, and the painter George Morland did so in art, though elite critics appreciated the idealised engravings made for sale by his printers more than his original paintings.[21] Ian Dyck argues that a similar change can be seen in popular culture: by the end of the eighteenth century popular culture became ideological, prescribing how the world should be rather than simply describing how it was.[22]

In terms of songs themselves, Dyck has argued that by 1815 rural popular songs became a class genre and were sung by labourers as a form of protest in pubs, while farmers sang loyalist and drawing-room songs in their homes, although there was still some overlap.[23] Roy Palmer has argued that ballads increasingly became the art form of the marginal or those excluded from other forms of public discourse. In addition, the element of opposition to elite culture, which had always been present in ballads, became stronger.[24] Martha Vicinus thinks the change involved an emphasis on the common man as hero in more and more ballads: in 'early' ballads the common man was seldom a hero, but in the 'late ones' he was often the hero.[25] Thus, while historians disagree about the precise nature of the change, they all agree that popular songs did change. I want to add to this debate by describing both traditional and new elements in songs. Thus chapters will make references to the Pepys ballads, but they are for the purpose of understanding the genre, rather than for the purpose of adding to historians' knowledge of the seventeenth century. The book seeks to make a contribution to historians' work in the eighteenth and the early nineteenth centuries.

The themes I have chosen have been dictated in part by the historiography of rural social relations and labour, in part by the songs themselves. Studies already exist of songs' representation of social relations, of songs' representation of gender relations, and of Hannah More's attack on popular culture.[26] This book will add to these studies and also introduce some less explored themes such as songs about the moral economy, songs' celebration of labourers' sexuality, the problem of women's agency in popular songs, and songs' celebration of agricultural labour, which we also find in painting and pastoral verse. I have included a range of moods: anger, sadness, humour and 'happiness' or 'content', and shown how each group of songs can lend itself to a reading that would have made it pleasing to a labouring audience.

Popular songs constitute a popular voice that in many ways differs from other kinds of discourse in the eighteenth and nineteenth centuries. They can add another dimension to the debate about rural social relations in this period. Historians disagree about how agricultural labourers' culture and sense of identity changed at the end of the eighteenth century. The extent to which agricultural labourers' resentment against their social superiors was new at this time, the growing discomfort with labourers' sexuality, the extent to which women were allowed sexual expression in popular culture, the role of philanthropy and elite propaganda in the lives of labourers, the way the poor saw enclosure and the loss of access to land, the contemporary understanding of the role of agriculture in the British economy – these are all issues that have been extensively written about but there is no consensus on them. When compared to other sources, popular songs confirm historians' arguments that social relations deteriorated at the end of the eighteenth century. While popular songs always defined labourers' culture against the culture of the elite and mocked the aristocracy, animosity toward the privileged and anger about social injustice grew greater by 1800.

One of the reasons why the genre of the ballad could be used more freely to voice rural discontent at the end of the eighteenth century could have to do with what some literary scholars have called the 'ballad revival' in elite literary culture. Thanks in part to Percy's *Reliques of Popular Antiquity*, the ballad was rediscovered by collectors and by the Romantics.[27] When speaking of the new respectability of the ballad, we must keep in mind the distinction between the traditional and the street or broadside ballad. Most of those who admired ballads were interested in the former. As late as 1827 the scholar William Motherwell saw the 'traditional' popular ballad of the Child canon as valuable and the broadside ballad as vulgar. Indeed, Child himself viewed ballads in this way. On the other hand, the respectability of the traditional ballad slowly made room for greater appreciation of the broadside ballad. Poets such as Robert Burns and William Wordsworth imitated broadside ballads and had some of their poetry circulated in this way.[28] This exchange between popular and elite culture must have allowed balladeers a broader range of expression and a greater confidence in giving their ballads a political message.

Chapter 1 discusses the problem of using popular songs and poetry as primary sources, as well as the role of the ballad singer in popular culture. The following chapter turns to social relations. It argues that there is a tradition of complaint in ballads that dates back to the Pepys ballads and that was rediscovered, after a period of silence from the late seventeenth century to the 1730s. Printers' renewed interest in these songs suggests a popular demand. Changing social conditions may account for this new demand, as well as for some of the new elements grafted on to an older genre. The chapter on enclosure takes further the theme of songs as social criticism by exploring the various arguments made by song writers and poets against enclosure. This chapter relies more heavily on the work of self-taught and rural poets, whose objection to enclosure was remarkably similar to that made by song-writers. All these texts emphasised the economic and social loss brought about by enclosure as well as the loss of an aesthetic experience.

This takes us to the second part of the book, which deals with songs as celebrations of identity. Chapter 4 deals with the celebration of agricultural labour during the period 1790–1815 and tries to explain why these songs were so popular at a time when the countryside experienced great distress. Chapter 5 discusses the construction of a rural labouring sexuality that contrasted the sexuality of agricultural labourers with that of their masters or the gentry. Finally, chapter 6 explores one kind of elite reaction to popular culture and to the popular ballad, that of the writer and Evangelical Hannah More. Her efforts to suppress ballads offer another proof of their importance as a form of popular artistic expression and their potential for subversion.

Notes

1 'Resolute Dick', in *Resolute Dick's Garland. Composed of Several Excellent New Songs* (Early nineteenth century?) John Bell Ballad Collection, Houghton Library.

2 Ann Bermingham, *Landscape and Ideology: The English Rustic Tradition 1740–1860* (Berkeley, Los Angeles and London: University of California Press, 1986), 3.

3 John Barrell, *The Dark Side of the Landscape: The Rural Poor in English Painting, 1730–1840* (Cambridge and New York: Cambridge University Press, 1980), 2.

4 Christiana Payne, *Toil and Plenty: Images of the Agricultural Landscape in England, 1780–1890* (New Haven, CT: Yale Centre for British Art and Yale University Press, 1993), 8.

5 Martha Vicinus, *The Industrial Muse. A Study of Nineteenth-Century British Working-Class Literature* (London: Croom Helm, 1974), 13, 44.

6 Alun Howkins and C. Ian Dyck, '"The Time's Alteration": Popular Ballads, Rural Radicalism, and William Cobbett', *History Workshop Journal* 23(2) (1987): 20–39. Ian Dyck continues this argument in his book on Cobbett and the popular ballad, where he sees the white-letter ballad as expressive of new concerns about class. He also sees songs as a form of popular protest. Ian Dyck, *William Cobbett and Rural Popular Culture* (Cambridge: Cambridge University Press, 1992), 1, 86.

7 Vic Gammon, *Desire, Drink and Death in English Folk and Vernacular Song* (Aldershot: Ashgate, 2008), 7–10.

8 Peter Burke, *Popular Culture in Early Modern Europe* (London: Temple Smith, 1978), 270.

9 Barry Reay, *Popular Culture in England 1550–1750* (London and New York: Longman, 1998), 199.

10 Tim Harris, 'Problematising Popular Culture', in Tim Harris, ed., *Popular Culture in England, c.1500–1850* (New York: St Martin's Press, 1995), 6–7.

11 Reay, *Popular Culture in England*, 56.

12 Barrell, *The Dark Side of the Landscape*, 3.

13 Bermingham, *Landscape and Ideology*, 75, 83.

14 On high versus low culture and how the two can no longer be seen as distinct see Reay, *Popular Culture in England*, 198. Reay says the elite participated in popular culture but not vice versa; see also his p. 200. Also Roy Palmer, ed., *A Touch on the Times: Songs of Social Change, 1770–1914* (Harmondsworth: Penguin Education, 1974), 8. Dyck, *William Cobbett and Rural Popular Culture*, 1.

15 Linda Colley, *Britons: Forging the Nation, 1707–1837* (New Haven, CT: Yale University Press, 1992).

16 Anna Clark, *The Struggle for the Breeches: Gender and the Making of the British Working Class* (Berkeley, Los Angeles and London: University of California Press, 1995).

17 Raymond Williams, *The Country and the City* (New York: Oxford University Press, 1973), 2.

18 John Lucas, *England and Englishness: Ideas of Nationhood in English Poetry, 1688–1900* (Iowa City: University of Iowa Press, 1990), 9.

19 Reay, *Popular Culture in England*, 201.

20 Barrell, *The Dark Side of the Landscape*, 31.

21 Barrell, *The Dark Side of the Landscape*, 102–3.

22 Dyck, *William Cobbett and Rural Popular Culture*, 85.

23 Dyck, *William Cobbett and Rural Popular Culture*, 89.

24 Roy Palmer, *The Sound of History: Songs and Social Comment* (Oxford and New York: Oxford University Press, 1988), 2.

25 Vicinus, *The Industrial Muse*, 9.

26 On social relations see Dyck, *William Cobbett and Rural Popular Culture*, 53–5, 58 ff.; on gender, Cathy Lynn Preston, '"The Tying of the Garter": Representations of the Female Rural Labourer in 17th, 18th, and 19th Century English Bawdy Songs', *Journal of American Folklore* 105(417) (1992): 215–341 and Anna Clark, *The Struggle for the Breeches: Gender and the Making of the British Working Class* (Berkeley, Los Angeles and London: University of California Press, 1995); and on Hannah More, Susan Pedersen, 'Hannah More Meets Simple Simon: Tracts, Chapbooks, and Popular Culture in Late Eighteenth-Century England', *Journal of British Studies* 25(1) (1986): 84–113.

27 Alan Bold, *The Ballad* (London: Methuen & Co. Ltd., 1979), 87.

28 Albert B. Friedman, *The Ballad Revival* (Chicago and London: The University of Chicago Press, 1961), 246, 257–8.

1

What are popular ballads and what can they tell historians?

Popular ballads are one of many kinds of text that survive from the past. It is natural to wonder why a historian would choose to use them instead of other documents. The answer is twofold: first, historians have studied these sources less than other kinds of documents, and they have much to add to historiographical debates; second, historians can contribute in a valuable way to the understanding of songs and poetry as well as their context. Anyone interested in how people saw their world in eighteenth- and nineteenth-century Britain must consider songs. As the great historian T. B. Macaulay pointed out, there is a great deal of ordinary people's history that can be learned only from their ballads.[1] Compared with our own, the culture of the eighteenth and nineteenth centuries was a 'verse-culture', which used verse for all purposes: news, political elections, celebrations, education, moral and religious instruction, entertainment, and social criticism. Ballads, as well as other poetic discourse about rural society, give us a view of what the countryside meant to contemporaries that we cannot obtain elsewhere. This is true of both polite literature and popular verse, and, as cultural historians have shown, the two are best understood when read side by side.[2] Thus, while focusing on ballads, we cannot ignore mainstream poetry and the way in which it approached some of the same themes as ballads.

First, I want to convey to readers unfamiliar with the genre what forms songs and ballads took on the printed page and how they can be dated. But ballads transcended print. They relate to both the oral and print culture of the eighteenth and nineteenth centuries. Print culture was national rather than local, allowing printed ballads to be seen as a coherent whole. Thus a printed ballad from Scotland looked much like a printed ballad from London. As they were both printed and oral, ballads related to both the rural and urban worlds. While they were printed in cities, ballads were very closely associated with

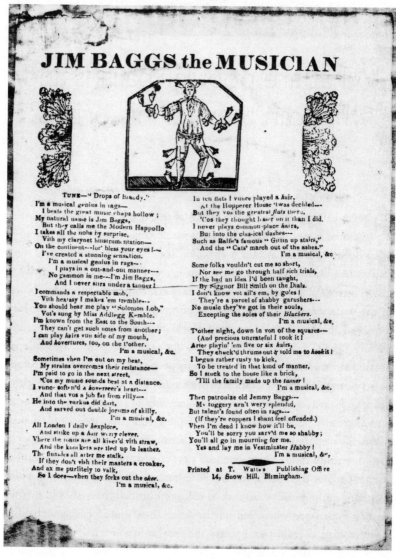

'Jim Baggs the musician' (1873)

the countryside, because the songs, the song writers and singers, and even the printers usually came from the country.[3] An examination of the literacy debate suggests that a significant proportion of the labouring class was able to read ballads. As literacy grew, so did the audience for broadsides and chapbooks as well as the trade in street literature. Changes in the audience and the trade, as well as social and cultural changes during the period, require us to read new meanings into ballads. It is within this context that the figures of the ballad seller and ballad singer acquire a particular significance in popular culture. Ballads themselves represented these artists as liminal figures who both appropriated and subverted elite culture. Thus it is useful to compare ballads to pastoral poetry, usually considered to be a polite genre, aimed at the middling sort and the gentry. Despite their more limited audience, pastoral poems, collected in books, were connected to ballads through the work of peasant poets like John Clare, who were familiar with both the literary canon and the oral tradition.[4]

What they looked like and how they can be dated

In simple terms popular ballads were songs that told a story. All popular ballads were songs but not all popular songs were ballads.[5] The term 'song' is thus more generic, but the two were often used interchangeably in the street literature of the eighteenth century and this is the way I use them in this book. There were two kinds of broadside and chapbook ballads at that time: traditional tales and 'new' ballads. Traditional ballads told the stories of folk heroes like Robin Hood and Jack of Newbury. They have been dated to the sixteenth century and appeared on the earliest black-letter (gothic type) broadsides.[6] Folklorists have often favoured these, arguing that they are of higher literary quality. While their survival is significant in that it shows broad continuities in popular culture, we will avoid them here because it is difficult to make a case for their historical specificity. The second kind, white-letter ballads, used a modern font and began to spread after 1700. In contrast to traditional ballads, they derive from the everyday life of working people and draw on themes such as courtship, labour, social relations and economic hardship. These songs tell us much about the ways in which working people perceived their world. New and traditional ballads existed side by side. Evaluating literary merit is not the purpose of this study, but I hope the lively and powerful language of the songs presented here will go some way to undermine any remaining prejudice against them.

The broadside or broadsheet and the chapbook or garland were slightly different formats but they often contained the same songs. Broadsides consisted of a single sheet often printed on both sides, while chapbooks (garlands) consisted of eight to twenty pages folded together. Originally broadside printers developed the tradition of printing a new and a traditional song or a comic and tragic one side by side. James Catnach's innovation of printing numerous songs on the same broadsheet brought the broadsheet closer to the chapbook songsters. It seems chapbooks were more likely to be read privately or in the home while broadsides, often displayed on walls, had a more public life. Also, broadsides circulated very widely, more so than chapbooks. The popular ones often sold in their thousands. Singers who sold the broadsides would sing them in pubs and on the street, reaching the illiterate as well as the literate.[7] Thus broadsides appear to have had more of a performative, oral life than chapbooks. However, the contents were very much the same and do not require separate analytical tools. Nevertheless, in citations I have indicated whether a song comes from a broadside or a chapbook – the titles of broadside songs are in quotation marks followed immediately by the place and printer while the titles of chapbook songs are followed by the name of the chapbook in italics and then by the place and printer. This gives the reader some sense of the degree of literacy assumed by the song's printers and vendors.

It should be noted here that broadside and chapbook ballads consisted of text, music and images. The experience of a broadside ballad would have been enriched by these different media. Each song came with a woodcut, albeit the woodcut was seldom directly connected to the content. Printers owned a fixed number of woodcuts that were quite expensive. It took less time to write a new song than to make a new woodcut and it also cost less. At the same time, printers believed their customers would much rather buy a ballad with a picture, even a very clumsy and irrelevant picture, than pure text. For these reasons the same woodcuts were reused with different songs. The music, or tune, was also more fixed than the text. We seldom get the music notation in broadsides and chapbooks but we are often told the name of the tune, which would have been well known at the time. New verses were often written to old tunes. Unfortunately, the analysis of images and music will have to be left to art historians and musicologists. Here we are going to deal primarily with the words.

It is difficult (sometimes impossible) to assign a specific place and date to broadsides and chapbooks. Many of them do not have imprints, and those that do often state the name and address of the printer but not the date. The historian must often rely on librarians and archivists (and occasionally folklorists and collectors) who have organised these items in broad chronological categories. For broadsides and chapbooks that name a known printer, it is possible to narrow down the date to twenty years or so, the years during which the printer was in business. If we know the printer we also know the place where each broadside was printed. However, since printers often borrowed each other's ballads, this would not tell us where a song originated and how far it circulated beyond its place of origin. Moreover, a large number of broadsides and chapbooks do not mention a printer. Another way to date ballads is to look for the title in the lists kept by some printers like the London Stationers' Company and John Pitts.[8] If a certain ballad comes from a collection we can use the date of collecting as evidence that it was still in circulation at this time but, again, we cannot know when it was first created and whether it was still popular when the collector found it. Furthermore, eighteenth-century collectors often depended on other collectors rather than using modern techniques of field research. Thus ballads compiled in book form by collectors are a more problematic source than those that come from broadsides and chapbooks. We cannot be certain about the oral life of the songs used here, but we can be certain that they were all printed during the period under consideration. The fact of their being printed testifies to a belief on the part of the printers that they were sought after.

I have eschewed an analysis based on local identities and have tried to consider the ballad culture as a coherent whole. I believe that this is a reasonable way to look at these sources. When British folklorists began recording folk songs in the 1900s they were often surprised by the degree to which the same songs appeared in different areas throughout Britain. This tendency was already present in the eighteenth century: the same ballads were printed in different places. This kind of exchange was true even with respect to the Scottish lowlands: in his study of the Scottish lyric Thomas Crawford points out that many songs printed in Scotland were written in England and vice versa.[9] It is true that the occasional ballad names a specific place, but this is seldom an indication that the author is trying to create a particular sense of place: 'The Oxfordshire Tragedy' could just as easily have taken place in any other county. This distinguishes ballads about the countryside from industrial ballads from places like Birmingham, which often make many references to the history and life of a particular city. Some sense of local identity is provided by the work of peasant poets, which will be examined together with ballads where possible.

Orality, print and collectors

The difficult nature of these sources is further complicated by their relationship to the oral tradition. 'The oral tradition seems to arouse in historians suspicion at best, loathing at worst', wrote Roy Palmer in 1988.[10] Unfortunately this is still largely true. Given the oral origins of some of our ballads we must consider the relationship between orality and print. In addition to their reliance on other printers and on individual ballad writers who worked for them, ballad printers relied in part on the oral tradition. Margaret Spufford and Ian Dyck have demonstrated that orality and print in the eighteenth and nineteenth centuries were not mutually exclusive. Poets like John Clare collected both oral and printed folk songs without making a distinction between them.[11] Ballads belonging to the oral tradition could get printed and, vice versa, ballads originating in print could enter the oral tradition.[12] Folk singers often learned songs from print, while broadside texts were sometimes taken down from songs already in oral circulation.[13] For example, James Rankin, a blind Scottish beggar who travelled through Scotland singing old songs and ballads, was employed in 1828 by the publisher Peter Buchan, whom he supplied with ballads.[14] Readers, but also illiterate listeners, would remember and repeat songs, while chapmen would record songs they heard and turn them to print.[15] This is why scholars studying popular songs often refer to them as 'folklore in print'.[16]

The verses themselves exhibit elements of both print and orality. Walter Ong distinguishes between oral narratives, which have an episodic narrative structure with parts of speech joined with 'and', and written narratives, which have a climactic structure and use subordinate clauses.[17] Popular songs are formulaic and tend to avoid subordinate clauses, but the narrative has a climactic structure. Also, the repetition of the refrain is an oral aspect of songs that we still have today. Songs often had an agonistic structure typical of oral verse: the milkmaid versus the squire, the agricultural labourer versus the landlord.[18] Oral poetry favours action rather than description – we do not see the detailed verbal descriptions of the visual world in oral verse that we see in written narrative.[19] Popular songs also tend to concentrate on the story. When they describe a person or a place it tends to be in generic terms. This explains the lack of a local sense of place and the use of stock characters. According to Ong, oral narrative can only produce a flat or type character.[20] Thus popular songs are 'on the edge of orality', forming a bridge between oral and written culture.[21]

Many famous men collected ballads: Dryden, Boswell, Burns, Macaulay, Clare. Collectors had an influence on the printing of ballads similar to the influence of print on oral culture. Leslie Shepard describes how seventeenth-century ballads entered the world of polite culture because collectors mistakenly thought they were part of ancient traditional minstrelsy. Ballads were often reprinted in books like *A collection of Old Ballads. Corrected from the Best and from Ancient copies Extant* (1723). The words 'corrected' and 'from the best' betray collectors' concern with propriety and literary merit and are to be found in folklore collections well into the twentieth century. Later these ballads made it back into broadsides.[22] Some pre-1800 collections of ballads are used here, but we must remember that collectors often edited ballads and omitted the ones they deemed offensive. An example is *The Aviary*, a collection of songs whose editor prides himself on having made corrections, restored the rhyme and supplied the missing lines.[23] I have used these songs because they were still in use when they were collected in 1750, but I have not put them in the same category as broadsides and chapbooks. If a collector specifies that he or she obtained the songs from broadsides or chapbooks and provides dates, I have not made a distinction between the collection and the loose broadside or chapbook. Where possible I have tried to substitute a loose broadside or chapbook version of the ballads for the collected one. I have used the Pepys collection for the purpose of evaluating which genre or trope was new to the eighteenth century and which had a longer history. This collection is substantial.[24] It does not contain bawdy songs, but it contains a surprising number of songs about poverty. It relies on earlier ballad collections as well as on ballads Pepys himself collected in his own time.

A word needs to be said here about some of the other collections which have served as sources for the loose broadsides and chapbooks used in this book. Information about collectors themselves is scarce. Some libraries, like the British Library and the Houghton Library at Harvard University, have not relied on a single great collector to acquire ballads and it is difficult to connect their holdings to an individual's bias or method of selection. In the case of the Bodleian Library we are fortunate enough to know the names of the major collectors who have donated their broadsides but, again, we cannot know for certain how they chose ballads. They come from different walks of life and from different periods. Walter Harding was a musician who collected opera and musical comedy scores, English popular songs, French songs of the eighteenth and nineteenth centuries and American popular sheet music from the 1790s to the 1960s. He died in the 1970s.[25] It is possible that he was attracted to ballads because of the music rather than the lyrics. Charles Harding Firth (1857–1936) was a historian of the seventeenth century who collected broadside ballads from the seventeenth to the nineteenth centuries.[26] But he has left no writing about ballads and we do not know his motivations and preferences. Francis Douce (1757–1834) was a collector of books, prints and street literature. Giles Barber has written about Douce's interest in French literature, allowing us to hypothesise about his attitudes toward English broadsides and chapbooks. According to Barber, Douce was interested 'in almost anything printed' regardless of subject matter.[27] He also finds that historians' analysis of the subject content of the *Bibliothèque bleue* in the seventeenth and eighteenth centuries accords well with Douce's holdings, meaning that his collection can be taken as representative of what was in circulation at the time.[28]

The problem of collecting can also be situated within the broader changes in the culture of collecting since the eighteenth century. Eighteenth-century collectors were primarily interested in rarity and curiosities rather than history or preservation for its own sake. Collectors of ballads, such as Boswell, hoped to discover the 'true', 'ancient' ballads, which were seen to contain the genuine voice of the people in contrast to the vulgar productions of street literature.[29] For this reason these collections are not used here. Douce lived in the eighteenth and nineteenth centuries, but he belonged more to the nineteenth-century culture of collecting, which emphasised historical significance and representativeness.[30] Barber describes Douce as a collector who was ahead of his time and who saw no separation between popular and elite culture.[31] Of course, nineteenth-century collectors of ballads such as F. J. Child and Sabine Baring Gould could still be prejudiced against street literature. But this prejudice did not keep them from collecting it.[32] Furthermore, different collectors have different ideas and approaches. By using a variety of collections one can avoid being a prisoner of the source. It is unlikely that there were many extraordinary and exciting broadside and chapbook ballads floating around that would not have attracted the attention of at least one of our collectors.

Since the concern of this study is the representation of rural life, one may wonder about the precise nature of ballads' relationship to the countryside. Most chapbooks and broadsides were printed in cities, but a large number of them reached the countryside. They were carried to country fairs, markets and even remote villages by pedlars and chapmen who, together with village poets or singers, played an important role in rural communities.[33] Aside from these distributors, broadsheets were often pasted onto the walls of country cottages and pubs. In fact, the reason why broadsides were often printed only on one side was to make them suitable for posting on walls in public places. This points to a readership larger than the simple number of sheets printed. The number of broadsides in circulation in the country in the eighteenth century was larger than the number of newspapers. Indeed, as many as twenty layers of broadsides have been found under the wallpaper of some cottages, perhaps suggesting the decline of singing in the house as well as the decline of the broadside trade after 1900.[34]

A further association between popular verse and the countryside can be made through song writers and printers. Many of these men were born in the countryside and started their businesses in provincial towns before they moved to London. This is the case with Doughal Graham, chapman and author, who was born in a Stirling village in 1724 and started as a farm worker. David Love, a chapman and ballad-writer born near Edinburgh in 1750, was also a farm labourer initially. While he lived in London for a long time, he later moved to Nottingham, where he sold broadsheets in his old age.[35]

A large number of English chapbooks from the south, especially for the first half of the eighteenth century, were printed in London. This is due in part to accidents of preservation but also to London's domination of the printing trade at that time. John Feather has pointed out that these chapbooks were meant largely for local consumption because financially it was not worth while for chapmen to sell them too far away. Since local production was more efficient and cheap, scholars speculate that there must have been a lot more chapbooks and broadsides printed in the provinces than we have today and that most local printers were involved in producing them.[36] We do know of a number of provincial printers who were major producers of chapbooks, ballads and other popular books, though the majority of them became important in the second half of the eighteenth century.[37] After 1711 Newcastle became a printing centre, after 1724 York and Birmingham. After 1760 Banbury, Nottingham, Coventry and Manchester can be added to the list.[38] Sheffield (after 1736), Worcester, Tewksbury and Leicester were not as significant but were also productive. Unfortunately, no ballads from these towns have been preserved. The first known local printer of ballads is S. Gamidge of Worcester, whose business opened in 1758. Thomas Davies opened a print shop in Hereford in 1788 or 1795, but only one of his ballads has been found.[39] Minor printing centres were Carlisle, Durham, Whitehaven, Stockton and Bath.[40] Newcastle-upon-Tyne became the major printing centre for the north in the early nineteenth century. At its annual fair, songsters would sell out quickly even if songs cost as much as 10s. a copy.[41] In Scotland, Glasgow and Edinburgh became major printing centres in the second half of the eighteenth century and today still contain some of the richest collections of popular songs and ballads. It is noteworthy that when we talk about provincial printing we are still talking about towns rather than villages, but the line between provincial towns and the countryside was often thin, especially in the north. For example, Glasgow and Edinburgh are often described as large villages by historians.[42] By the 1830s the printing press had begun to reach even villages and small towns like Exeter, where some songs about shepherds printed locally on single sheets have been discovered.[43]

Provincial printers aside, the major London printers themselves had links with the countryside. An example is William Dicey (1720–1765), whose first printing shop was opened in Northampton and who continued to supply the provincial chapbook trade after moving to London.[44] The two greatest London printers of street literature both had ties to the provinces. John Pitts was the son of a Norfolk baker and worked in the trade himself before moving to London in 1802.[45] He has been praised for reviving a declining folk music tradition as well as bringing urban culture to the countryside: 'He thus brought many old country songs to London and circulated the latest hits of stage and pleasure gardens in the countryside.'[46] James Catnach, the most successful London printer of street literature, came from a small Scottish town and started business in Alnwick, Northumberland. His biographer writes:

> It appears that this extraordinary man at one time contemplated devoting his life to rural pursuits; in fact, when a youth he served for some time as a shepherd boy, quite contrary to the wish and desire of his parents. Every opportunity he could get he would run away, far across the moors and the Northumbrian mountains, and, always accompanied by his favorite dog Venus, and a common-place book, in which he jotted down in rhymes and chymes his notions of a pastoral life.[47]

The reason why so many song printers have a rural background probably has to do with their growing up surrounded by a rich oral tradition of music and verse. It is curious that so many of these men retained their interest in popular songs after they had become successful as urban printers. Although the printed objects themselves (chapbooks and broadsides) were made in cities, the songs that covered their pages often came from the countryside. James Catnach and John Pitts reportedly sent their assistants to the countryside to collect songs.[48] Ballad singers who travelled around England might collect country songs and bring them back to London, selling them to publishers like Pitts and Catnach.[49] Thus, popular songs served as a link between the rural and the urban world.

Literacy and the audience in country and city

I am often asked how we know that anyone read broadsides and chapbooks. This is not a well-conceived question. As I will explain below, in addition to direct evidence of a readership for broadside and chapbook songs, the production of these objects was a commercial enterprise. There is no reason why printers would have continued to produce thousands of them if no one was reading them. It is more useful to ask who read them and how large the audience was. Evidence for literacy is fragmentary, especially for the peasantry, and one can make an argument for both a high and a low literacy rate. In some places literacy was very widespread: in the parish of St Mary, Islington, whose register recorded whether or not children could read, of 267 boys tested 205 or 74.5 per cent could read and of 228 girls 173 or 75.7 per cent.[50] While reading aloud was very common among rural labourers, there must have been many illiterate ones. Of those that could read few could afford books, but chapbooks and broadsides were more accessible.[51] John Brewer supplies figures (Table 1.1) for the growth of literacy in the first half of the eighteenth century based on signature counts.

Table 1.1 Growth of literacy in England, 1500–1750

Year	Males (%)	Females (%)
1500	10	1
1714	45	25
1750	60	40

Source: John Brewer, *The Pleasures of the Imagination: English Culture in the Eighteenth Century* (Chicago: University of Chicago Press, 1997), 167–8.

Brewer's argument that these figures concern largely the gentry and the middling sort leaves out an important group of readers, craftsmen and artisans and small farmers. For the north of England and Lowland Scotland in the period 1640–1770, R. A. Houston found high literacy among male craftsmen and tradesmen and low literacy for labourers and servants based on signature counts (Tables 1.2 and 1.3).

Because his study only extends to 1770, Houston does not deal with the impact of industrialisation on levels of literacy at the end of the eighteenth century. However, using signature counts from Lancashire, Michael Sanderson has shown that there was a significant decline in literacy from the 1780s to the 1820s.[52] He argues this decline was characteristic of areas undergoing industrialisation because the new mechanised methods of production were more heavily dependent on child labour than the traditional crafts.[53]

A second factor, affecting rural areas as well, was the inability of school endowments to keep up with the growth in the child population.[54]

Table I.2 Levels of occupational literacy for men, 1640–1770

	Four northern counties (%)	Yorkshire (%)	Lowland Scotland (%)
Craft and trade	73	65	81
Yeoman/tenant	60	66	69
Husbandman	57	38	–
Labourer	33	23	28
Servant	53	39	44

Source: R. A. Houston, *Scottish Literacy and the Scottish Identity: Illiteracy and Society in Scotland and Northern England, 1600–1800* (Cambridge and New York: Cambridge University Press, 1985), 41, 60. Percentages have been converted from illiteracy to literacy rates.

Table I.3 Levels of occupational literacy for women, 1700–70

	Northern England	Scotland
Craft and trade	31	28
Farmer/tenant	32	14
Labourer	12	10
Servant	25	12

Source: R. A. Houston, *Scottish Literacy and the Scottish Identity: Illiteracy and Society in Scotland and Northern England, 1600–1800* (Cambridge and New York: Cambridge University Press, 1985), 41, 60. Percentages have been converted from illiteracy to literacy rates.

But the Lancashire figures are contradicted by studies done in other areas. For the early nineteenth century Rex Russell provides figures based on signatures in marriage registers from twenty-eight Lincolnshire parishes (Table 1.4).

If in areas undergoing rapid industrialisation there was a downward trend in labourers' literacy at this time; in other areas literacy was on the increase.

In spite of their different emphases, all the above studies suggest a low literacy rate for labourers. But they are based on signature counts, and this method has come under criticism. Using evidence from three Kent parishes, Barry Reay has shown that signature counts tend to underestimate the number of readers.[55] Furthermore, it is possible to participate in political discourse without being literate. Historian E. P. Thompson describes how illiterate

Table 1.4 Literacy in Lincolnshire based on signature counts, 1800–29

	Bridegrooms (%)	Brides (%)
1800–09	66.2	39.9
1810–19	66.7	45.2
1820–29	67.6	48.2

Source: Rex C. Russell, *From Cock-Fighting to Chapel Building: Changes in Popular Culture in Eighteenth- and Nineteenth-Century Lincolnshire* (Sleaford: Heritage Trust of Lincolnshire, 2002), 79. I have changed the percentages to reflect literacy rather than illiteracy for the purpose of comparison with Brewer.

labourers visited pubs where Cobbett's editorial letters were read aloud. They might listen to radical orators or a friend reading the news.[56] In similar fashion, labourers must have engaged with printed popular ballads on different levels. The illiterate ones may have heard them in pubs, on the street or from friends, while the literate may have bought and read them themselves.

Broadside ballads often cost a penny or half a penny. This was a significant sum for working people but not unaffordable, and many of them considered ballads to be worth it.[57] The heavy damage caused to chapbooks by their being thumbed over and over again shows that one chapbook would be shared by many.[58] Specialists in street literature are convinced that the audience for songs was the lowest class of readers and that songs only became popular if they expressed the feelings of the community.[59] Contemporaries often commented on the popularity of ballads. This was true for both patriotic and 'subversive' songs.[60] Street songs were purchased by sailors, soldiers, labourers and women workers.[61] Paintings from the period often showed broadsides. Hogarth's engraving 'The Fellow Prentices Industry and Idleness at their Looms' of 1747 reproduced in Palmer's *A Ballad History of England*, showed a sleeping apprentice with a ballad about Moll Flanders pinned above him on the wall.[62] In his discussion of the Political Register of 1767 Francis Place pointed out that those among the lower classes who could read 'would not exercise their capacity beyond a ballad, a bawdy tract or a foolish story'.[63] Writing in 1819, he said ballads were sung and hung against the walls and also in clubs.[64] There is also some evidence for working-class readership in working-class autobiographies. For working people like Thomas Holcroft (1745–1809), who read broadsides on the walls of cottages and alehouses when he was serving as a stable boy in Newmarket, chapbooks and broadsides were a part of everyday life.[65] Dr Alexander Murray, who began as a shepherd in Scotland, recalled reading a lot of ballads when he was a shepherd boy. Self-taught poets like John Clare used their knowledge of ballads to create their own poetry.[66] It is probable that ballads not only provided entertainment, but spread literacy:

> Even the walls of cottages and little alehouses would do something; for many of them had old English Ballads, such as Death and the Lady and Margaret's Ghost, with lamentable tragedies, or King Charles' golden rules, occasionally pasted on them. These were at that time the learning, and often, no doubt, the delight of the vulgar.[67]

Broadsides and chapbooks were consumed primarily – but not exclusively – by the labouring classes.

While we have evidence that the labouring classes read and enjoyed popular songs, it is hard to tell what they made of them – in other words, how they read them. If we accept Walter Ong's argument that peasants eschew abstract analysis and categorical thinking, interpreting phenomena in terms of the immediate world, it is likely they would have related to songs whose characters they could recognise, and would have thought of stock characters such as ploughmen in terms of their experience of real ploughmen.[68] That is not to say they would have immediately accepted any story, only that they would have looked for a link between the story and real life.

According to Ong, print commodifies the word.[69] In their printed form popular songs were commodities that functioned within a literary market. The eighteenth century is a key period in the growth of the trade in popular literature. As the Licensing Act expired in 1695, restrictions on printing were lifted and the monopolist power of the Company of Stationers was destroyed, allowing many independent printers to flourish.[70] The trade became so widespread, that some chapmen banded together to form fraternities with rules of government and penalties for misbehaviour, holding a gala day once a year. The Fraternities of Chapmen of Stirling, Fife and Perth kept minute books dating from the beginning of the eighteenth century.[71]

The growth of the audience as the century progressed, due both to population growth and improving literacy rates, made the trade increasingly profitable.[72] Though Richard Altick has suggested that there was no new audience but only a desire on the part of the existing one to buy more books, the larger number of working-class autobiographies and self-educated working-class poets suggests that more working people took an interest in literature.[73] There was a large growth in publications throughout the period. The total number of items published per year grew from 2,000 to 6,000 from 1740 to 1790.[74] Ballad printing increasingly became a commercial enterprise. A comparison between the printers John Catnach and his son James Catnach illustrates the kinds of commercial practices that were coming to dominate printing. John Catnach was a printer in Alnwick, where he specialised in printing the standard poets like Burns and James Thomson in high-quality, carefully designed editions. Occasionally he printed popular ballads but they were 'traditional' ones, which he valued for their literary merit. He made a modest income from his trade, being forced to go to debtors' prison towards the end of his life and then moving to London, where he was not successful.[75] James Catnach, his son, set up business in London in 1813 and, unlike John, was primarily concerned with what would sell. He printed street literature: reports on crime, dying confessions, popular songs both new and old. His biographer, perhaps reflecting a particular kind of Victorian prejudice, felt that Catnach was

> incessant in his endeavours in trying to promulgate and advance not the beauty, elegance, and harmony which pervades many of our national airs and ballad poetry, but very often the worst and vilest of each and every description – in other words, those most suitable for street sale.[76]

James was less scrupulous than his father and immensely more successful, leaving £10,000 at the end of his life.[77] In the nineteenth century it became possible to make money from street literature in the provinces also: Joseph Russell, a radical printer from Birmingham who was in the business from 1815 to 1837 both printing and selling ballads in his own ballad store, is said to have made £12,000.[78]

In the eighteenth century the chapman David Love observed a high demand for his ballads but both he and the Irish pedlar Magee noted that by the 1820s deteriorating economic conditions made it harder for the poor to spend money on print.[79] On the other hand, the number of annual publications continued to increase and some of the largest collections of street literature in existence today date from this period. Self-taught peasant poets were more likely to attract elite subscribers at this time, and this may be why their number was also larger than before. The expansion of the printing trade may be explained in part by population growth, but since most of the new ballads after 1800 came from the north, it is likely that any decline in readership was a phenomenon confined to the more depressed south.

Developments in the printing trade, such as the expansion of provincial printing, are one of many changes that affected ballads at the end of the eighteenth century.[80] The 1790s also saw the beginning of the anti-ballad campaign waged by reformers like Hannah More and Francis Place. Fears about political stability made middle-class contemporaries associate the ballad trade with labourers' tendency to insubordination. According to Roy Palmer, 'Balladry was once favoured as a vehicle for the views of a wide social cross-section, but it increasingly became the voice of those who felt themselves to be excluded from other means of public self-expression'.[81] Ian Dyck also believes ballads became more radical, drawing a distinction between old ballads expressing traditional values and new ballads expressing class concerns, both of which were sold by the same people. He argues that by the end of the Napoleonic Wars popular culture in general became less willing to adopt the values of elite culture and was thus more ideological.[82] Rural popular songs were now sung by labourers in pubs as a form of protest while loyalist and drawing-room songs were sung by farmers in their homes.[83] While some ballad writers like Joseph Mather of Sheffield (1737–1804) and Michael Wilson of Lancashire (1763–1840) were clearly radical, this may be too black and white.[84] Douglas Jerrold, writing in 1841 about the period of the Napoleonic Wars, described patriotic war songs being sung by ballad singers in the street rather than only in drawing rooms.[85]

Did the change in the context and cultural meaning of popular ballads lead to a change in their language and content? Even if the ballad form had remained completely static, it would have acquired new meanings within a new cultural context. To show that the range of subjects discussed in ballads increased and that the language of song also changed, one can use Braudel's temporal frame-work of the long term, the mid-term and the event, which helps distinguish between the static and changing elements within popular songs. The music, images and verse structure belong to the long term, as do certain kinds of themes, like 'contentment is to be found in the cottage'. Language belongs to the mid-term and it changed to reflect the mood of popular movements like Luddism and Captain Swing. Content belongs to the event level and it changed constantly to address new grievances. The Braudelian model and the ways in which ballads changed will be discussed in later chapters.

The ballad singer and seller in popular culture

Although the content of songs shifted to reflect cultural change, the percep-tion of the ballad seller, writer and singer (sometimes the same person, sometimes three distinct occupations) remained constant in the eighteenth and nineteenth centuries. Certain associations seem to have been attached to these individuals throughout the period. While printing was becoming a commercial and profitable trade, at all other stages of the production and consumption of popular songs poverty was the norm. A study of pedlars' autobiographies shows that they were extremely poor. Many of them were beggars who turned to selling chapbooks as a last resort.[86] In fact, chapmen were deemed to belong to the same category as vagrants. They were targeted together with vagrants by Elizabethan repressive legislation and were referred to as 'vagabonds' throughout the eighteenth century. On the other hand, they were necessary and numerous because not every village had many shops and as well as chapbooks they also sold diverse household items such as needles, pins, thread and ribbon.[87] Hoh-Cheung Mui and Lorna Mui estimate there were 1,290 licensed hawkers in 1784–85 in England and Wales but these were only one of many different kinds of itinerant traders.[88] There are fewer sources referring to unlicensed or local pedlars.

While propertied men like the innkeeper Joseph Freeth sometimes wrote and performed popular ballads, most ballad-writers known to us were as poor as the pedlars described above. While it has been argued that the authorship of ballads is not important and that consumption should interest us more than production, a knowledge of the authors' social circumstances where possible can help us understand the context out of which the poems emerged.[89] Ballad writers could be amateurs who practised a trade and wrote ballads in their spare time, or professionals who made a living from their songs. For instance, Joseph Mather of Sheffield (1737–1804) worked as a filemaker and performed his ballads for extra money. Though he could read, he could not write so he had to memorise all the ballads he created, only two of which were made into broadsides. His songs were very popular in Sheffield, and his funeral was attended by thousands.[90] George Davis of Birmingham (1768–1819) was sent to grammar school with money donated by a benefactor and later worked as a printer at the *Birmingham and Staffordshire Chronicle*. He abandoned his job when his family died, became a drunk and lived off selling his ballads at public houses. He died in a workhouse.[91] Michael Wilson (1763–1840) of Lancashire was the son of a handloom-weaver and worked as a calico printer, then a furniture broker.[92] Even John Morgan, who was one of Catnach's poets and lived solely off writing ballads, did not benefit from his employer's success. Charles Hindley, who interviewed Morgan for his Catnach biography, noticed the poet's poverty, suggested by his dilapidated hat, his love of drink, and his anxiety that he be paid for discussing his memories of Catnach.[93]

The ballads themselves provide some evidence for the poverty of ballad singers. Most songs describe the ballad singer as suffering privation and hardship. 'The Ballad Singer' is an example. The narrator begins by explaining that his song is not a sign of jollity:

Gentle people as ye throng
Listening to a beggar's song,
Think ye mirth inspires the strain?
Think ye pleasure and joy reign?

Ah! No, the strain that beggars chaunt,
Issue from the breast of want,
Ah! The strains that beggars sing,
Not from mirth but misery spring.

The singer then explains that in wealthy households the entertainer may indeed be enjoying himself, but this cannot be expected of the wandering minstrel who suffers hunger and cold. He ends by inviting his listeners to feed him, so that his song too might acquire a more cheerful note.[94] 'Little Bess the Ballad-Singer' describes a child singer placed in similarly dire circumstances. She tells of how her parents are suffering poverty and how crucial it is for her to sell the ballads in order to sustain her family.[95] The ballad 'The Wandering Bard' provides an unusually detailed description of the singer's lifestyle.[96] Originally from Manchester, this bard is compelled to wander from town to town. He complains his poverty is so great he has to continue his travels even in the rain. He seems to take little joy in his trade. He also complains about the times being very hard and asks for charity. To move the listener to compassion, he describes his shabby clothes, apparently his sole possession, which would offer scant protection during the fast-approaching winter. The clothes are so old, it is impossible to tell where they were made and they consist of a coat he bought six years ago from an old Jew for ten and sixpence; a greasy old hat whose lining has been torn, bought from a soldier; an old oil skin worn thin bought seven years ago; an old handkerchief worn about his neck bought from a whore at a gin shop door at the corner of Drury lane; a waistcoat bought for three-pence; an old shirt he found in the dirt; a pair of breeches he begged; stockings he bought in 1792 costing four-pence; and shoes, one bought at St Giles's and the other at Rag Fair.[97] The story of Melina, 'The Disobedient Daughter', gives us a glimpse of a female hawker. She sells hymns rather than popular songs and thinks of the trade as a punishment for disobeying her parents rather than a vocation. Again, she is very poor. Often ballads that portrayed women ballad sellers and singers took the form of a plaintive cry for charity.[98]

Because everyone connected with the trade in chapbooks and broadsides (except successful printers) was poor, in the eighteenth century the trade continued to be viewed with suspicion by social commentators. Ballad singers were often seen as criminals, and the ballads as a corrupting influence on the mind of the poor.[99] In 1716, John Gay put it this way:

Let not the ballad singer's thrilling strain
Amid the swarm thy lis'ning ear detain,
Guard well thy pocket, for these syrens stand
To aid the labours of the diving hand;
Confed'rate in the cheat, they draw the throng;
And cambrick handkerchiefs reward the song.[100]

In 1794 Birmingham officials stated that 'The Offices of this Town give this public Notice, that they are come to a determined Resolution to apprehend all strolling Beggars, Ballad Singers, and other Vagrants found within this Parish'.[101] The efforts of Hannah More to replace existing ballads with new loyalist ones, discussed in chapter six, also show us that they were seen as subversive.[102] Concerned observers thought ballads made more impression on the poor than anything else and should, instead of serving the purposes of subversives and criminals, be used as a vehicle for church and king propaganda.[103]

Ballads themselves often linked the street poet with the vagabond or thief. 'Down the Dark Arches near the Adelphi' tells the story of a charming female ballad singer and seller who is also part of a team of thieves.[104] Enchanted by her song, the narrator buys a ballad from her and takes her to a pub to treat her to a drink. He spends five shillings on lobsters, salmon and brandy trying to please her. As he notes to himself that she drinks the brandy rather freely a 'gent with a black eye and a stick' walks in, drinks up the narrator's brandy, smokes his cigar and before he knows it he finds himself surrounded by five thieves who tear off his coat, steal his watch and strip him of everything, leaving him naked in a ditch.

If ballad singers were pitied for their poverty and feared for their association with vagabonds, in songs they were also envied for their freedom to move where they liked, their carefree lifestyle. 'The Travelling Chapman' expresses the contradiction between the chapman's hard life and the joy he takes in his freedom. Although he is poor, sells little, and sleeps in the field or in barns, he still has 'contentment'.[105] A number of songs about strolling singers promoted a philosophy of being content with one's lot and not worrying about the morrow.[106] 'Beggars and Ballad-singers', while equating the trade with begging, points out that balladeers are better off than the queen because they have no responsibilities and can drink as often as they like. The song also says that a nobleman's dignity and honesty is no better than that of the beggar and the ballad singer.[107]

Other ballads illustrated ballad singers' liminal position between elite and popular culture. These songs satirised ballad singers' pretensions to artistic greatness but in so doing allowed the possibility of such a claim. Furthermore, by placing a ragged ballad singer in the company of great poets, they mocked not only the ballad singer but also the literary tradition. What we see in these songs is a juxtaposition of the singer's material poverty with his firm belief in the value of his art. In this sense the ballads appropriated the claims made by Romantic poets, although the songs were much more humorous and self-deprecating. One of them, 'The Dustman's Brother', begins by endowing the street poet with a kind of moral stature:

> My moralizing muse attunes
> Mankind ven [sic] in their cradles,
> That some are born to wooden spoons,
> And some to silver ladles.[108]

The poet claims the right to make moral judgements. He sees the world as divided between rich and poor. His own social status appears to be liminal: on the one hand he places himself with Apollo and the muses, stating that he is known as Apollo Bell. On the other hand, the very next line reveals that he is 'brother to the dustman', claiming kinship with the poor. Thus the language of polite literature is mixed with the language of the street, and the exalted claims of poetry are thrown together with the lifestyle of the beggar. It is somewhat ironic that, because of his literary talent, the poet sees himself as a social climber:

> In early life I always seemed,
> To feel an hinclination,
> To rise above the common class,
> Of mortals in my station,
> At Sunday school, I could the boys
> All round my finger twist 'em
> For readin – and I larn'd to write
> By the Lanky-steerin system.

Literacy has given him an advantage over others of his class, allowing him to 'drive a roaring trade' as both a ballad singer and ballad seller. This commodi-fication of poetry reflects the growing profitability of the ballad trade, as well as mainstream poets' growing dependence on the market after 1800.[109] But pecuniary gain is only one motivation for the street poet. Like the Romantics he claims a poetic vocation is a fulfilment of his destiny: his mother, a fortu-neteller, prophesied a poetic future for him.[110] Like great poets he expects to be honoured after death: he thinks statues of him would be made to speak his praise, 'The Appollo Bell-vi-de-re'.

Of course there is a great deal of irony in this boast of the street poet. The very juxtaposition of 'poet' and 'brother to the dustman' puts in question the greatness of his verse. Later in the ballad he gets the literary canon all wrong:

> But larnin' is a dangerous thing,
> Lord Byron he determines,
> I've read Joe Miller's Iliad,
> And Mister Shakespeare's sarmons,
> The Pilgrim's Progress, done by Boz,
> And Bunyan's Jest Book handy,
> Sterne's work on Shipping Coke on gas
> And Milton's Tristram Shandy.

This undermines all his previous claims to poetic greatness. He mixes up the poets because he does not truly belong to this literary tradition. On the other hand, he appropriates the literary canon to suit his tune and his rhyme and his careless treatment of the authors and their work makes a mockery of them. Thus the poem both exalts and mocks the street poet, emphasising his liminal position between an artist and a pauper.

Ballads' relationship to pastoral poetry

While polite literature did not have as large an audience as popular verse, the growth in readership affected the audience for pastoral poetry too.[111] Even the more sceptical of literary scholars agree that in the eighteenth century a middle-class audience for pastoral verse emerged.[112] Even some working-class autobiographies mention the poets Goldsmith, Thomson, Cowper and Pope.[113] Still, editions of the great poets were very expensive and difficult for a working person to afford until the 1830s. Between 1800 and 1830 eighteenth-century poets were easier to come by than the Romantics.[114] Evidence for a middle-class audience for poetry comes from the circulation of provincial newspapers, which grew steadily throughout the period. Newspapers not only printed poetry, but distributed lists and catalogues of books. Editors would order and sell books as well as lend them.[115] Goldsmith's poems frequently appear in editors' lists.[116] Books were often issued in weekly numbers of instalments to make them more affordable. Thomson's *Seasons* came out in this form.[117] Poetry was the most frequently published type of literature, comprising 47 per cent of all titles.[118]

Self-taught peasant poets probably had the smallest audience of all the genres examined in this book. They did not have the reputation of established poets and could not appeal to polite audiences in the same way. At the same time few of them seem to have considered it worthwhile to try to get their poetry published in chapbook or broadside form. Their work was not 'representative' in the same way as popular verse or pastoral poetry. Even though their social station was humble, they were certainly not 'ordinary people' in the sense that social historians use this term. Nevertheless, this does not render their verse insignificant. However unusual they may have been, they were not anomalous. They were members of rural communities and their writings gave voice to feelings and attitudes that were shared by their neighbours. In contrast to the self-taught working-class writers studied by Vicinus, the works of poets like John Clare and Robert Bloomfield were not mere inoffensive portrayals of established values but social critiques.[119]

Subscription lists give us a sense of the supporters for peasant poets and their geographic distribution but they do not give us a complete picture of the audience. Those who became successful and were published by influential publishers, like Robert Bloomfield, sold in large numbers outside the circle of their subscribers. However, less prominent ones would often sell and recite their own verse in pubs.[120] They might write for newspapers, magazines and local events, but ultimately their success depended on patrons and friends rather than the market.[121]

Regardless of who the author was, books were very expensive in the first half of the eighteenth century. However, after the 1774 court decision against perpetual copyright, cheaper books, such as John Bell's series *Poets of Great Britain*, began to be produced. A volume of Bell's edition cost 1s. 6d. The success of the bookseller James Lackington – he sold books at half-price and in 1790 and 1791 had an annual turnover of 100,000 books – shows a growing demand for books.[122] For a long time the book trade was centred in London and Edinburgh. Indeed, scholars like Brewer refuse to acknowledge that a literary culture of any value or a plebeian audience for it existed outside these centres.[123] However, researchers have found evidence for the presence of numerous books in the countryside. Throughout the eighteenth century circulating libraries were spreading to the provinces and extending middle-class readership, though working people still could not afford the fees.[124] Book clubs were very popular in the country both in England and Scotland at the end of the century.[125] By 1800 the English provinces were highly literate.[126] Though most books were produced in London, provincial printers distributed them all over the country.[127] The eagerness of London booksellers to capture the market in the provinces, evident in their numerous advertisements in country newspapers in the 1770s, suggests a high demand for books.[128] Curiously, if we turn our attention to Scotland it appears that the more books reached the countryside, the more artificial the contents of pastoral poetry became. In Scotland there was less separation between city and country early in the period, resulting in a much closer connection between pastoral poetry and actual rural life. David Craig has argued that by the end of the century a polite urban culture emerged in Edinburgh destroying the 'authenticity' of pastoral poetry.[129] Of course, this argument should not be carried too far, since Scotland's most important poet, Burns, came from the country.

I do not want to give the impression that popular ballads were entirely confined to a working-class audience, while pastoral poetry belonged exclusively to the elite. Cultural historians have shown that an exchange took place between high and low culture. Song collectors organised chapbook and broadside ballads into books read by middle-class and antiquarian readers.[130] Great poets were not unfamiliar with this literature. Wordsworth spoke of chapbook and broadside ballads:

> Oh! give us once again the Wishing-Cap
> Of Fortunatus, and the invisible Coat
> Of Jack the Giant-killer, Robin Hood,
> And Sabra in the forest with St. George!
> The child, whose love is here, at least, doth reap
> One precious gain, that he forgets himself.[131]

Craig argues that in Scotland there was a more intensive exchange between high and low culture. There was less separation between different social orders.[132] For instance, in Edinburgh, different classes would occupy different floors in the same house: the first floor was reserved for the elite, the higher floors were given to middling-sort professionals, and attics were rented by artisans or servants.[133] People belonging to different social stations would come in contact with each other more often. The great Scottish poets of the eighteenth century – Robert Burns, Robert Fergusson and Allen Ramsay – had a closer relationship with popular culture than most English poets.[134] They wrote in a language little different from that of ordinary Scots. Ramsay liked popular tunes very much. He used cheap broadside-verse as a model for his vernacular elegies, and these were later read among the gentry.[135] But his readership extended further: apparently his 'The Ever Green' and 'The Gentle Shepherd' were 'universally read by the peasantry'.[136] Robert Fergusson actually sold his verse in the form of street ballads.[137] Burns both collected and wrote folk songs. He rewrote many of the popular songs he collected, though one scholar has complained that he was 'driving the devil out of Scottish folksong' much like a minister setting hymns to folk tunes.[138] Burns' poetry also turned up in chapbooks and broadsides.[139]

He was very popular among farmers and labourers in Scotland and in northern England.[140] Even ploughboys, harvest workers and shepherds would spend the little money they had to buy chapbooks with Burns's verse. Later in life Burns collected popular songs.[141] This kind of interaction between pastoral poetry and popular verse suggests a wider and more diverse audience for both genres.

In conclusion, broadside and chapbook ballads formed a cohesive whole, a culture of print with strong links to an oral culture that transcended local identity. They connected a literate with an illiterate world. They bore a complex relationship to the countryside. While produced in cities, they were taken to villages by pedlars. Some of them may have originated in villages enjoying an oral life before they made it to the printed page. Although the rural characters found in songs are stock characters or tropes recognised by a general audience, real tradesmen, artisans and agricultural labourers who could read might have identified with them. In the case of songs that originated in the countryside, they may have been informed by the real experiences of rural working people. For instance, a complaint about low wages makes little sense without the experience. While the language used may take conventional forms, it is hard to imagine such songs having resonance without some connection to reality.

In the course of the eighteenth century the audience for ballads and for poetry grew. In areas where literacy increased there were more new readers. Areas that experienced a decline in literacy may have still provided a larger market due to population growth and a more politically engaged audience. This changing audience was parallel to a change in the ballads themselves. Ballads became more antagonistic and more critical by 1800. However, the representation of the figure of the ballad singer remained a constant. Poor, with no fixed residence, the balladeer was seen as dangerous and subversive both by ballad writers and by the elite.

Pastoral poetry and the work of self-taught poets had a different audience than popular songs but underwent some of the same changes. They came to enjoy a larger audience and they became more sensitive to the negative side of the developments that were transforming the countryside. Thus we find agreement between poetry and songs on issues like the moral economy and enclosure. A study of the issues discussed in songs and rural verse will yield a more profound understanding of the nature of rural Britain, of the changes it experienced, and of what contemporaries thought about all this. The inevitable difficulties associated with using literary sources and with dating and placing street literature should not keep us from trying to situate these in their historical context and using them to learn more about it.

Notes

1 T. B. Macaulay, *History of England*, Vol. 1 (London: Longman, Green and Co., 1906), 437.

2 Some historians like Margaret Spufford think a division between popular and elite culture already existed in the seventeenth century. She thinks farmers read full-scale books while cottagers read chapbooks, and blames enclosure for this growing gap. However, the elite practice of collecting and the familiarity of poets like Wordsworth with popular ballads show that popular and elite culture were connected quite closely much later than Spufford supposes. See her *Small Books and Pleasant Histories: Popular Fiction and its Readership in Seventeenth-Century England* (Cambridge and New York: Cambridge University Press, 1985), 14, 46–7. The process of enclosure was not completed until the middle of the nineteenth century, which means that the interaction between popular and elite culture may have retained its earlier quality in unenclosed areas.

3 On how broadside and chapbook ballads were widespread in the countryside see Leslie Shepard, *The History of Street Literature: The Story of Broadside Ballads, Chapbooks, Proclamations, Newssheets, Election Bills, Tracts, Pamphlets, Cocks, Catch-pennies, and Other Ephemera* (Detroit: Singing Tree Press, 1973), 36, and Robert Collinson, *The Story of Street Literature, Forerunner of the Popular Press* (London: Dent, 1973), 2.

4 John Clare was a fiddler and a song collector. For his song collecting see George Deacon, *John Clare and the Folk Tradition* (London: Sinclair Browne, 1983).

5 M. H. Abrams, *Glossary of Literary Terms*, 5th edition (Chicago: Holst, Rinehart and Winston, 1988), 11.

6 On the distinction between black-letter and white-letter ballads and how the latter replaced the former, see Roy Palmer, *A Ballad History of England from 1588 to the Present Day* (London: B. T. Batsford, 1979), 5.

7 Martha Vicinus, *The Industrial Muse: A Study of Nineteenth-Century British Working-Class Literature* (London: Croom Helm, 1974), 14, 19–20.

8 Parts of the London Stationers' Company's list and Pitt's list have been reprinted in Leslie Shepard, *John Pitts, Ballad Printer of Seven Dials, London, 1765–1844* (London: Private Libraries Association, 1969).

9 On the influence of English songs on Scottish ones see Thomas Crawford, *Society and the Lyric: A Study of the Song Culture of Eighteenth-Century Scotland* (Edinburgh: Scottish Academic Press, 1979), ix, 6–7.

10 Roy Palmer, *The Sound of History: Songs and Social Comment* (Oxford and New York: Oxford University Press, 1988), 1–2.

11 Ian Dyck, *William Cobbett and Rural Popular Culture* (Cambridge: Cambridge University Press, 1992), 85. Spufford, *Small Books and Pleasant Histories*, 13. Spufford thinks print affected orality adversely because people remembered the fixed printed version and lost the ability to improvise.

12 Palmer, *A Ballad History of England*, 5.

13 David Atkinson, *The English Traditional Ballad: Theory, Method, and Practice* (Aldershot: Ashgate, 2002), 20–2.

14 Some of these later made it into F. J. Child's *English and Scottish Popular Ballads*: Shepard, *The History of Street Literature*, 93.

15 Collinson, *The Story of Street Literature*, 9.

16 Victor E. Neuburg, *Popular Education in Eighteenth-Century England* (London: Woburn Press, 1971), 121. See also Shepard, *John Pitts*, 26.

17 Walter Ong, *Orality and Literacy: The Technologizing of the Word* (London and New York: Methuen, 1982), 81.

18 On the agonistic character of oral verse see Ong, *Orality and Literacy*, 111.

19 Ong, *Orality and Literacy*, 127.

20 Ong, *Orality and Literacy*, 151.

21 Ong, *Orality and Literacy*, 159. On ballads' belonging to both oral and print culture see also Cathy Lynn Preston, 'The Tying of the Garter: Representations of the Female Rural Labourer in Seventeenth-, Eighteenth-, and Nineteenth-Century English Bawdy Songs', *Journal of American Folklore* 105(417) (1992): 318.

22 Shepard, *John Pitts*, 27.

23 Preface, *The Aviary: Or Magazine of British Melody Consisting of a Collection of One Thousand Four Hundred and Forty-Three Songs* (London, 1745).

24 Pepys collected street literature, including ballads, in the period 1682 to 1687. The ballads he collected were black-letter broadside ballads from the sixteenth and seventeenth centuries. I have only used ones from the seventeenth century. Edward Hyder-Rollins, to this day the only editor of the Pepys ballads, believed that many of them were about real historical events though others were fictional. He also thought that in Pepys' time and earlier, ballad writers were clearly writing for money, and were expecting to satisfy a market. See Preface to volume 1 of *The Pepys Ballads*, ed. Edward Hyder-Rollins (Cambridge, Mass.: Harvard University Press, 1929).

25 Michael L. Turner, 'Who was Walter Harding? Some Preliminary Notes on his English Antecedents, Part I', *Bodleian Library Record* 15 (1996), 439.

26 On Charles Firth as a historian see Maurice Ashley, 'Sir Charles Firth: A Tribute and a Reassessment', *History Today* 7, no. 4 (1957): 251–6. Ashley does not discuss Firth's interest in ballads.

27 Giles Barber, 'Francis Douce and Popular French Literature', *Bodleian Library Record* 14, no. 5 (1993), 403.

28 Giles Barber, 'Francis Douce and Popular French Literature', 407.

29 Diane Dugaw, 'The Popular Marketing of 'Old Ballads': The Ballad Revival and Eighteenth-Century Antiquarianism Reconsidered', *Eighteenth-Century Studies* 21, no. 1 (1987), 71.

30 Heather MacLennan has described the new collecting culture with respect to prints. She argues these collectors resembled cultural historians in their range of responses to prints. She also sees Douce as belonging to the new culture, 'Antiquarianism, Connoisseurship and the Northern Renaissance Print: New Collecting Cultures in the Early Nineteenth Century', in *Producing the Past: Aspects of Antiquarian Culture and Practice 1700–1850* (Aldershot and Bookfield: Ashgate, 1999), 149–50.

31 Barber, 'Francis Douce and Popular French Literature', 410.

32 Roy Palmer, ' 'Veritable Dunghills': Professor Child and the Ballad', *Folk Music Journal* 7, no. 2 (1996), 157.

33 Collinson, *The Story of Street Literature*, 1; Shepard, *John Pitts*, 36; Ian Maxted, 'Single Sheets from a Country Town: The Example of Exeter', in Robin Myers and Michael Harris, eds, *Spreading the Word: The Distribution Networks of Print 1550–1850* (Detroit: St Paul's Bibliographies, 1990), 118.

34 Collinson, *The Story of Street Literature*, 2, 9.

35 Shepard, *The History of Street Literature*, 91, 93.

36 John Feather, 'The Country Trade in Books', in Myers and Harris, eds, *Spreading the Word*, 165–72.

37 Feather, 'The Country Trade in Books', 166.

38 Neuburg, *Popular Education*, 140.

39 Roy Palmer, *The Folklore of Hereford and Worcester* (Herefordshire: Logaston, 1992), 188.

40 Neuburg, *Popular Education*, 141; Shepard, *The History of Street Literature*, 64.

41 Vicinus, *The Industrial Muse*, 33.

42 David Craig, *Scottish Literature and the Scottish People 1680–1830* (London: Chatto and Windus, 1961), 28. Also E. P. Thompson, *The Making of the English Working Class* (New York: Penguin Books, 1980; first published Victor Gollancz, 1963), 445.

43 Maxted, 'Single Sheets from a Country Town',128.

44 Shepard, *The History of Street Literature*, 62.

45 Shepard, *John Pitts*, 35–7.

46 Shepard, *John Pitts*, 44–5.

47 Charles Hindley, *The History of the Catnach Press* (London, 1887), 38.

48 For a discussion of John Pitts see also Vicinus, *The Industrial Muse*, 15. Vicinus points out that Pitts acted as a link between high and low culture, as well as between country and city, bringing old country songs to London and sending 'copies of the latest hits from the pleasure gardens and supper clubs out to the rural villages'.

49 Shepard, *The History of Street Literature*, 46.

50 Neuburg, *Popular Education*, Appendix III.

51 Richard D. Altick, *The English Common Reader, A Social History of the Mass Reading Public, 1800–1900*, 2nd ed. (Columbus: Ohio State University Press, 1998; first published University of Chicago Press, 1957), 35, 39.

52 Michael Sanderson, 'Literacy and Social Mobility in the Industrial Revolution in England', *Past and Present* 56 (1972), 75.

53 Sanderson, 'Literacy and Social Mobility', 79.

54 Sanderson, 'Literacy and Social Mobility', 80.

55 Barry Reay, 'The Context and Meaning of Popular Literacy: Some Evidence from Nineteenth-Century Rural England', *Past and Present*, 131 (May, 1991): 112. Reay demonstrates that those able to read were one-and-a-half times the proportion able to sign.

56 Thompson, *The Making of the English Working Class*, 782–3.

57 Shepard, *The History of Street Literature*, 25; Collinson, *The Story of Street Literature*, 1.

58 Collinson, *The Story of Street Literature*, 24.

59 Neuburg, *Popular Education*, 118; also Dyck, *William Cobbett and Rural Popular Culture*, 219–20.

60 Douglas Jerrold, writing in 1840, commented on the popularity of patriotic songs during the Napoleonic war: 'It was his [the ballad singer's] narrow strips of history that adorned the garrets of the poor; it was he who made them yearn towards their country, albeit to them so rough and niggard a mother', Quoted in Roy Palmer, *A Touch on the Times: Songs of Social Change, 1770–1914* (Harmondsworth: Penguin Education, 1974), 8. For subversive songs, or what Francis Places called 'lewd songs and songs in praise of thieves', see The Francis Place Papers, Vol. I, Shelfmark Add 27825, vol. xxxvii, 144.

61 Palmer, *The Sound of History*, 6.

62 Palmer, *A Ballad History of England*, 5. Palmer has found evidence that broadside ballads were often attached to looms. Apparently the workplace was yet another space where broadside ballads would be read and perhaps sung.

63 The Francis Place Papers, 108.

64 The Francis Place Papers, 144.

65 Altick, *The English Common Reader*, 38.

66 Shepard, *The History of Street Literature*, 112. Deacon, *John Clare*, 10.

67 Thomas Holcroft, *Memoirs of the Late Thomas Holcroft* (London, 1816), quoted in Shepard, *John Pitts*, 28. See also p. 14.

68 Ong, *Orality and Literacy*, 81. Ong's arguments concern primarily oral cultures rather than cultures affected by print, but in this instance he used the work of Luria, who conducted his research in the early 1900s among Russian peasants who were aware of print and many of whom were literate. A second important feature of peasants' way of thinking is an emphasis on the group rather than the interior life of the individual. Most characters in the ballads lack interiority. Ong refers to rural communities who had retained an oral culture, but were also familiar with print as possessing 'residual orality' and I think this applies well to eighteenth-century rural communities.

69 Ong, *Orality and Literacy*, 131.

70 Shepard, *The History of Street Literature*, 62.

71 Shepard, *The History of Street Literature*, 92.

72 Neuburg, *Popular Education*, 140.

73 Altick argues that the growth was not in literacy but in people interested in reading, *The English Common Reader*, 30. Further support for this idea can be found in James Raven, *Judging New Wealth: Popular Publishing and Responses to Commerce in England, 1750–1800* (Oxford: Clarendon Press, 1992), 56.

74 Raven, *Judging New Wealth*, 32.

75 Hindley, *The History of the Catnach Press*, 36.

76 Hindley, *The History of the Catnach Press*, 222.

77 Palmer, *The Sound of History*, 13.

78 Palmer, *The Sound of History*, 13.

79 Michael Harris, 'A Few Shillings for Small Books: The Experience of a Flying Stationer in the Eighteenth Century', in Myers and Harris, eds, *Spreading the Word*, 93.

80 Shepard, *John Pitts*, 28.

81 Palmer, *The Sound of History*, 5.

82 Dyck, *William Cobbett and Rural Popular Culture*, 74.

83 Dyck, *William Cobbett and Rural Popular Culture*, 89.

84 On these two balladeers see Palmer, *The Sound of History*, 25, 27.

85 Regretting the decline of ballad singing in the 1840s, Jerrold thought the war period had been the last great age of the ballad singer. News of battles were instantly turned into ballads, inspiring the poor with hatred for the French., Hindley, *The History of the Catnach Press*, xxxix.

86 Shepard, *The History of Street Literature*, 93. Martha Vicinus also argues that singers of ballads were working class: *The Industrial Muse*, 22. Michael Harris sees a close link between hawking and begging: 'A Few Shillings for Small Books', 89.

87 Neuburg, *Popular Education*, 115.

88 Hoh-Cheung Mui and Lorna H. Mui, *Shops and Shopkeeping in Eighteenth-Century England* (Kingston, Montreal and London: McGill University Press, 1989), 99.

89 For a discussion of the importance of consumption rather than production in the study of popular culture see Dyck, *William Cobbett and Rural Popular Culture*, 219–20.

90 Palmer, *The Sound of History*, 25.

91 Palmer, *The Sound of History*, 24–5.

92 Palmer, *The Sound of History*, 27.

93 Charles Hindely, *The History of the Catnach Press*, xix.

94 'The Ballad Singer', *The New Vocal Harmony, or the Merry Fellow's Companion. Being a Choice Collection of Songs, Sung at all the Places of Public Entertainment.* (London: J. Davenport, n.d.) British Library Chapbook Collection, Shelfmark 11643.bbb.33.

95 'Little Bess the Ballad-Singer', *A Garland of New Songs* (Newcastle: J. Marshall, 1801–c.1824), B.L., Shelfmark 11621.c.4.

96 'The Wandering Bard' (Liverpool: W. Armstrong, 1820–24), Bodleian Library, Harding B28(82).

97 There were multiple versions of this song including a version printed by J. Pitts where the reference to the whore was omitted, but the prices of the clothes were identical. 'The Wandering Bard' (London, 1819–44), Bodleian Library, Harding B 25(1997). Catnach also printed this song. This suggests it was very popular. The reference to 1792 in the song suggests this was a 'new' song, or at least its content was new.

98 'The Disobedient Daughter' (Berkeley: Lewis Povey, 18–), Bodleian Library, Firth B. 26(6). Compare this to 'Little Bess the Ballad Singer' (see note 75). To all the ills suffered by the ballad singer was often added that of blindness, perhaps a tribute to the tradition of the blind bard.

 99 Palmer, *A Touch on the Times*, 12.

100 John Gay, *Trivia: Or, the Art of Walking the Streets of London* (1716), quoted in Palmer, *A Ballad History of England*, 5.

101 J. A. Langford, *A Century of Birmingham Life, 1741–1841*, vol. 2 (1868), 44, quoted in Palmer, *A Touch on the Times*, 13.

102 Anon., Letter to John Reeves from Fidelia, 4 December 1792, B.L., Add. MS 16920, fol. 119, Quoted in Palmer, *The Sound of History*, 17. The letter also points to the ballads' popularity: 'Every serving Man and Maid, every Country Girl, and her Sweetheart, in Towns and Villages will buy a halfpenny ballad to a popular tune...'

103 Anon., Letter to John Reeves, secretary to Association for Preserving Liberty and Property Against Republicans and Levellers, quoted in Palmer, *The Sound of History*, 16–17.

104 'Down the Dark Arches near the Adelphi' (n.p., 18–), Bodleian Library, Harding B11(1645). There is an allusion to the police in the song so it must be after 1829.

105 'The Travelling Chapman', *Five Popular Songs* (Edinburgh, 1824), L.C. 2815.

106 'Pedlar's Song', *The Delight of the Muses. Being a Choice Collection of Dibdin's Favourite Songs* (London, 18?), B.L., Shelfmark 1077.g.47.

107 'Beggars and Ballad Singers', *Sweet Echo, or the Vocalist's Companion* (London: John Pitts, n.d.), L.C. 2087. There is no date, but Pitts was in business 1819–44.

108 'The Dustman's Brother' (London: J. Pitts, 1819–44), Bodleian Library, Harding B11(1264).

109 For a discussion of poets' dependence on the market see Raymond Williams, *Culture and Society, 1780–1950* (Harmondsworth: Penguin Books, 1962), 50.

110 For a celebration of the ballad singer's trade see also 'Chanting Benny, or the Batch of Ballad' (London: J. Catnach, 1813–28), Bodleian Library, Harding B36(7).

111 See pp. 22–3.

112 Altick, *The English Common Reader*, 41.

113 Altick, *The English Common Reader*, 57.

114 Vicinus, *The Industrial Muse*, 142–3.

115 Roy McKeen Wiles, 'The Relish for Reading in Provincial England Two Centuries Ago', in Paul J. Korshin, ed., *The Widening Circle: Essays on the Circulation of Literature in Eighteenth-Century Europe* (Philadelphia: University of Pennsylvania Press, 1976), 91.

116 Wiles, 'The Relish for Reading in Provincial England', 93.

117 Wiles, 'The Relish for Reading in Provincial England', 98–9.

118 But literature was preceded by religion and the social sciences. Brewer, *The Pleasures of the Imagination*, 172.

119 Vicinus, *The Industrial Muse*, 6.

120 Vicinus, *The Industrial Muse*, 164–5.

121 Vicinus, *The Industrial Muse*, 159.

122 Altick, *The English Common Reader*, 41.

123 See Brewer, Chapter 4, 'Readers and the Reading Public', *The Pleasures of the Imagination*. Brewer thinks of peasants as largely illiterate. Also Pat Rogers,

Literature and Popular Culture in Eighteenth Century England (Brighton: The Harvester Press, 1985), 6.

124 Altick, *The English Common Reader*, 41.

125 Altick mentions this but his overall opinion is that reading was an urban activity and he does not think it reached the countryside until the end of the eighteenth century: *The English Common Reader*, 65.

126 Wiles, 'The Relish for Reading in Provincial England', 88.

127 Feather, 'The Country Trade in Books',165.

128 Wiles, 'The Relish for Reading in Provincial England', 95.

129 Craig, *Scottish Literature and the Scottish People*, 23.

130 Shepard, *The History of Street Literature*, 113.

131 William Wordsworth, *The Prelude* V, l. 341–6, in *Complete Poetical Works*, ed. Ernest De Selincourt (Oxford and New York: Oxford University Press, 1988).

132 Craig, *Scottish Literature and the Scottish People*, 20.

133 Craig, *Scottish Literature and the Scottish People*, 29–30.

134 Craig, *Scottish Literature and the Scottish People*, 19.

135 Craig, *Scottish Literature and the Scottish People*, 21, 33.

136 Craig, *Scottish Literature and the Scottish People*, 70.

137 Craig, *Scottish Literature and the Scottish People*, 32.

138 G. Legman, *The Horn Book: Studies in Erotic Folklore and Bibliography* (New York: J. Cape, 1964), 234.

139 Shepard, *The History of Street Literature*, 103; also, Craig, *Scottish Literature and the Scottish People*, 112.

140 Craig, *Scottish Literature and the Scottish People*, 113.

141 Craig, *Scottish Literature and the Scottish People*, 104.

2

The language of complaint:
ballads as social criticism

This is a story about complaining – complaining about people on whom one is dependent, as well as people for whom one is responsible. It is about the popular use of verse from the late seventeenth century to the 1830s to express dissatisfaction with the prevailing social relations in the countryside. The use of poetry and ballads to comment on social and economic conditions was not new to the eighteenth century, but what was new were the particular grievances voiced and the manner in which they were expressed.

When discussing social relations during this period, historians have created a narrative about the tension and mistrust between different social groups often erupting in protest on the part of plebeians. This tension decreased during good times and increased during hard years. The agricultural depression between 1730 and 1750 due to low corn prices was good for agricultural labourers. Population was low enough that there was plenty of work, and the standard of living in the countryside was relatively high compared to the second half of the century.[1] Things got worse after 1770 partly due to a growing fear on the part of the gentry of the plebeian potential for social disorder and partly caused by plebeians' increasing dissatisfaction with deteriorating standards of living. At the same time E. P. Thompson has pointed out that, despite the worsening social relations, labourers also gained some advantages by the eighteenth century: the breakdown of paternalism left them more independent, and free to move around and organise.[2]

Nevertheless, agricultural labourers experienced serious economic difficulties in the second half of the eighteenth century. Evidence suggests real wages started declining in the 1760s. Despite a temporary increase in the 1780s, they continued to fall in the 1790s.[3] The low wages at the end of the eighteenth century coincided with poor harvests and scarcity. Roger Wells has described these as famine conditions.[4] For much of the period, population growth made it more difficult for labourers to find employment. The oversupply of labour made it easy for farmers to treat workers badly and pay low wages. In the 1790s and early 1800s there may have been more work because so many able-bodied males were in the army, but war-time price inflation made it difficult to afford the necessities of life and the rise of the poor rates caused animosity between rate payers and those dependent on poor relief. Increasingly, the responsibility for relieving the poor was taken off employers, making the rural poor more dependent on parish authorities.[5] The role played by enclosure and the loss of common rights in the growing immiseration of agricultural labourers is still debated, but the sources examined here lend support to historians like the Hammonds and Jeanette Neeson who have shown that these problems were yet another reason for labourers and peasants to feel they had been unfairly treated.[6]

After the Napoleonic Wars the agricultural depression meant that the life-style of rural workers continued to deteriorate. Contemporary writers also noticed the growing poverty of agricultural labourers and their growing resent-ment of their superiors:

> When the 'Ploughman homeward plods his weary way' ruminating on his forlorn situation, degraded to the condition of a pauper, by those who should have cherished in him a spirit of independence; and in addition to this, forced to a great distance (in some instances miles) from the scene of his labour, to obtain lodgings; those persons must be little acquainted with human nature, who would persuade themselves that one so mal-treated, should not be disaffected to such as are termed of the upper orders. It is no surprise that persons so unfeeling and unreasonable should have excited throughout the land an outcry against the salutary regulations of the Corn Bill.[7]

Other observers noted the wretchedness of agricultural labourers as well as employers' resentment of having to pay wages and poor relief.[8] In the counties of Cambridgeshire, Huntingtonshire and Bedfordshire, for example, agricul-tural labourers and shepherds made as little as five or six shilling a week.[9] Skilled artisans who lived in the countryside also had cause to complain of low wages, high prices and mechanisation.[10] I will say more about economic hardship in chapters 3 and 6.

The evidence of songs and poetry cannot show that in real economic terms there was a decline in the standard of living or suggest a precise date when the change may have occurred. However, it does show in more general terms that labourers and commoners thought both economic and social conditions were getting worse.[11] In this case the songs are supported by other sources and do bear a relationship to experience or rather to the perception of experience. In fact, any attempt to explain them without reference to the work historians have done on the moral economy and on rural social relations is bound to be unsatisfactory.

It is useful to categorise songs in terms of Fernand Braudel's three-tiered temporal framework, according to which historical time moves at a different pace (slow, medium and quick) depending on the aspect of society one is looking at. We can relegate the poetry celebrating an idealised rural life and criticising the evils of London or of wealth to the *longue durée*, meaning that it is a long-enduring structure that changes very slowly. Such verses were produced in large numbers throughout the period and exhibited little change or development. Their number grew together with the expansion of the printing industry at the beginning of the nineteenth century, but their content was static. It may be that the sources of pride or pleasure for agricultural labourers and small farmers were the same in the eighteenth as in the nineteenth century. To these optimistic songs (which I will discuss in later chapters) we may add conjunctures – in Braudel's model these are social and economic phenomena that exhibit cyclical behaviour and have a mid-term duration of a century or a few decades. 'Conjunctures' are songs critical of rural conditions. These can be found in the Pepys ballad collection. After 1700 they stopped appearing until mid-century.[12] Then they slowly resurfaced, really taking off after 1800. Clearly printers found a market for these angry ballads and, therefore, they must have resonated with a broad popular audience. Braudel's last stage is the *histoire événementielle* – that is, the history of events. In song terms these are songs that complain about particular events affecting country life such as the dearth of 1801 and the corn bill of 1814. In many ways the two latter types of ballad are the most interesting because they are more likely to inform us about cultural and social change. Songs of protest not only found a growing audience at the end of the eighteenth century, but were transformed by a change in representation in terms of language, content and rhetoric. Indeed, I would argue that, like elite poetry, they constituted a significant departure from earlier forms.[13]

If we look at how eighteenth-century people talked about their rural social structure and social relations in songs and ballads, we will see that, as I have already suggested, plebeian representations of social tensions were balanced by a far larger body of literature portraying a socially harmonious rural world. Must we dismiss these representations as 'idealised' or as having been written by a self-serving elite in order to preserve the social order? This may be true of some of them, for instance the ballads explored in the chapter dealing with Hannah More. But on the whole it is too simplistic to assume that pessimism is always real while optimism is naïve and idealised. Also, it is unfair to presume that all songs and tales that represented the rural world as harmonious originated with the elite, while all social criticism originated with plebeians. Optimistic songs may have had a certain appeal for a plebeian audience. Some of them may also have had a prescriptive function. For instance, the songs about paternalism that I deal with later may be trying to show how things should be rather than describing how things really were.

But except for the issue of paternalism, I will leave the question of happy songs to chapters 4 and 5, where I will discuss them in connection with representations of agricultural labour and sexuality.

When popular songs complained about social relations in the countryside, they spoke of landowners, middlemen, farmers and agricultural labourers. This model of rural society is familiar to rural historians, who have tried to nuance and refine it. While songs do not explicitly distinguish between 'household producers' and 'capitalist farmers' (as historians do), it is possible to deduce from the content whether the farmers described were small farmers who worked on the land themselves or large wealthy farmers who employed labour.[14] Songs cannot offer the kind of sophisticated analysis of rural social structure provided by tax rolls, militia lists and other such sources, but they do reveal considerable complexity in their use of the word 'farmer', which we will examine below.

The second thing that will strike us is that, like riot, popular songs could be a powerful form of protest.[15] Murray Pittock has demonstrated this in his study of Jacobite songs. Pittock uses these to show that a subversive popular culture existed in the early eighteenth century, using the language of Jacobitism to question the Whig plutocracy. Often songs that had no direct Jacobite references, such as 'Chevy Chase', were used as a symbol of Jacobite sympathies. This is a very sophisticated and subtle form of political commentary and criticism of the establishment. Evidence for where and when protest songs were sung is hard to come by and I have not found any direct evidence for moral economy songs being sung during food riots, where plebeian notions of a moral economy were usually invoked. However, Len Smith discovered that during the Kidderminster carpet weavers' strike in 1828 protesters used printed ballads like 'The Carpet Weaver's Lamentation' and 'Weavers Never Will Be Slaves' to voice their grievances.[16] Songs about social relations and labourers' economic circumstances had a similar function.

In this chapter we will look at a tiny portion of the vast body of critical popular songs: songs that criticised the relationship between the gentry, farmers and agricultural workers during the long eighteenth century.[17]

Ian Dyck has illustrated that rural songs became more radical and sensitive to issues of class in the nineteenth century.[18] This new emphasis on class conflict amounted, in his view, to a new genre of song. It replaced a 'countryman consciousness' which had defined the rural interest as a whole against an urban interest.[19] Prior to 1810 songs were accepting of farmers but after 1810 the figure of the hated 'new-fashioned farmer' came to dominate.[20] Nineteenth-century songs contrasted benevolent squires with evil farmers.[21] Farmers' culture also changed. Instead of singing songs that praised the unity of countrymen they started singing drawing-room songs by Charles Dibdin. After 1820 the old country unity songs were only sung to celebrate the harvest.[22]

Songs' growing antagonism towards farmers cannot be disputed, but the change may have taken place earlier than 1810. Also, Dyck may underestimate the extent to which nineteenth-century songs about social conflict grew out of an existing tradition of protest in song. Finally, Dyck does not discuss the new anti-gentry songs that were circulated in this period. Anti-gentry songs were much more numerous by 1800 than songs about paternalistic squires. Far from expecting the gentry to step in and defend the poor, popular songs written in the voice of tradesmen or agricultural labourers saw the farmers and gentry as in league with each other.

The use of ballads to express social protest was an old practice. In the Pepys collection we find songs complaining about high prices, unemployment, taxes, and the cruelty of the rich to the poor. Most of these songs were organised around the theme of the 'rich' oppressing the 'poor'. This form can be dated to the sixteenth century and perhaps even to the Middle Ages, particularly when 'the rich' were defined as being wicked misers.[23] Pepys' 'The Poor Folks Complaint' of 1675 makes use of this trope but also refers to specific social conditions: high prices of provisions, low wages and long working hours. The oppressed 'poor' appear to be labourers dependent almost solely on the wage. Despite his hard work, the labourer in the ballad can barely sustain himself and his family: 'Yet his Labour not suffice, / His wages are so small and slender.' The ballad makes it clear that the poor it is defending are deserving rather than undeserving:

> I speak of such poor honest ones
> As will take pains in Town or City,
> For those that live like lazy Drones,
> I think that they deserve no pity.[24]

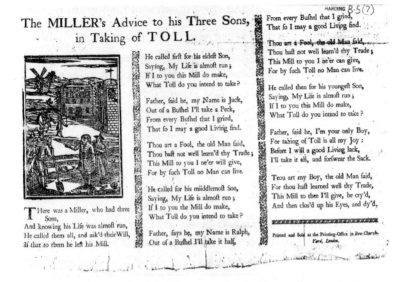

'The miller's advice to his three sons, in taking of toll' (between 1736 and 1763)   **2**

After 1700 this use of songs appears to have declined, but did not disappear. A ballad from 1713 supported weavers and spinners and criticised the nobility for ordering clothes from Paris and thereby starving the poor.[25] 'The Pope's Pedigree' from the period 1719–57 was very critical of the whole elite, but particularly of bailiffs and jailers:

> A Dog he got a Bayliff,
> Who Cerbrus like could roar,
> And daily hunt about the Town,
> To terrify the poor.
> The Bayliff got a Turnkey,
> The Turnkey got a Jailor,
> Who hellhound like to suck the Blood
> Of those the Bums do hail there.[26]

The song's theme is in part the corruption of the elite, but it connects all the ranks to one another, thus saying all of mankind is the same – they are all sinners. Nevertheless, it does deal with social injustice. It is noteworthy that these songs cannot be classified as 'rural'. As the second line of the Pepys ballad quoted above suggests, they were more explicitly associated with towns and cities. Critical songs about the countryside began to be printed or reprinted by the Diceys in the period 1736–66.

The moral economy and the injustice of high grain prices

The moral economy, defined as the expectation of fair market practices and resentment against speculation in grain, is very old and it naturally found its way into balladry. A large number of the socially critical songs were about the injustice of high grain prices. Like Pepys' 'The Present State of England', they denounced the activities of greedy millers and corn dealers during times of scarcity:

> Each Meal-man is a cunning elf,
> The corn they engrose and buy,
> Thus ev'ry man is for himself
> The poor they may starve and dye.[27]

The meal-men in the song not only buy up the corn, they hoard it until the price is high enough to make a handsome profit. The narrator contrasts the productivity of the land with the dearth in grain – clear proof that the high prices are unnatural. The exporting of grain and the use of grain by brewers are also condemned. Curiously, in this instance, farmers are said to be innocent – they bring their corn to market and sell it as soon as they can regardless of the price.[28] However, another Pepys song makes farmers share the blame for high grain prices, accusing them of refusing to sell their corn because they are waiting for the price to go up:

> Curmudgeons will not sell their Corn,
> Though poor Men's cryes about 'em thunder,
> To serve themselves, they do but scorn
> The burden that poor men lies under.
> It is a thousand pities that
> Such things are suffered in this Nation.
> That Farmers to enrich themselves
> Should starve the poor in such a fashion.
> If corn were sold at easie Rate,
> now there is plenty in each Chamber,
> Then it would very much abate
> The sorrows that the poor lyes under.[29]

If one surveys the Bodleian Library's Broadside Ballads catalogue, one will find no songs about the moral economy or rural social relations printed during the period 1700–36. The first song that resembles the moral economy songs is an anti-miller song of 1736–63.[30] Studies such as E. P. Thompson's *Whigs and Hunters* have shown that the period 1700 to 1736 was not one of complete harmony. Thompson describes the conflict over customary rights between yeomen and labourers on the one side and the crown and manorial lords on the other in Windsor Forest and Hampshire, which escalated to disruptive acts perpetrated by the labourers and the passing of the Black Act.[31] Using evidence from the Peak Country, Andy Wood has argued that plebeians in the countryside at this time were defiant, independent and ready to voice their grievances.[32] He shows how miners after 1700 established a tradition of riot in defence of their mining rights and in opposition to high food prices and government interference.[33] However, if songs of rural complaint were sung at this time, they were not published. It may be that despite these local conflicts there was no market for such songs large enough to make it worth printers' time.

Donna Landry, when explaining the emergence of the georgic in the 1740s, connects it to real changes happening in the English countryside and defines it as a form of plebeian protest against the way neoclassical pastoral poetry ignored labour.[34] The growing popularity of the georgic may be related to the resurgence of moral economy songs in the second half of the eighteenth century. The amount of such poetry produced after 1770 increased significantly, as did the directness of the protest.[35] Moral economy ballads became particularly widespread after 1800. It makes sense that this should be so. It was in the late eighteenth century that the view of the market as benevolent and beneficial if unhindered became the norm. In 1772 the old statutes forbidding forestalling and regrating were repealed.[36] The tension between the old belief that the market required regulation and the new popularity of unfettered market practices was fertile ground for both riots and songs of protest. It is also possible that worsening living conditions and rising bread prices after 1800 made the moral economy a more salient problem. Just as poets seem to have become more keenly aware of nature with the advent of industrialisation so do 'the bards of the poor' seem to have become more concerned about the moral economy at a period which historians have identified as its breakdown.

Ballads' anger at middlemen, farmers and the gentry, and support for paternalistic landlords

Historians of grain riots and the moral economy have pointed out that the target of anger over dearth and high grain prices were most often middlemen, bakers, millers and anyone associated with grain distribution. That has led them to look for the formation of middle-class identity in the discourse against forestallers and engrossers.[37] The numerous popular songs against badgers (dealers who act as middlemen between producers and consumers) and millers (as well as against farmers) suggest that songs represented the voice of the same people who participated in grain riots.

The song 'Forestalling Done Over' opens with the following verse:

Come, all you poor people, I pray lend an ear,
And of the roguish Badgers you quickly shall hear:
It's their daily study, and long they've contriv'd,
To raise our provisions, and starve us alive,
So you Farmers, and Badgers, and Millers I'm sure
You all deserve hanging for starving the poor.[38]

In the early 1800s satire became a popular weapon directed at middlemen. Dealers and badgers were always shown sulking when everyone else was happy, and rejoicing when everyone else was starving. In 'The Corn-Factor's Dream' the dealer is distraught about the good harvest which is bound to ruin him and goes about praying for rain, which would rot all the grain. He has a dream that 'his friend the devil' grants his wish: a storm destroys a significant portion of the crop. His joy upon waking is quickly dispelled when his wife tells him the harsh truth:

No, love, if I must be so plain
What you took for rain was me using the pot
And the wind which you heard was in fact but a f-t.[39]

The song 'The Badger Completely Done Over' also made fun of middlemen. This badger is also miserable when everyone else is happy. The narrator is enjoying the sight of the lush wheat while walking through a rich field, but is shocked when he runs into a 'lank pallid wretch with a skance evil eye'. The miserable fellow is scowling and is so thin one can see his bones. The narrator learns that when others are well this wretch is full of 'spite, rancour, and spleen' and, vice versa, when others suffer he is in excellent health. Of course, the wretch is a badger, the wickedest of men.[40]

After 1800 poets who wrote about the countryside also came to be concerned about the ability of corn dealers to adversely affect grain prices. One of the angriest condemnations of corn dealers from the period came from the poet Samuel Jackson Pratt and is worth quoting here at length. It is a contrast to the more humorous idiom used in the songs:

Plund'rers abhorr'd! If your dark threats portend,
Another season from the poor to rend;
Ye jobbers' vile! Or by whatever name,
Ye stand recorded on the lists of shame;
Ye who ne'er labour on the teeming plain,

But like dire locusts, only eat the grain!
Ye more than savage cannibals, who feed
Upon your kind, without the savage need;
Devour in fulness, and with truant art,
Suck the warm life-blood of your country's heart;
With more than demon wiles can undermine,
Gifts of the Gods, and make creation thine;
Its fruits increase, diminish or supply,
While captive earth shall at your mercy lie;
If all a poor man's hopes must be o'erthrown,
But yet another famine of your own.[41]

The next verse continues to denounce corn dealers, inviting them to perform the work of agricultural labourers and cottagers so they can experience the same hardship, calling them 'wanton locusts', and accusing them of 'sordid gluttony', describing their 'fiend-like joy' at the sight of peasant corpses on the plain.

Songs about millers' greed were as numerous as those condemning corn dealers. The earliest example of a moral economy song after 1700 that I have been able to find is an anti-miller song called 'The Miller's Advice to his Three Sons, in Taking of Toll'. It is listed in the Bodleian Library catalogue as having been printed between 1736 and 1766. This song tells the story of a miller on his deathbed who summons his three sons to decide who should inherit the mill. He asks each how much toll he would take. The eldest replies he would take a peck out of a bushel, the middle one that he would take half of every bushel, but the youngest and smartest son says he would take the whole bushel and 'forswear the sack', before he would give up a comfortable living. The father is delighted with this answer and praises the boy for having learned the trade so well. He leaves the mill to his youngest son.[42] But we also have the song 'The Crafty Miller' from the same period, in which the miller is a hero. So the condemnation of millers was not yet a matter of course in popular songs.[43] When moral economy songs began to be reprinted in the early 1800s the character of the fraudulent miller became more deeply entrenched. Take, for example, 'The Covetous Miller', which tells of an avaricious miller living in the north of England. When one of his neighbours finds a pot of gold, the miller is jealous and unhappy out of all proportion. He begins to neglect his work and lose customers. After having a dream of finding a pot of gold under the mill, he starts digging and undermines the mill's foundations, causing it to collapse.[44] 'The True Joke, Or, the Poor Man's Complaint' categorically denies the existence of any but corrupt millers, arguing that all millers are 'honest men' until they are found out.[45]

In addition to millers, popular songs became increasingly critical of farmers. However, their use of the term 'farmers' is problematic. Before we deal with the poor's grievances against farmers, we must establish who exactly fell into this category. The identity of farmers in popular songs is not fixed. Sometimes it appears that they are a sub-category of 'the poor', sometimes they are indistinguishable from the gentry, and at yet other times they appear to be a separate group, engaged in activities like imitating the gentry or hiding corn. In some songs the farmers are the protagonists and the voice of the narrator is that of a farmer. 'The Farmer's Song. A New Song Sung At Sadler's Wells' is one such example. It juxtaposes the farmer against the 'fine folks in London'. As in many pastorals, the farmer is judged to have greater moral integrity and superior knowledge of what constitutes a good life. He is an honest patriot who honours his king and Church, but has no use for 'the great'. Significantly, he is very kind to the poor:

> I ne'er was at law in the course of my life,
> Nor injure a neighbour in daughter or wife;
> To the poor have lent money, but never took fees,
> But your fine folks at London may do as they please.[46]

The growing protest against farmers in song coincided with a distinction between small and large farmers made in other texts. 'Honest Ploughman, or 90 Years Ago' is about the farmers' transformation from peasants to capitalists. It starts off with a description of the narrator's parents: the father is labelled a 'farmer', but he relies on family labour. The mother does the dairying. A plough boy is hired until the son is old enough, at which point the son takes on the work. No other help is hired. The father and son do all the agricultural tasks. This description sounds exactly like Mick Reed's definition of the peasant or 'household producer'. In the narrative of the song, small farmers are replaced by large, affluent farmers whose wives ride fine horses, instead of milking the cows. The result is that the narrator, who has been a hard-working husbandman all his life and never had to rely on poor relief, is pauperised in his old age and has to spend his last days in a poor house.[47] The strain on small farmers is confirmed by many contemporary documents. While prosperous farmers surrounded themselves with more and more luxuries, poor farmers were becoming more and more like the labourers. In some cases, those who had been used to supervising hands now had to 'put their hands to the plow'.[48] In contrast, the new-fashioned farmers whose rise was deplored by songs like 'The Apron Farmer' engaged in large commercial enterprises, employing 'a multitude of hands'.[49]

The distinction between small and large farmers was also clearly made in pamphlets about the state of agriculture and autobiographical writings of the late eighteenth and early nineteenth centuries:

> Perhaps there is none which can bring forwards an aggregate of more excessive industry, harmless inoffensive manners, and, sorry I am to say, of dire poverty, than the little farmer. With scanty provision and excessive toil he can vie with the labourer in industry, but not like him can he in the hour of distress apply for parish relief.

According to this writer, the small farmer often had more need of aid than those who styled themselves paupers and received parish relief. These modest men were desperate to get their corn to market as quickly as possible and had to thresh it as soon as it was brought in, even if it was not ready for threshing. They had to sell quickly regardless of the price of corn, because they needed cash to pay their rent and buy provisions. They could not even think of hoarding grain.[50] Because times were difficult small farmers often lost their farms and were compelled to become landless labourers. This was the fate of William Lawrence's father, who lost his farm in Dorset. William also had to contribute to the family by working as a bird scarer for 2p a day, and later as plough boy for 6p a day.[51]

In what purports to be an autobiographical poem, the peasant poet William Hersee described the hard fate of his parents, small farmers near the town of Colchester. He described his parents as 'peasants'. A hard winter destroyed their crops and their landlord seized their small farm. The landlord, categorised as a 'yeoman', appears to have been a large farmer of a 'churlish mind'. Spoiled by wealth and luxury and incapable of compassion, he mistreated his poor tenants. The poem shows the conflict that could arise between large farmers and small farmers who were their tenants.[52]

The songs' anger against farmers was primarily directed at large farmers, who failed to observe the moral economy, making every effort to inflate the price of grain. This complaint was older than the critique of 'new-fashioned farmers'. As we have learned – thanks to the work of Andrew Charlesworth, Adrian Randall and others – conflict over grain prices was not confined to the countryside – on the contrary, towns seem to have suffered more from it.[53] However, moral economy songs dealt with both the country and the city. When the farmers were denounced in these songs, the voice or the point of view from which the song was performed was that of an artisan or agricultural labourer. It is unlikely that so many complaints against farmers would originate with farmers themselves and the only context in which the gentry are known to have written and printed popular ballads was as propaganda to prevent social disorder.[54]

There were examples of blaming farmers for high grain prices in Pepys, but songs written specifically against farmers were new. There are no ballads against farmers from the first half of the eighteenth century. The first anti-farmer broadside ballad in the Bodleian library's catalogue is 'The Farmer's Lamentation', and it could have been printed as late as 1774. The title may lead one to think that this song was written in support of farmers, but in fact, they were mocked for their exaggerated reaction to low grain prices:

> Sad dreadful cries and mourns we hear
> In market towns you know,
> The farmer stands with watery eyes,
> Crying, corn sells very low!

This song contains all the elements of anti-farmer songs discussed below: the farmers' perception of labourers' wages as a burden, their love of luxury, their daughters' pride and unwillingness to do manual labour.[55]

A very striking example of the poor's condemnation of farmers is 'A New Song Called the Farmer's Rant or Jockey's Dream'.[56] The narrator has a dream about two farmers meeting at market and complaining about being compelled to put all their corn on sale and about the restriction of their 'underhand dealing'. The farmers' indignation about the label 'engrossers' being attached to their 'brave buyers', and their plans to petition the crown to repeal anti-engrossment legislation, reinforce the impression that they are a separate interest group whose needs were a polar opposite to those of the poor, but in accord with the interests of corn dealers. These two farmers prefer to sell the grain to the factors, apparently out of sheer spite. Whatever is left over will be exported. It is a malicious and deliberate ploy to starve the poor. Farmers' unfair treatment of the poor is described with greater bitterness here than in earlier moral economy songs.

The song is quite specific about the relationship between farmers and agricultural labourers:

> For we can take down the Hind's Wages,
> And grind the proud face of the Poor;
> And he that can't hold in House keeping,
> I welcome to go to the door.
>
> Our Barn-men have far too much Wages
> When Corn give such a good price;
> They'll take less before they have nothing,
> For this is no time to be Nice.

Two labouring men overhear the farmers' conversation and use Biblical language and imagery to condemn their greed. Here the song reverts to earlier rhetoric about greed, rich versus poor and Christian charity. The solution proposed is divine justice. The concluding verse points out that many share the narrator's views but not all are brave enough to speak out. In 'New Corn Laws' the farmers are accused of hoarding grain until the price rises and of trebling the price of cheese, eggs, butter, beans and peas, whenever the price of grain goes down.[57]

Perhaps it is apparent by now that the farmer's reputation seems to have sunk lower and lower in the eyes of the poor in a manner inversely proportional to his own self-esteem. It is not only grain prices that provoked angry invectives against farmers. Their shaky relationship with their hired labourers and their growing tendency to inhabit a separate social space were a similar source of anger. Such complaints often described the eighteenth century as a better time, a time when amicable relations between farmers and agricultural servants were possible. As late as the 1780s James Paterson described his parents as having been 'old-fashioned enough' to let servants live with them and eat at the same table, treating them as part of the family.[58] They did hire seasonal help during harvest but many labourers also lived in and the table was 'greatly extended in autumn' to make room for the reapers. This is precisely what seems to have been lost in the nineteenth century, particularly in the south. In 'Cottage Pictures', the poet Samuel Jackson Pratt made this argument, reminiscing about the days

> When hind and husbandman, and lord and swain,
> Were softly blended on the social plain;
> Or in the good old hall assembled free,
> To join and share the poor man's jubilee?
> The good times were over:
> Ah change severe! The ancient customs fail,
> And loftier manners, prouder modes prevail;
> Tyrant o'er tyrans, lord o'er lords are seen,
> That once were friends and neighbours of the green.[59]

To song writers, farmers' embrace of a new lifestyle was signalled by their increasing love of luxury and abhorrence of the 'simple' lifestyle practised by Paterson's parents. This issue was largely absent from pre-1800 ballads but became central after 1800. 'Times Altered, or, the Grumbling Farmers' complains about the gentrification of the farmers, especially about the expensive tastes of their wives and their sons' imitation of squires' dress. Before, farmers ate with their servants but now they take tea separately in the parlour, even when their income places them closer to labourers than to the gentry.[60] The famous song 'When My Old Hat Was New' makes a similar point about farmers wearing velvet caps and red cloaks, so as to declare their difference from the poor.[61] Poets agreed with song writers. In 'Cottage Pictures' the rich farmers decorate their homes to resemble those of the gentry, filling their gardens with temples, naked statues of Venus and Bacchus, and fake ruins. Pratt referred to these farmers as 'farmer-gentry'.[62] At the same time as they are growing in luxury, they are neglecting their paternal duties toward the poor; as their wealth grows, their sympathy for the poor diminishes.

Disgust with the farmers' new luxurious lifestyle often fell most heavily on farmers' daughters in popular songs.[63] Songs tended to blame rich farmers' daughters for high food prices, or explore their failures to attract suitors from among the village youth. In 'The Farmer's Daughter' the young lady is dressed up in finery, but this places a barrier between her and other villagers, leading young men to avoid courting her. She no longer belongs to the village community, having alienated her neighbours through her love of luxury.[64] In the song 'Father and I', two farmers, father and son, have trouble finding wives because the farmers' widows and daughters are too refined, busying themselves with hobbies such as painting instead of picking a cabbage or making a pie.[65] In the poem *Cottage-Pictures* both farmers' wives and daughters are decked with finery and luxury. How upset, thought the poet Pratt, would the 'pale peasant' be if he could catch a glimpse of the rich farmer's daughter beautifying herself for the ball:

> To see the wealth, thy industry has made
> Fruit of thy scythe, thy sickle, and thy spade.[66]

In songs, farmers' love of luxury not only created a barrier between them and their workers, it also became a direct cause of their unjust treatment of the poor. 'The True Joke, Or, the Poor Man's Complaint' points out that the lust for an extravagant style of life leads farmers to raise the prices of provisions – they need more money to maintain their daughters' expensive tastes.

> The old farmer's daughter to her mother cry'd,
> An air-balloon bonnet you must me provide,
> And all the new fashions for me shall be found
> Tho' butter you sell at fourteen-pence per pound.
> The second young miss on her mother did frown,
> Saying, remember the fair I must have a gown,
> The mother cries daughter I won't you control,
> I'll lay double tax on the eggs and the fowl.[67]

Farmers' aspiration to be a leisured class is sometimes corroborated by other sources. It appears prosperous farmers were less willing to do the manual work they used to do in the past and needed to hire more servants for the purpose.[68]

After all this it may seem hard to believe that farmers were guilty of yet other transgressions after 1800, but such was indeed the case. Their zeal for agricultural improvement was yet another source of annoyance to the poor and their bards. In his *Autobiographical Reminiscences*, Paterson claimed his father's agricultural improvements made him popular in the parish because he hired agricultural labourers to help him. But popular songs had little praise for improvement. 'The Apron Farmer' mocks the farmer's zeal for agrarian innovation. The motivation for it is seen as deriving largely from greed – expecting 'the stubble-stumps to sprout'. Like Paterson's father, this farmer employs a lot of hands to help with improvement, but far from making him popular this breeds resentment, because he is a demanding master, and because 'We who can hardly pay our debts, / Hear him and grudge him what he gets'. Many of the improvements are geared toward creating a picturesque landscape, rather than producing more food.[69] The song alludes to hedges, posts and gates being thrown down and to burning ricks (arson), showing how deep-rooted the general dislike of his ways is among his labourers. The farmer emulates the gentry, expecting praise from them for his activities.[70] Eventually his ambition grows so large that he spends more on improvement than he can get a return for and loses the farm. The narrator sees this as just punishment for his pride and greed.

The problem of farmers imitating the gentry shows how the two classes were conflated in the mind of song writers. Not that they did not recognise them to be separate – obviously, in order for one to imitate the other the two must be distinct. However, they were seen to be of one mind in their treatment of the poor. This was new to the early nineteenth century. 'A New Song Called the Farmer's Rant or Jockey's Dream' shows that songs were often quite explicit about this when it makes the wicked farmer say to his fellow:

> We have a good Friend in a Justice,
> I know he will lend us his Aid;
> We'll take all our corn to his Store house,
> And who is to make us afraid.[71]

Often both squires and farmers were lumped together under the category of 'the rich' or 'the great'. Sometimes the words 'farmers' and 'landlords' were used, but the two were seen as collaborating to bring about the destruction of the poor.

Historians have argued that forestallers and regraters were scorned by all including the gentry and the middling sort, and that in 1800 there were still many paternalist gentlemen who adhered to customary market practices.[72] Thompson believes the Tories naturally tended to ally with the crowd prior to 1760. In *Whigs and Hunters* he shows how Justices of the Peace frequently upheld the rights of farmers and peasants against encroaching gentry. But he is more skeptical about paternalism after 1760, calling it 'theatre' and suggesting it was only used to maintain the peace.[73] More recently Douglas Hay has written about Lord Kenyon's continuing support for market regulation at the end of the eighteenth century, and Peter King has shown that local magistrates continued to support the poor's customary right to glean after the 1788 verdict which could be used by farmers to restrict it.[74] However, popular songs have little sympathy for gentlemen. This evidence supports Hay and Rogers' argument that the gentry were less willing to uphold custom after mid-century. Their avoidance of service on the bench and reluctance to uphold custom point to a decline in paternalism.[75] Perhaps by 1800 justices who upheld the moral economy were not common enough to appear in ballads. Landowners' collaboration with farmers was seen as a neglect of the sacred duty of great men to defend and protect the poor, a duty that was practised by Job and that was now being forgotten.[76] The song 'The Corn Laws' accuses farmers and landholders of only looking to increase their wealth while tradesmen were suffering:

> For farmers and Landholders all should make rich,
> If tradesmen of all kinds should die in a ditch.[77]

In 'A New Song Called the Farmer's Rant or Jockey's Dream', the Justice of the Peace is depicted as in combination with the farmers – he aids them to the extent that he allows them to hoard grain in his house.

The song 'The Corn Laws' goes further. The gentry are seen as the principal culprits behind the Corn Law of 1814. Farmers are blamed only insofar as they were compelled to raise prices to pay the high rents demanded by landlords:

> O then, said the Landholders, we must proceed
> To get a bill pass'd with all possible speed,
> For we are determin'd our rents to uphold,
> As we must ride in our chariots of gold.

The tradesmen's numerous petitions against the new Corn Law meet with no response because the statesmen and landholders have made a pact to starve them:

For statesmen and landholders all did agree,
To starve the poor tradesman, you plainly may see;
Yet without such people they never could stand,
[As] that they will find, when they're forc'd from this land.[78]

The song appeals to JPs to uphold the old laws that punish forestallers, but it has little faith that the petitions of the poor would be heeded. The judges have failed to pay attention to petitions for higher wages, so why should they honour petitions to reinstate forestalling laws?

It is not many years since petitions were sent,
From all kinds of tradesmen, their wages to stent,
So that they might live by the sweat of their brow;
But these you rejected, and why not this too?

The critique of the gentry and the aristocracy could go beyond faulting them with the responsibility for high grain prices. In 'A Man's a Man for A'That', which appeared in numerous broadsides, Burns labels the whole aristocracy as dishonest and contrasts this with the poor man's honesty:

The honest man, tho' e'er sae poor,
Is king o'men for a'that.

Ye see yon birkie, ca'd a lord,
Wha struts, and stres, and a'that;
Tho' hundreds worship at his word,
He's but a coo for a'that,
The man of independent mind,
He looks and laughs at a'that.

A prince can mak a belted knight,
A marquis, duke, and a'that;
But an honest man's aboon his might,
Guide faith he mauna fa' that!
The dignities, and a'that,
The itch o'sense, and pride o'worth,
Are higher ranks than a'that.[79]

The poor man here is said to have an 'independent' mind, 'sense' and 'pride of worth'. These qualities, not titles, are what make him 'king of men'. The song 'The Plough Boy' provides further evidence of the poor's dislike of the gentry. It tells the story of 'a flaxen headed cow boy' who climbs the social ranks by first becoming 'a saucy footman' to a wealthy gentleman, then steward, member of parliament, and finally a peer. His corruption becomes progressively more severe. He attains the position of peer by accepting bribes and selling his votes. 'And when I'm tir'd on my legs / Then I'll sit down a peer', says he, perhaps an allusion to the inefficiency of the House of Lords. Once he is a peer, he believes no one would remember the little plough boy 'That whistled o'er the lee'. The plough boy is a symbol of goodness and innocence or honest poverty, while the peer, his opposite, is a symbol of corruption.[80]

Up to this point I may have presented a somewhat one-sided picture of the representation of farmers and gentry in popular songs. Even as late as the nineteenth century songs were still printed about farmers and landlords who were kind and generous to their inferiors. In 'The Happy Farmer' we meet a wealthy farmer who appears not to work in the fields but only to supervise the work of his labourers, and who is proud of his prosperity, delighting in the ripe corn, flocks and golden fruits which exude health and pleasure. However, he shares his wealth with his labourers, for whom he has a paternal concern. He always visits them at noon to treat them with home-brewed ale and listen to their jokes and tales.[81] The same type is found in 'The Golden Farmer'. Here the farmer's interest in landscaping and improvement is not seen as a problem because he is so generous:

> While my farm thus cuts a dash, too,
> Poor folks daily labouring on't,
> Who plough, sow, reap, and thrash, too,
> I'll be thrashed if they shall want.

The farmer feels a responsibility to share his treasures with the poor. It is curious here that despite all this wealth the farmer still distinguishes himself from 'greater' and richer folks and speaks of his abode as 'the cot'.[82] James Bruce's poem 'The Farmer' advises farmers about proper behaviour. They must be good to their industrious labourers:

> Just at the term, pay rent or feu,
> An' sevants' fees, – gi'e a' their due:
> But to the lads wha're best at pleugh,
>   Gi'e something mair;
> Wi' half-a-crown or pickle woo'
>   Reward their care.[83]

Good farmers must look after the whole village as well as their labourers, aiding widows, orphans, the old and the sick, as well as those fallen on hard times. Ian Dyck has argued that in the south this ideal was no longer a reality in the nineteenth century and that such songs were no longer popular even if they were occasionally printed. Indeed, songs about good farmers are much less numerous than critical songs. However, the fact that at least in the early 1800s they were still circulated suggests that the market for them wasn't completely extinguished.[84] Two of the four nineteenth-century songs about good farmers I have referred to were printed in Scotland. There they may have had a greater relevance, because the survival of service in husbandry until 1815 may have lent force to the ideal of the generous, paternalistic farmer for longer.[85]

Songs about generous landlords were even more rare than songs about generous farmers both in the eighteenth and nineteenth centuries. This was in part because ballads were a popular form of expression. In the Pepys collection a good landlord is the Bountiful Knight of Somersetshire, who cares about the poor so much that his last advice to his son as he lies on his death bed is to take care of them.[86] A prose tale from 1746 depicted a magistrate, who distributes the perquisites from his office among fifteen poor villagers about to leave their homes to look for subsistence elsewhere, enabling them to return home and till their land.[87] In nineteenth-century songs the ideal of the pater-nalistic landlord could occasionally be found side by side with angry denuncia-tions of the gentry, as a kind of afterthought. The song 'The New Corn Laws' begins with pessimism about the likelihood of justices paying attention to the petitions of the poor, but then goes on to praise Lord Archibald, who, unlike his peers, always looks out for the good of his country.[88] So the paternalistic ideal did exist but it was rarely invoked in song.

The depiction of farmers' anger at both the gentry and the poor

Here we must return to the problem of how songs served as a site of social conflict. We have seen that a certain genre of popular song described the conflict between labourers or tradesmen and farmers. A different group of songs spoke about the tensions between farmers and gentry or tenant and landlord. Because of the multiple definitions of the term 'farmer', popular songs can be found to support both contentions: that farmers worked with the gentry against the poor, and that farmers were in conflict with the gentry. This must have depended on the kind of farmer song writers had in mind. What cannot be found in songs, though it obviously happened in reality, are examples of farmers or the gentry defending the poor against each other. There was a tradition of confrontation between landlords and tenants that dated as far back as the Pepys ballads and that concerned the relationship between farmers and gentry. 'The Poor Man's Distress & Tryal, Or, Fortune Favours after her Frowns' is about this relationship.[89] The ballad is a narrative about a wicked landlord who refuses to defer the rent for his poor tenant whose wife has just died. When the poor tenant inherits land from his brother, the landlord apologises and offers his friendship, but the tenant proudly rejects it. The landlord lacks compassion and is thus condemned by the ballad. It is noteworthy that the landless tenant could not make ends meet in the country, but as he moves to London he 'live[s] content'. When he inherits land, he returns to the country. There is an implication here that only those with land could be happy in the country. In contrast to nineteenth-century anti-gentry songs, not all landlords are denounced, only the uncharitable ones, who do not fulfill their obligations to their tenants. The tenant in this ballad is not referred to as 'the farmer', even though he lives off the land, but is rather called 'the poor man'. So this is a small rather than a large farmer.

After Pepys we have a hiatus again until the period 1736–66 when we find 'The Farmer', a song of complaint about the hard life of farmers. As in Pepys, the farmers in this song are clearly small farmers who employed some labour, but also worked in the fields themselves:

> There's hunting and hawking is gentlemens game,
> While we poor farmers must toil on the plain,
> Thro' cold wind, and rain, we must toil all the day.
> We slave like negroes, and nothing dare say.

The narrator further complains that the law favours gentry over farmers:

> If any poor Farmer is forced by law,
> Then on the pursuit of his gold he must draw,
> Without that companion his case is not heard,
> His suit is cast out, and thrown overboard.
> The lawyers and attornies are full of policy,
> If they're not brib'd they'll never comply.[90]

Other ballads from the Douce collection depict the relationship between tenant and landlord as a continuous contest of wits. 'The Crafty Miller' is about the conflict between a miller and his landlord. The 'poor, honest' miller is the hero of the story. Having fallen on hard times, the miller is unable to pay rent for two years, but because of his attractive wife the landlord makes him the following proposition: he will let the miller keep the mill if he lets the landlord have his wife. The miller obtains a written deed to the mill and makes a verbal agreement about the wife, asking if they could pretend the landlord has received a she-ass for the mill, so that the neighbours would not get suspicious. The landlord agrees with predictable results: he ends up in bed with the she-ass and the miller gets to keep the mill.[91] A similar story about a clever subordinate tricking the landlord is told in the ballad 'The Case is Alter'd' where the squire's bull gores Hodge's cow (Hodge is a small farmer). The squire happens also to be the local justice. Hodge tricks him by saying it was the squire's cow that has been killed by Hodge's bull. The squire wants to use his position as justice to wreak vengeance upon Hodge, until he finds out what really happened. Then he sends Hodge away hastily, promising to think about the case.[92] Like 'The Farmer', this song exposes the flaws of the legal system.

Tension between farmers and gentry continued in the late eighteenth century. In his autobiography William Johnston described how in 1785 agricultural improvement led the local squire to take away his father's farm in Petershead, Scotland. The family was allowed to reside there until 1792, when they were ordered to leave. Johnston's father refused, saying he would die on his own farm, as indeed he did that same year. Johnston concluded that 'we should not be oppressive to our poorer neighbours nor use the power we have over them for their injury. Both rich and poor must leave all they have in this world and be no more seen.'[93] Agricultural improvement occasioned disputes between farmers and landlords.[94] This was perhaps due to what Robert Allen has called 'the landlords' agricultural revolution', which was happening throughout the eighteenth century. In Scotland a very heated agricultural revolution was taking place by 1800. Although it did not affect farmer–labour relations until after 1815, the Scottish agricultural revolution appears to have caused considerable tension between tenants and landlords.[95]

Nineteenth-century popular songs echoed some of the tensions described in Johnston's autobiography. Songs in which a farmer voices a complaint about a landlord were far fewer than labourers' complaints about farmers, but they did exist. While they may have tried to imitate the gentry, farmers (or at least, farmers as depicted by song writers) clearly saw themselves as a group whose interests were different from and often opposite to those of the gentry. The numerous songs celebrating the farmer's occupation often contrasted his lifestyle with that of the landlord, to show how superior the former was to the latter. 'The Farmer's Song. A New Song Sung at Sadler's Wells' was of this kind. The narrator, a farmer, places himself on the side of the poor, against the gentry. He prides himself on his independence and professes not to care about fine folks in London. He is not one of the gentry (but nor is he of the poor, though he claims to be constantly helping them).[96]

Unease about one's dependence on the landlord and fear of being unable to pay the rent increasingly found their way into farmers' complaints. 'The Muirland Farmer' celebrates the end of the harvest because the profit made from it would ensure the farmer's continuing independence from the laird, to whom he owes rent.[97] 'The Farmer's Wish' shows that while the farmers and landlords might drink together in good times, farmers lived in fear of landowners' lack of charity when grain prices were low.[98]

Concerns about the rent could escalate into deeper tension. The song 'A New Song on the Farmer's Glory' emphasises the landlords' dependence on farmers' labour for survival, making the landlord's callousness in demanding the rent all the more appalling:

> The Farmers by their Landlords are slighted,
> And for their Labour thus requited:
> But if they did not occupy their Land,
> The Landlords would be at a stand.[99]

And, indeed, after 1800 tenant farmers had ample reason to complain about landlords. Rents were rising steadily. One contemporary observer wrote about a Nottinghamshire landlord, who in the year 1810 forced all his tenants to bring in their leases before they expired and take them out again at a higher rent. If they refused he threatened not to renew the lease when it expired:

> Now reader, laying aside prejudice and partiality, what would be the epithets and character, applied to a Poor Man acting in the same way? Would he not have to sustain the appellations of wretch, rascal, scoundrel, and villain; and would he not merit such names?[100]

In 'New Corn Laws', both the farmers and the landlords make life hard for tradesmen but they also fight each other. The farmers want to shut down the ports to prevent the importing of grain and increase its price, unless landlords agree to lower their rents. The landlords refuse, forcing farmers to increase the price of grain.[101]

So far our discussion may have given the impression that all the complaining in the late eighteenth century was done by the 'lower' orders against their superiors. In fact, farmers and improving landlords complained about their dependants quite as much. I have not found this point of view in Pepys or during the early eighteenth century. It was new to songs in the second half of the eighteenth century. Again, the earliest ballad containing it is from the Douce collection and dates to 1736–66. Before this time one encounters the Hodge stereotype, a satire on the peasantry, but not the kind of anger at the poor we see in later material.

Verse was not the vehicle most often used by farmers to complain about labourers – they preferred the agricultural treatise or polemical pamphlet where they pointed out that the poor were saucy and disrespectful and used all extra wages to buy luxuries, instead of saving (thus wages should not be increased). Also farmers often argued it was wrong to give land to agricultural labourers, because they would become even more insolent when given a little independence. An anonymous writer who styled himself 'One who pities the oppressed' identified the oppressed as farmers, oppressed by both landlords and insubordinate labour. The farmers suffered intensely due to a too rapid expansion in cultivation, high taxes and the burden of maintaining the poor.[102] He also complained about the bad character of the peasantry, particularly their lack of economic independence. Apparently they were no longer ashamed of getting poor relief, as decent persons should be, but considered it their due. This had baneful effects on their morals:

> To say nothing of the effects of this feeling upon their habits of industry and economy; to pass over this fatal influence on their character, and especially on their spirit of independence; only observe how it removes all check upon imprudent marriages, and tends to multiply the number of people beyond the means of subsistence – that is, to multiply the numbers of the poor.[103]

The evidence for farmers' grievances against the poor in songs is not always direct. Anti-farmer songs often depicted farmers as hating the poor. The song we discussed above, 'A New Song Called the Farmer's Rant', shows the farmers refusing to lower grain prices because 'The poor is growing so spiteful / I think they deserve none at all'. These farmers are also upset about grain riots: the 'damned mobs' who 'laugh them to scorn' and seize their goods are said to belong in jail. This is followed by a verse about refusing charity to beggars and instructing wives and daughters to drive them away from the door: they should go back to their parish or be placed in a workhouse.[104]

An earlier song, which I have discussed in connection with farmers' animosity toward the gentry, directly voices farmers' concerns about agricultural labourers. Although these farmers work in the fields, they also employ farm servants. Having to pay wages to the latter makes their life harder. In a kind of reversal of the association of farmers with luxury, the song condemns the pride and luxury of servant girls, though it is not clear whether this refers to servants working for the farmers or servants working for the London rich. The song also complains that the poor were now drinking tea. All of these luxuries make it obvious 'the poor farmers have all to maintain'.[105] After 1800, while songs in which the small farmer was a protagonist continued to be printed, no song ever portrayed a farmer preoccupied with financial gain or engaged in large-scale agricultural enterprise in a positive light.

The lack of representations of the gentry's point of view

The voice of the third rural social category, the gentry, is missing from this discussion because I have found no popular songs that assume this point of view.[106] Of course, writers on agriculture frequently took the side of the gentry. Writers on Wales seem particularly sympathetic to them. Ben Heath Malkin, for instance, saw agricultural improvement in Wales, a necessary and positive activity, as the prerogative of the gentry, especially those of a persevering character, willing 'to conquer the prejudices of the natives'.[107] The Rev. J. Evans had a very similar position: he was critical of backward Welsh farmers who failed to improve. For Evans, the enlightened practitioners of agriculture were the proprietors of estates who improved the land and took on a huge tax burden to prevent their tenants from becoming paupers.[108] Many were the reasons the reverend was unhappy with the farmers. They were stubborn, prejudiced and unwilling to deviate even slightly from the customs of their forefathers. They were poorly educated, poorly read and unenlightened. They were hostile to all improvements because their narrow-mindedness rendered them incapable of making intelligent decisions.[109] These must have been small subsistence farmers, because Evans thought they were too similar to peasants to be worthy of the name of 'an industrious and respectable yeomanry', whom Evans considered to be the 'pride and sinews of a country'.[110]

In his introduction to his work the poet Thomas Maude explained why the pastoral genre was no longer appropriate to depicting the countryside, but, unlike most rural poets appearing in this book, his explanation involved not the growing luxury and oppression of landlords over peasants, but the growing vice of the peasantry:

> If we bring the innocence, knowledge, or happiness of the peasantry to the measuring line of truth, we shall but too frequently find that they differ little from depravity, ignorance, and wretchedness; at least some qualities contrary to what the poets usually draw, too often mingle themselves in the pompously figured scene.

Maude then spoke of a golden age when shepherds were bards, which had been replaced by vice and luxury.[111]

Thus writers who spoke for the gentry expressed no less hostility toward their inferiors than the writers of popular songs did toward wealthy farmers and cruel landlords. This is all I will say about the gentry's complaints about farmers and the poor here. Chapter 6 deals with the elite's concerns in more detail. To a large degree, Hannah More represented the voice of the conservative gentry. She never identified with farmers, whom she saw as beneath her.

Her attitudes toward the poor were in many respects the attitudes of a large segment of the gentry and her complaints were shared by her class.

Popular songs become increasingly critical over time

In the nineteenth century songs went beyond the moral economy and farmer–labourer relations to demand the punishment of 'oppressors' and justice for everyone. In 'The Corn Laws', after the narrator has given up hope because the Prince Regent had approved the Corn Law bill, he invokes divine vengeance. God could punish oppressors in this world:

He many a time has oppressors brought low,
For proof you may look into Judges, and know
How Sisera and Eglon and many beside,
By him were destroyed for oppression and pride.

Now let us request him to grant us relief,
From all our oppressions, our sorrows and grief,
For this he has promis'd, and will not deny,
But give to his people who on him rely.[112]

The famous late eighteenth-century song by Burns, 'A Man's a Man for A' That', is even more violent in its language. It contains an angry condemnation of an entire social order and its way of life:

For a'that, and a'that
Our toils obscure, and a'that,
The rank is but the guinea's stamp,
The man's the gowd for a'that.
What tho's on hamely far we dine,
Wear hoddin grey, and a'that:
Gie fools their silks, and knaves their wine,
A man's a man for a'that.

The song is very striking in concluding with a utopian hope for a new world where there will be no inequality:

Then let us pray that come it may,
As come it will for a'that,
That sense and worth, 'er a' the earth,
May bear the gree, and a'that.
For a'that, and a'that,
It's comin yet for a'that,
That man to man, the warld o'er,
Shall brothers be for a'that.[113]

These were highly unusual sentiments. Most songs that criticised the rich never went so far as to suggest reforming the social order. Nevertheless, these songs were more radical than their post-Restoration seventeenth-century ancestors.

It would be well if we could access the oral life of popular ballads or find evidence of how each of them was interpreted by people from different walks of life, or if we could find more detailed and persuasive reasons as to why printers produced so few broadside ballads in the first half of the eighteenth century. Our evidence is imperfect. But with the evidence we have, we can still draw some useful conclusions. Ballads of social protest were an old art form. Moral economy songs in particular date at least to the seventeenth century. Printers stopped printing these songs in the early decades of the eighteenth century, but then slowly brought them back.[114] To them were added new anti-farmer songs, distinguishing between small and large farmers and empha-sising farmers' love of luxury and fancy dress, as well as anti-gentry songs. These new songs resembled the old ones in certain ways, but they were more outspoken. In contrast, songs praising good farmers and landlords appeared quite rarely at the end of the eighteenth century. Perhaps the audience saw them as old-fashioned and perhaps they no longer reflected popular senti-ments about paternalism. Critical ballads were circulated within a context of general animosity among the different ranks in the countryside. Farmers were unhappy with landlords and with labourers, landlords had grievances against farmers and the poor. While excluding the voice of the gentry, ballads provided a space in which social relations among small farmers, large farmers, labourers and gentry could be negotiated. Thus songs of protest exhibit considerable complexity. However, the amount of ballads expressing the point of view of labour dwarfed those written from other points of view. That is, the voice of agricultural labourers and tradesmen dominated critical popular songs.

These ballads were subject to convention, like all other songs. The new-fashioned farmer and the spoiled farmer's daughter became new stock characters at the end of the eighteenth century. Ballads alone cannot tell us whether social relations deteriorated. However, when ballads are compared to other sources from the time, common concerns and a common language can be identified. This overlap can make us feel more confident about our under-standing of both ballads and the social history of the late eighteenth century.

Notes

1 Roger Wells, 'The Development of the English Rural Proletariat, 1700–1850', in Mick Reed and Roger Wells, eds, *Class, Conflict and Protest in the English Country-side, 1700–1880* (London: Frank Cass, 1990), 32. This view is shared by E. P. Thompson, 'The Patricians and the Plebs', in *Customs in Common* (New York: The New Press, 1993), 40.

2 On growing poverty and discontent among agricultural labourers see K. D. M. Snell, *Annals of the Labouring Poor: Social Change and Agrarian England 1660–1900* (Cambridge: Cambridge University Press, 1985), 2. Thompson, 'The Patricians and the Plebs', 38. Thompson's argument is that agricultural labourers had a higher standard of living in the first half of the eighteenth century because they had more customary rights which gave them some degree of independence from the wage.

3 George R. Boyer, *An Economic History of the English Poor Law 1750–1850* (Cambridge: Cambridge University Press, 1990), 45–6. See also M. J. Daunton, *Progress and Poverty: An Economic and Social History of Britain, 1700–1850* (Oxford and New York: Oxford University Press), 427, 434. Daunton's data suggests wages increased much slower than prices.

4 Roger Wells, *Wretched Faces: Famine in Wartime England 1793–1801* (Gloucester: Alan Sutton, 1988), 36–9. See also Appendix 5, which shows the proportion of agricultural labourers' wages spent on grain.

5 On the sharp rise in bread prices between 1794 and 1801 as well as the coercive behaviour of parish authorities see Wells, 'The Development of the English Rural Proletariat, 1700–1850', 35.

6 For the negative impact of enclosure in the south of England see J. L. and Barbara Hammond, *The Village Labourer, 1760–1832: A Study in the Government of England before the Reform Bill* (1911; reprinted London: Longman's, Green, 1980), 97; E. P. Thompson, *The Making of the English Working Class*, 237–43; Jane Humphries, 'Enclosures, Common Rights, and Women: The Proletarianization of Families in the Late Eighteenth and Early Nineteenth Centuries', *Journal of Economic History* 1 (1990): 18–21; J. M. Neeson, *Commoners: Common Right, Enclosure and Social Change in England, 1700–1820* (Cambridge: Cambridge University Press, 1993), 5–6. This issue will be dealt with more extensively in chapter 3.

7 William Harris, *On the Present Distress of the Country and Suitable Remedies* (London, 1816), 58–9.

8 George Dyer, *The Complaints of the Poor People of England* (London, 1793; reprinted Oxford and New York: Woodstock Books, 1990), 2.

9 Dyer, *The Complaints of the Poor People of England* (1793), 188.

10 On the economic hardship faced by rural industrial labour during the second half of the eighteenth century, see Franklin F. Mendels, 'Proto-Industrialization: The First Phase of the Industrialization Process', *Journal of Economic History* 32, no.1 (1972): 242–3. Mendels argues the real wages of rural industrial workers were at the bottom of the social scale.

11 An example of a poem about growing poverty is Samuel Jackson Pratt, 'Bread; Or the Poor, Part I', in *Cottage-Pictures; Or, the Poor: A Poem, With Notes and*

Illustrations (London, 1803), 18–19: 'The social level of the land is gone, / Alike the farm and farmers are o'ergrown; / While the spurn'd cottagers and cottage, whirl'd / With all their claims, are into chaos hurl'd. / No morning carol now regales the ear, / And nought at eve but sounds of grief you hear; / And nought but haggard shapes and forms you see, / And spectres thin of hollow penury.' For a song about difficult economic conditions see 'The Request of the Poor' (London: J. Pitts, 1819–1844), Bodleian Library. The song talks about unemployment, the parish vestry's stinginess and contempt for the poor, its discrimination against those who are young and single, and the high price of meat.

12 This is not a precise date. The first songs of rural complaint I have found in the eighteenth century come from the Douce collection and could have been printed anywhere between 1736 and 1766.

13 In elite poetry we see a change from idealized Augustan pastoral to Wordsworthian depictions of wandering vagrants. See Gary Harrison, *Wordsworth's Vagrant Muse: Poetry, Poverty and Power* (Detroit: Wayne State University Press, 1994), 46–9.

14 Mick Reed uses the term 'household producer' to apply to the peasantry. He criticizes the inadequacy of the tripartite model of agricultural labourers, farmers and landowners because it leaves out peasants. See his 'Class and Conflict in Rural England: Some Reflections on a Debate', in Reed and Wells, eds, *Class, Conflict and Protest in the English Countryside*, 9–10.

15 See Murray G. H. Pittock, *Poetry and Jacobite Politics in Eighteenth-Century Britain and Ireland* (Cambridge: Cambridge University Press, 1994), 34–5.

16 Len Smith, *The Carpet Weaver's Lament: Songs and Ballads of Kidderminster in the Industrial Revolution* (Kidderminster: Kenneth Tomkinson, 1979), 38, 42.

17 Figures are difficult to come up with and they may not be useful in this instance. Up to 1770 critical songs are rare, but after 1770 one runs into them all the time. The proportion of critical to non-critical songs is something like one to ten. There is a similar development in poetry about the countryside. After 1800 there are many more poems critical of rural social and economic conditions.

18 Ian Dyck, *William Cobbett and Rural Popular Culture* (Cambridge: Cambridge University Press, 1992), 9.

19 Dyck, *William Cobbett and Rural Popular Culture*, 56.

20 Dyck, *William Cobbett and Rural Popular Culture*, 53.

21 Dyck, *William Cobbett and Rural Popular Culture*, 55.

22 Dyck, *William Cobbett and Rural Popular Culture*, 56–8.

23 In his study of London crowds, George Rude observed that an animosity toward the rich was a characteristic that riots throughout the eighteenth century had in common, regardless of the particular issue that sparked them. Being seen as belonging to the affluent class was sufficient reason for being harassed by the crowd on many occasions. George Rude, *Hanoverian London 1714–1808* (London: Secker & Warburg, 1971), 226–7. For the tradition of protest in song see Roy Palmer, Forward to *The Sound of History: Songs and Social Comment* (Oxford: Oxford University Press, 1932).

24 'The Poor Folks Complaint' (1675), *The Pepys Ballads*, ed. Hyder Edward Rollins,

Vol. 3 (Cambridge, MA, 1930). See also 'The Poor Peoples Complaint of the Unconscionable Brokers and Talley-Men' (c.1680) in *The Pepys Ballads*, Vol. 3.

25 'An Excellent New Ballad, Giving a Full and True Relation How a Noble Lord Was Robb'd of his Birth-day Cloaths' (1713), B.L., Johnson Ballads, fol. 342.

26 'The Pope's Pedigree: Or, the Twining of the Wheel Band, Shewing the Rise and First Pedigrees of Mortals Inhabiting beneath the Moon' (Northampton: William Dicey, 1719–57), B.L., Johnson Ballads, fol. 342.

27 Pepys relied both on broadsides of his own time and on earlier ballad collections. Some of the moral economy songs in his collection may be as old as the sixteenth century, although most were probably printed closer to his own time. The idea of the moral economy certainly predates Pepys, as Buchanan Sharp has shown in his 'The Food Riots of 1347 and the Medieval Moral Economy', in Adrian Randall and Andrew Charlesworth, eds, *Moral Economy and Popular Protest* (Hampshire and London: Macmillan Press, 2000), 33–55.

28 'The Present State of England: Containing the Poor Man's Complaint in a Land of Plenty, Occasioned by the Many Abuses Offer'd by the Ingrossers of Corn, and Likewise Brandy-Stillers, which Makes a Scarcity in a Time of Plenty' (1688) *The Pepys Ballads*, Vol. 4.

29 'The Poor Folks Complaint' (1675).

30 'The Miller's Advice to his Three Sons, in Taking of Toll' (London: W. and C. Dicey, 1736–63), Bodleian Library, Harding B 5(7).

31 E. P. Thompson, *Whigs and Hunters: The Origins of the Black Act* (New York: Pantheon Books, 1975).

32 Andy Wood, *Riot, Rebellion and Popular Politics in Early Modern England* (Basingstoke and New York: Palgrave, 2002), 191. See also Robert W. Malcolmson, '"A Set of Ungovernable People." The Kingswood Colliers in the Eighteenth Century', in John Brewer and John Styles, eds, *An Ungovernable People: The English and their Law in the Seventeenth and Eighteenth Centuries* (New Brunswick, NJ: Rutgers University Press, 1980), 87, 89 for the independence and rebelliousness of the coal miners of Kingswood Chase between 1720 and 1750. Andrew Charlesworth, ed., *An Atlas of Rural Protest in Britain 1548–1900* (London and Canberra: Croom Helm, 1983), 44 describes land and deer park protest in forest areas between 1702 and 1739.

33 Andy Wood, *The Politics of Social Conflict: The Peak Country, 1520–1770* (Cambridge: Cambridge University Press, 1999), 314–15.

34 Donna Landry, *The Muses of Resistance: Labouring-Class Women's Poetry in Britain, 1739–1796* (Cambridge: Cambridge University Press, 1990), 24.

35 We need to bear in mind that the number of all publications increased dramatically after 1800. Nevertheless, printers' decisions to produce and circulate certain kinds of material have significance.

36 Adrian Randall, Andrew Charlesworth, Richard Sheldon and David Walsh, 'Markets, Market Culture and Popular Protest in Eighteenth-Century Britain and Ireland', in Adrian Randall and Andrew Charlesworth, eds, *Markets, Market Culture and Popular Protest in Eighteenth-Century Britain and Ireland* (Liverpool: Liverpool University Press, 1996), 10.

37 See Peter King, 'Edward Thompson's Contribution to Eighteenth-Century Studies: The Patrician Plebeian Model Re-Examined', *Social History* 21, no. 2 (1996): 226; Paul Langford, *A Polite and Commercial People: England 1727–1783* (Oxford: Clarendon Press, 1989), 442–7.

38 'Forestalling Done Over', *A Garland of New Songs* (Newcastle upon Tyne: J. Marshall, 1801–c.1824), B.L., Shelfmark 11621.a.2. The Bodleian Library has a version of the song dated 1810–31. The mention of Napoleon suggests that it must indeed come from this period. Another song condemning millers and farmers for making a profit at the expense of the poor is 'A Touch on the Times', *The Bold Sailor* (Glasgow: J. & M. Robertson, 1800), B.L., Shelfmark 11621.b.13: 'The first is the Farmer that soweth the corn, / I'm sure they're as big rogues as ever was born. / They are not content with their going on, / Tho' the grain turns out nine hundred to one. / The next is the miller that grinds in the mill / He's sure to take care his own bags to fill; / The Devil's so busy at taking his toll, / First with his dish and then with his bowl.' The song also criticizes bakers and gardeners for keeping prices high.

39 'The Corn-Factor's Dream. A True Story' (Newcastle: H. Watson, 1817), B.L., Shelfmark 11621.i.2,vol.ii. For criticism of corn dealers buying the grain before it leaves the field see Pratt, *Cottage-Pictures* (1803), 55.

40 'For experience has prov'd in the days of distress, / That even the Mealman and Cadger, / To him when compar'd, might their innocence bless, / And thank God they were Saints – to a Badger!': 'The Badger Completely done Over, an Extemporary Dash of the Pen, in the Year 1801', *Scripscrapologiea; or, Collins's Doggerel Dish of all Sorts. Consisting of Songs Adapted to Familiar Tunes* (Birmingham: Published by the Author, Printed by M. Swinney, 1804), B.L., Shelfmark 11633.aaa.10.

41 Pratt, *Cottage-Pictures* (1803), 72.

42 'The Miller's Advice to his Three Sons, in Taking of Toll', (1736–63): 'Thou art my Boy, the old Man said, / For thou hast learned thy Trade, / This Mill to thee I'll give, he cry'd, / And then clos'd up his Eyes, and dy'd.'

43 'The Crafty Miller, or, Mistaken Batchelor' (London: W. and C. Dicey, 1736–63), Bodleian Library, Douce Ballads 3(13b).

44 'The Covetous Miller', *The Covetous Miller with Other Tales* (London: Dean and Munday, n.d.), L.C. Folio.79.rb.s.435. The printers Dean and Munday were in business between the years 1811 and 1841.

45 'The True Joke, Or, the Poor Man's Complaint', *The True Lovers' Garland; Consisting of Three Good Songs* (Warrington, W. Eyres, n.d.), L.C. 2837.

46 'The Farmer's Song. A New Song Sung at Sadler's Wells' (n.p., n.d.), B.L., Shelfmark HS.74.11250. See also 'The Muirland Farmer' (n.p., n.d), B.L., Shelfmark 11621.c.10, another song that has a protagonist who is a farmer.

47 'Honest Ploughman, or 90 Years Ago' (n.p., n.d.), B.L., Shelfmark HS 74 1250.

48 Harris, *On the Present Distress of the Country* (1816), 5.

49 'The Apron Farmer' (Birmingham: Grafton and Reddell, n.d.), B.L., Shelfmark 992.g.11.

50 Anon., *An Address to the Good Sense and Candour of the People* (1800), 38.

51 William Lawrence, *The Autobiography of Sergeant William Lawrence, A Hero of the Peninsular and Waterloo Campaigns* (London, 1886). Working as a bird scarer was a common experience for children in the countryside. See also M. K. Ashby, *Joseph Ashby of Tysoe 1859–1919: A Study of English Village Life* (Cambridge: Cambridge University Press, 1961), 24.

52 William Hersee, 'A Cottage Picture. Drawn from Life', in *Poems, Rural and Domestic* (Colchester, 1810), 29.

53 John Stevenson has argued that grain riots happened mostly in ports, market towns and transhipment points, but mobs could move from rural districts to market towns and vice versa. John Stevenson, *Popular Disturbances in England, 1700–1832*, second edition (London and New York: Longman, 1992), 124.

54 See chapter 6.

55 'The Farmer's Lamentation' (Newcastle: Angus, 1774–1825), Bodleian Library, Harding B 25(629).

56 'A New Song Called the Farmer's Rant or Jockey's Dream Shewing the Pride and Ambition of the Farmers and Factors, and the Distressed and Deplorable Condition of the Poor at this Day' (Newcastle, 1800), L.C. 2851.

57 'The Corn Laws – A Song. Tune: The Factor's Garland' (Glasgow: R. Hutchinson, 1815–30), L.C. 2842.

58 James Paterson, *Autobiographical Reminiscences* (Glasgow, 1871), 5. On the decline of the custom of Harvest Home, where farmers and labourers ate supper at the same table, see David H. Morgan, *Harvesters and Harvesting 1840–1900. A Study of the Rural Proletariat* (London & Canberra: Croom Helm, 1982), 170–4. Morgan argues the custom began to decline in England in the early nineteenth century. It was replaced by the Harvest Festival, which was a public celebration that maintained the separation between farmers and labourers. Morgan connects this cultural shift to the loss of community and the deterioration of rural social relations. The Harvest Home custom may have persisted longer in the north.

59 Pratt, *Cottage-Pictures* (1803), 36–7.

60 'Times Altered or, the Grumbling Farmer' (London: S. Paul, n.d.), B.L., Shelf-mark 1876.l.41. There is a version by J. Catnach which the Bodleian library lists as 1813–38.

61 *Luckidad's Garland; Or, When my Old Hat was New* (n.p., n.d.), L.C. 2846. There is a version in the Bodleian Library from 1820–24 printed by W. Armstrong in Liverpool, Harding B 28 (56). The song also talks about how small subsistence farmers had been transformed to large capitalist ones.

62 Pratt, *Cottage-Pictures* (1803), 42. An example of such a song is 'The New-Fashioned Farmer' (J. Catnach, 1803–38), B.L., Shelfmark 1876.l.41.

63 For a discussion of farmers' daughters see also Dyck, *William Cobbett and Rural Popular Culture*, 62.

64 'The Farmer's Daughter', *A Garland of New Songs* (Newcastle upon Tyne: J. Marshall, 1810–31), B.L., Shelfmark 11621.a.2.

65 'Father and I' (London: J. Pitts, 1819–44), L.C. Folio.79.rb.m.168.

66 Pratt, *Cottage-Pictures* (1803), 42.

67 'The True Joke, Or the Poor Man's Complaint', *The True Lovers' Garland; Consisting of Three Good Songs* (Warrington, W. Eyres, n.d.), L.C. 2837.

68 *The Beggar's Complaint, Against Rack-Rent Landlords, Corn Factors, Great Farmers, Monopolizers, Paper Money Makers, and War, and Many Other Oppressions, by One Who Pities the Oppressed* (Sheffield, 1812), 58.

69 'The farmer makes / Fine grottos, walks, and water-falls; / Improves the garden, plants and gilds; / Stuccos, white-washes, paints and gilds; / And when the whole is quite compleat, / Mounts hills to view his 'Country-seat'; / On tiptoe to the very top, / Forgets he ever kept a Shop.': 'The Apron Farmer' (Birmingham: Grafton and Reddell, n.d.), B.L., Shelfmark 992.g.11.

70 'Expects the king of compliments, / A medal from a club of gents!': 'The Apron Farmer'.

71 'A New Song Called the Farmer's Rant or Jockey's Dream' (Newcastle, 1800), L.C. 2851.

72 Randall, Charlesworth, Sheldon, and Walsh, 'Markets, Market Culture and Popular Protest in Eighteenth-Century Britain and Ireland', 16.

73 Thompson, 'The Patricians and the Plebs', 46, 80.

74 Douglas Hay, 'The State and the Market in 1800: Lord Kenyon and Mr Waddington', *Past & Present* 162 (1999): 101–62; Peter King, 'Gleaners, Farmers and the Failure of Legal Sanctions in England 1750–1850', *Past & Present* 125 (November 1989), 123–4.

75 Douglas Hay and Nicholas Rogers, *Eighteenth-Century English Society: Shuttles and Swords* (Oxford and New York: Oxford University Press, 1997): 147–8, 197.

76 For a complaint about the low wages of agricultural labourers see 'Times are Altered' (n.p., n.d.), B.L., Shelfmark 1876.d.41. Another version of this song was printed by J. Pitts in London, 1819–44, Bodleian Library, Harding B 11 (1930): 'When Buonaparte was in vogue, poor servants could engage / For sixteen pounds a year, my boys, and that was handsome wages, / But now the wages are so low and what is worst of all,   / Masters cannot find the cash which brings them to the wall.' Some of the later versions of this song from the 1840s substituted a line about high bread prices for this last line. See 'The Cries of the Poor Against the Oppression of the Rich &c', *Two Excellent Old Songs* (n.p., n.d.), B.L.

77 'The Corn Laws – A Song.'

78 'The Corn Laws – A Song.'

79 Robert Burns, 'A Man's a Man for A'That' (n.p., E. Hodges, c.1840), B.L., Shelfmark HS 74 1250.

80 'The Plough Boy', *Three Celebrated Songs* (Newcastle: J. Smith, c.1800), B.L., Shelfmark 11621.b.9.

81 'The Happy Farmer' (n.p., n.d.), B.L., Shelfmark 11622.a.46.

82 'The Golden Farmer' (n.p., Collins, n.d.), B.L., Shelfmark 11661.eee.22. There is another version: 'The Golden Farmer, A Song' (Birmingham, M. Swinney, 1804).

83 In the next verse, however, he advised them to be harsh with lazy labourers. James Bruce, *The Farmer, A Poem* (Dundee, 1813), 15.

84 Dyck points out that Roast Beef songs were still circulated in the nineteenth century

but were not popular with labourers. Songs accepting of farmers were still popular with a plebeian audience until 1810. Thus protest verse coexisted with traditional songs, Dyck, *William Cobbett and Rural Popular Culture*, 132, 53, 60. See also the song 'Popular Opinions, or a Picture of Real Life, Exhibited in a Dialogue Between a Scottish Farmer and a Weaver' (Glasgow, 1812). The song described a generous farmer who lent his poor companion, the weaver, 50 shillings, even though he lectured him on frugality.

85 T. M. Devine, ed., *Farm Servants and Labour in Lowland Scotland 1770–1914* (Edinburgh: J. Donald Publishers, 1989), 2.

86 'The Bountiful Knight of Somersetshire' (1685), *The Pepys Ballads*, Vol. 3. A similar ballad celebrating paternalism and generosity is 'A Brave Old Country Gentleman', *The Merryman Songster* (Glasgow, n.d.), L.C. 2847.

87 This story was told in A.F., 'Tale LXV', *The General Entertainer* (London, 1746).

88 'The Corn Laws – A Song.'

89 'The Poor Man's distress & Tryal, Or, Fortune Favours after her Frowns', (1685), *The Pepys Ballads*, Vol. 3.

90 'The Farmer' (London: W. and C. Dicey, 1736–66), Bodleian Library, Douce Ballads 3(30a).

91 'The Crafty Miller, or, Mistaken Batchelor' (London, W. and C. Dicey, 1736–63), Bodleian Library, Douce Ballads 3(13b).

92 'The Case is Alter'd: A Tale' (Salisbury: Fowler, 1770–1800), Bodleian Library, Harding B14 (11).

93 William Johnston, *The Life and Times of William Johnston, Horticultural Chemist, Gardener, and Cartwright,* ed. Reginal Alenarly, Esq. (Petershead, 1859), 10.

94 See Rev. J. Evans, *Letters Written during a Tour Through South Wales, In the year 1803, and at Other Times, Containing Views of the History, Antiquities, and Customs of that Part of the Principality* (London, 1804), 194.

95 T. M. Devine, *The Transformation of Rural Scotland: Social Change and the Agrarian Economy, 1660–1815* (Edinburgh: Edinburgh University Press, 1994), 127–8.

96 'The Farmer's Song. A New Song Sung at Sadler's Wells', (London, S. Paul), B.L., Shelfmark HS.74.11250.

97 'The Muirland Farmer' (n.p., n.d.), B.L., Shelfmark 11621.c.10.

98 'The Farmer's Wish', *Mad Tom's Garland. Composed of Six Excellent Songs* (n.d., n.p.), B.L., Shelfmark 11621.c.4.

99 'A New Song on the Farmer's Glory', *Bonny Jockey's Garland Beautified with several merry new songs* (Newcastle: Angus, 1774–1825).

100 *The Beggar's Complaint* (1812), 58. Note that the 'beggars' and the 'poor' are here synonymous with small tenant farmers in contrast to the 'great farmers' of the title. Though we do not see this in songs, in pamphlets and tracts from the nineteenth century farmers or their spokesmen sometimes complained that the gentry were taking the side of the mob in times of grain riots. See, for example, Anon., *An Address to the Good Sense and Candour of the People* (1800), 6. On growing rents and landlords' refusal to renew leases see Robert C. Allen, *Enclosure and the Yeoman* (Oxford: Clarendon Press, 1992), 20.

101 'Next season this grand committee did report, / That no farmer could live without shutting each port, / When the quarter of grain was sold under four pounds, / Unless the landholders would lower their grounds': 'The Corn Laws – A Song'.

102 *The Beggar's Complaint* (1812), 36–7, 41.

103 *The Beggar's Complaint* (1812), 52–4. The same view was expressed by the MP Henry Brougham. He was concerned that the young no longer waited until they could support themselves to get married because they knew the parish would take care of them. He felt the peasantry viewed relief as a regular part of their wages, while in the past they had hated the thought of it. Speech of Henry Brougham, Esq., MP on Tuesday, the 9th of April, 1816; in Committee of the Whole House, upon the State of Agricultural Distress (London, 1816), 52–4.

104 'A New Song Called the Farmer's Rant or Jockey's Dream Shewing the Pride and Ambition of the Farmers and Factors, and the distressed and deplorable Condition of the Poor at this Day' (Newcastle: 1800), L.C. 2851.

105 'The Farmer' (London: W. and C. Dicey, 1736–66), Bodleian Library, Douce Ballads 3(30a).

106 Thompson has found that complaints about the insubordination of labour were common among the writings of the gentry throughout the period: 'The Patricians and the Plebs', 41.

107 Ben Heath Malkin, *The Scenery, Antiquities, and Biography of South Wales, from Material Collected during two Excursions in the Year 1803* (London, 1804), 59.

108 Evans, *Letters Written during a Tour Through South Wales* (1804), 326.

109 Evans, *Letters Written during a Tour Through South Wales* (1804), 324. Evans describes these farmers as accustomed to manual labour: 'The country is divided, for the greater part, into small farms, so that the farmer and his hind are nearly upon an equality, and precedency at table may easily be dispensed with.'

110 Evans, *Letters Written during a Tour Through South Wales* (1804), 327.

111 Thomas Maude, Introduction to *Wensley-Dale, Or, Rural Contemplations: A Poem* (London, 1780), xi. He was referring to the luxury of the shepherds.

112 'The Corn Laws – A Song.'

113 Burns, 'A Man's a Man for A'That' (n.p., E. Hodges, c.1840), B.L., Shelfmark HS 74 1250. Traditional songs of complaint that used the language of rich versus poor were still printed in the nineteenth century. However, no bitter, angry songs like 'A Man's A Man for A'That' were printed early in the period.

114 The lack of ballads about rural social condition in the first half of the eighteenth century will be noticed by anyone searching for them in broadside and chapbook collections. It was also observed by William Chappell, who wrote that 'Political songs seem to have been the only kind of poetry in general favour, after the reign of Queen Anne.' William Chappell, *The Ballad Literature and Popular Music of the Olden Time* (1859; republished New York: Dover Publications, 1965), 624.

3

Ballads' and poems' condemnation of enclosure

In his discussion of enclosure in *The Country and City*, Raymond Williams associates pastoral poetry at the end of the eighteenth century with nostalgia: a celebration of the English countryside gave way to a fond remembrance of how good life used to be in the past, when land was more evenly divided.[1] We see something of this in the popular song 'The Land'.[2] The first verse praises the richness and beauty of the land:

> The land, the land, the rich and solid land.
> The hills, and dales, and fields so grand
> All fill'd with flowers, and fruits, and trees,
> And back'd by rocks and surrounded by seas.

But in the last verse all this glory is associated with the past:

> The fields were green, and ripe the corn,
> On the summer's day when I was born;
> The reapers reap'd, and the gleaners glean'd,
> The harvest was rich, and no one complain'd.

A feeling of nostalgia is created both by the change of tense and reference to childhood. Significantly, readers are told that in the old days no one complained, either because all were prosperous enough to be content or because there was still amity between those who reaped or gleaned and those who farmed. Popular songs and poetry both celebrated the richness of the land and objected to the changes that were making access to it more difficult.

Studies of artistic representations of the changing relationship between peasants and the land have tended to emphasise artists' and poets' ambivalent attitude towards enclosure. Some scholars have done this more successfully than others. One of the earlier artistic representations of enclosure, that of Oliver Goldsmith, has provoked suspicion because he did not belong to the peasantry. Raymond Williams made too much of the idea that Goldsmith was writing about the condition of the poet rather than a real situation and that he was more concerned about his own economic independence than the economic independence of the dispossessed villagers. Goldsmith's inability to retire to the country may be a theme associated with 'The Deserted Village', but the main theme is certainly the negative effect of enclosure on the peasantry.[3] Furthermore, there is nothing wrong with Goldsmith identifying his own sufferings with those of the dispossessed peasantry. How else was a poet of his class supposed to express sympathy with the poor? Ann Bermingham's more nuanced analysis of Gainsborough's landscape paintings and their discomfort with enclosure is more persuasive. Gainsborough painted his native east Suffolk, whose landscape was characterised by the irregular pattern of sixteenth-century enclosure (hedged small fields). Bermingham argues that these looked more natural than the new parliamentary enclosures but more 'pastoral' than the sweeping wastes and that they embodied an idealised past that was kinder to the small farmer.[4] Painters were ambivalent about enclosure and their landscapes could also be read as supportive of the new land pattern because, instead of showing sweeping fields and woods, they only showed small pieces of the countryside with trees blocking the view, which evoked the new enclosures. While this improves our understanding of the landscapes, those interested in a more explicit artistic opposition to enclosure still have to look elsewhere.

The poetry of John Clare is a good place to look, and a number of studies have been done on his relationship with the land. John Barrell, Jeanette Neeson and Johanne Clare have all shown that John Clare, though avoiding the argument that enclosure impoverished the peasantry, took a strong stance against the enclosing class.[5] This chapter seeks to add to this body of work by bringing into the discussion some popular songs and some less known poets.[6] These were very definitely against the loss of access to commons and wastes. Like John Clare, they were outraged by the social cost of enclosure, but they also perceived its economic impact on the poor. Poets and song writers also tried to expose what they saw as the selfish motives of enclosers.

In the chapter on social relations I described how songs complained about the behaviour of both large farmers and the gentry. Songs and poems about enclosure and engrossment more often identified the gentry as the guilty party, but they also blamed wealthy new farmers for the changes in landholding patterns. My criteria for including songs and poems in this chapter has been whether they spoke directly about the economic and social meaning of access to the land and the loss of it, and whether they have been thoroughly analysed by other historians and literary scholars. As in previous chapters, I have included anonymous broadside and chapbook ballads but also some verses written by the Bloomfield brothers, a few minor pastoral poets from the early nineteenth century and a poem by Wordsworth. It is curious how often the ballad genre was used to criticise loss of common right (both Nathaniel Bloomfield and Wordsworth employed it). It is also striking how similar the language is of these different kinds of verse and how similar the issues are that concerned both poets and popular ballad writers at the time.

Songs and poems made the economic argument, according to which enclosure impoverished the peasantry and enriched the gentry, but they were equally concerned about the social cost, particularly the poor's loss of liberty, a home, a community, and an aesthetic experience. Poets and balladeers also expressed their opposition to enclosure through praise and sympathy for those who broke the post-enclosure laws.

The economic argument: enclosure makes the poor poorer

The economic importance of common right to peasants has been convincingly demonstrated by historians like the Hammonds, Jane Humphries, Keith Snell, E. P. Thompson and Jeanette Neeson. Despite contemporary arguments from supporters of enclosure that commons and wastes could only sustain poor breeds of animals and that commoning allowed for no agricultural improvements to be made, peasants' opposition to enclosure shows they found access to land to be very valuable.[7] Jeanette Neeson in particular has illustrated the importance to the household economy of wasteland commodities such as fuel, and plants for food, medicine and manufacture.[8] In unenclosed areas access to the land helped sustain poor people from squatters to small farmers.

Songs and poems frequently referred to the economic significance of customary practices like gathering and gleaning. Gathering was seen as part of a peasant way of life and a source of extra income, usually for the poorest segment of rural society. The Cornish peasant-poet, Henry Quick, recalled gathering broom with his mother, which they bound and sold.[9] A similar experience of a poor single parent was described by the poet William Holloway in the story of poor Susan and her son, who could eke out a living before enclosure by gleaning, fishing in the river, and weaving baskets. Of course after enclosure they are evicted and their little hut is deserted.[10] The farmer Nathaniel Dale's memory of gathering mushrooms as a boy to sell at the market and his depiction of female farm servants gathering wild strawberries from the meadows in his poem 'My Favorite Girls' show that farmers also found such activities beneficial.[11] Aside from food and commodities for sale, the rural poor's dependence on fuel from the common was also noted by Holloway:

> The common, clad with vegetative gold,
> Whose well-dried stores allay the wintry cold;
> Whence ev'ry family its portion claims,
> To fence the hovel, or recruit the flames…[12]

In songs, the gatherer is usually an attractive young woman or little girl, probably in order to arouse the pity or sympathy of the audience but also illustrating Jane Humphries' argument that the wasteland had a special significance for women.[13] Some of these heroines suggest the ideology of the picturesque, according to which poverty and ragged clothing were seen as somehow romantic and appealing.[14] The songs 'Lilies and Roses' and 'Helen the Fair' seem to belong to this genre. In the former the beautiful Nancy sells her flowers in the village until she is espied and married by a young nobleman. In the latter young Helen meets with exactly the same lucky fate.[15] Here the gathering of flowers is perhaps used to convey the girls' picturesqueness and appeal to the noble young men who are schooled in the rules of taste and artistic appreciation. But other songs more clearly link gathering activities to economic survival. In 'The Song of Phoebe' a girl gathers flowers and sells them in town to support her poor mother and little sister.[16] Similar is the work of the beautiful orphan Frances, who gathers nuts to sustain her five little siblings.[17]

Gleaning also carried ideas of the picturesque with it, perhaps more so than gathering, which is why it more often found a place in polite art (Gainsborough painted his wife as a gleaner, for instance). Its depiction in popular ballads and pastoral poems, however, often suggested its economic significance. Though assumed to be the right of the poor, it could be of use to anyone who had fallen on hard times. The Rev. W. Huntington remembered how, when he was not earning enough to make ends meet, his wife went gleaning to supplement their diet, but farmers drove her out of the fields as did other gleaners, saying that a parson's wife should not glean (presumably because she was well-off). She persevered and kept gleaning. This was before the court ruling that decided gleaning was not a universal right under common law.[18] Things had changed by 1812 when a pamphleteer lamented the loss of gleaning rights:

> It has been legally determined, not long ago, that no one has any right to glean in any field without the owner's permission! Poor Beggars! You have got the strait Jacket on at the last: there will soon be nothing you can call your own but air and water!'[19]

Here we see a slight difference in emphasis between popular ballads and pastoral poems. Though written (or at least printed) at the same time, popular ballads contained a greater sense of entitlement to gleaning than pastoral poems.[20] In songs, gleaning was often taken for granted:

See, content the humble gleaners,
Take the fetter'd ears that fall,
Nature all her children viewing,
Kindly bounteous cares for all.[21]

The song suggests gleaning was a matter of course, a natural activity, rather than a kindness that a landlord allows the peasants. Interestingly, in this song the gleaner is male, in contrast to the numerous female gleaners found in other songs, as well as in polite art. In 'The Cottager's Daughter' Mary helps her father (a cottager who lives off the produce of his cottage) by gleaning. Again, this custom is presented as a matter of course.[22] Despite the 1788 ruling, in many regions small farmers and commoners continued to glean, so the popular songs may have had a more accurate understanding of the practice than the pastoral poets and pamphleteers who regretted its loss.

In contrast, pastoral poems showed a greater awareness of the disputes surrounding gleaning and often saw gleaning as a privilege that kind and paternal landlords should allow the poor, rather than a right. In the following verses the narrator urges landlords to allow gleaning and pity the poor:

Rake not the Land (the Peasant cries)
Touch not the scatter'd Ear;
Can Gratitude with such supplies,
Refuse the Gleaner's share?

No, rather let your pity leave
Some straggling spikes behind;
Who that with generous heart can give,
A comfort fails to find?[23]

To whom are these words addressed? Very likely to the landowner of the fields, or the capitalist farmer for whom the 'peasant' works. The fact that the landlord needs this reminder suggests that gleaning is no longer taken for granted by everyone. Still, the peasant has some say in the matter.

The poet D. Hurn describes the gleaners picking the stubble and compares them to birds that have to live off this meagre fare. He issues a stern warning to farmers who might be tempted to restrict gleaning:

Grudge not; but freely let them have a share,
Ye Farmers, blest with store of wealth and ease.

Can these poor partners of your kind displease?
Forbid them not to glean the scatter'd grain,
While Heaven with plenty crowns the fruitful plain;
While last year's corn, unthrash'd, augments your store,
Grudge not this yearly pittance to the poor.[24]

Hurn, a farmer himself in the Lincolnshire fens, invites the farmers to reflect on how often they lose grain to mice and how insignificant the loss to gleaners is by comparison. Then he warns that even the greatest men can fall on hard times and it may come to pass that the sons of the now wealthy farmers will one day have to make ends meet by gleaning. All of this suggests that the farmers who opposed gleaning were seen as cruel and ungenerous. The good farmer would allow gleaning:

No rake takes here what Heaven to all bestows –
Children of want, for you the bounty flows!
And every cottage from the plenteous store
Receives a burden nightly at the door.[25]

This belief in the economic usefulness of gathering and gleaning makes logical the conviction, shared by most poets and song writers, that enclosure further impoverished the poor. Other contemporary sources spoke of economic dependence rather than outright impoverishment. According to one observer, enclosure and engrossment caused small farmers to become day-labourers, day-labourers to became beggars, and beggars to grow in misery and in number (while farmers were 'elevated above their proper level').[26] Though they disagreed on whether this was a good thing or not, most commentators agreed that enclosure and engrossment caused agricultural labourers to become more dependent on the wage.[27] This was partly due to parishes' refusal to grant new settlements, but also partly due to 'The practice of enlarging and engrossing of farms, and especially that of depriving the peasantry of all landed property…'[28] The resulting large farms were seen by some to be wasteful and unproductive, making England a net importer of grain, causing scarcity and high grain prices, further augmenting poverty.[29] The proposals to give land allotments to the poor often acknowledged that a measure of economic independence was important in ensuring a decent lifestyle.[30] Thus songs and poems' argument that loss of access to land caused poverty would have resonated with other contemporary writings.

Songs against enclosure were rare, as Roy Palmer has already observed, in part due to the local nature of opposition.[31] Johanne Clare has pointed out that the enclosure elegies were John Clare's most local poems.[32] Because most of the popular ballads that have been preserved were printed in printing centres like London and Newcastle-upon-Tyne, many anti-enclosure songs may be lost or buried in local archives. But enclosure was never popular among the poor and there is a ballad tradition linking enclosure to poverty that probably goes back to the sixteenth century. The old ballad of Thomas Hickathrift found in the Pepys penny dreadful collection tells the story of a hero who kills a giant and confiscates his land to provide commons for the poor.[33] We find more direct and explicit complaints against enclosure in some of the songs that criticised the existing social conditions and that we already encountered in chapter 2. An old song from the Roxburghe collection about corruption and various social ills contains the following verse:

> There be many rich men,
> Both Yeomen and Gentry,
> That for their owne private gaine,
> Hurt a whole Countrey
> By closing free Commons;
> Yet they'le make as though
> 'Twere for common good,
> But I know what I know.[34]

The same argument can be found in 'The cries of the poor against the oppression of the rich', though this song contains some apocalyptic imagery and has a more menacing mood:

> Against poor folk they still prevail,
> With all their wicked works,
> For they inclose both muir and dale,
> And turn corn field to parks,
> Within their power they compass all,
> And fast their wings they spread,
> But God shall make their Dragon fall,
> And lose both hands and heads.

The enclosers here are not large capitalist farmers but the gentry, who have no intention of busying themselves with agriculture, but are only interested in pleasure and sport, thus turning corn fields to parks. The sin has almost biblical proportions and the enclosers are cast in the role of a dragon to be smitten. The tone is threatening, particularly the reference to the loss of heads. The loss of hands may be a symbolic punishment of the hand that does the enclosing or it may refer to 'hands' as in hired workers. Naturally, this kind of enclosure has to be followed by the eviction of tenants:

Yea, they are more forward to starve,
Poor people in the land,
Than Israel was the heathen folk,
At Moses' strict command,
The lords and lairds who cast them out
From houses where they dwell
The poor man cries, where shall I go?
They bid me go to hell.[35]

Again we see more biblical imagery, a parallelism between Israel's treatment of the heathens and the landlords' treatment of the poor, perhaps to emphasise how low the tenants stand in the eyes of the enclosers. The Israelites are also relevant here because they were driven away from their land, just like the English poor will now be. But, unlike in Israel, the poor Englishman has no prophecy to look forward to and feels he has been condemned to go to 'hell'. Such songs do not tell us whether enclosure actually caused poverty, whether this was how it was seen by the peasantry, or whether song writers who opposed enclosure felt they might make a more convincing case against it by depicting it as the cause of such extreme suffering as starvation and homelessness. They do, however, tell us that a connection between enclosure and poverty existed in the minds of ballad writers and their audience.

The economic argument against enclosure continued to be made at the end of the eighteenth century. The ballad about the enclosure of Nun's Green, discussed in more detail below, was written in the 1790s, and it too associated lack of access to commons with poverty. The two following songs, both printed in numerous versions around 1800 and frequently found in histories of enclosure, speak of the loss of pasture for one's animals:

In old times I have heard 'tis true,
That a poor man kept a pig and a cow,
Their commons and places to feed them on,
That a poor man might live happy then,
But now they are all taken in,
And the rich do reap the gain,
Workhouses and gaols then they have made,
And to send them there is quite a trade.[36]

In 'My Old Hat' the same point is made:

In former times it was not so,
For this was all the due,
The poor to have both milk and woo'
When my old hat was new.
When the Romans liv'd in our land,

These commons they did give,
Unto the poor for charity,
To help them for to live:
They've ta'en from them their proper right
Which makes them for to rue,
Although the same to them belong'd,
When my old hat was new.[37]

The narrator here regrets the loss of milk as part of the diet as well as the loss of a little bit of extra income through the wool of a sheep that could be kept on the common. The song seeks to legitimise common right by tracing its origins to Roman antiquity.

The poet James Templeman agreed that enclosure and engrossment brought poverty, though he focused more on the high prices of provisions that could result from it. The engrossing activities of his hero, the selfish farmer Hobson, cause the disappearance of the small farmer from his lands and give him complete control over all the grain, allowing him to jack up the price and make a huge profit at the expense of the poor. The guilty party here is not the gentry, but the large capitalist farmer, Hobson, who, we learn later in the poem, eagerly annexes more and more fields to his already large holdings.[38] For the poet Samuel Jackson Pratt, enclosure and engrossment impoverished cottagers. He described impoverished villages, 'haggard shapes' and 'spectres thin of hollow penury'.[39]

The economic argument extended not only to the effects of enclosure but also to the motivations of enclosers. Ballads and poems concerned with this problem refused to grant enclosers their claim that they were acting in the national interest.[40] The major motive, in their view, was avarice.[41] Nathaniel Bloomfield blamed gentlemen's avarice for enclosures that converted pasture to arable, causing shepherds to lose their employment, and increasing the gap between rich and poor. 'Great men's' greed and lack of charity in regards to this matter are seen as a neglect of duty in the popular ballad 'The cries of the poor against the oppression of the rich &c':

It is the duty of great men
Poor people to defend
But worldly interest moves them more,
They mind no other end.

The process described here is engrossment rather than enclosure. Though we know engrossment might follow or precede enclosure, the former was more often and more explicitly denounced in poetry and in popular songs. Adding farm to farm was seen as a particularly selfish thing to do:

> Woe to them that addeth house to house,
> And addeth field to field,
> This dreadful curse he cannot miss
> For they deserve it well.
> There's many lairds within this land,
> Of judgement have no fear,
> If cattle with them pasture have,
> The meal it is so dear.[42]

This song was written at the end of the seventeenth century, when meat prices were higher than grain prices, and the last two lines are probably an allusion to the conversion of arable to pasture, a process that was reversed, causing similar poetic outrage, at the end of the eighteenth century.[43] In contrast to the previous verse, this time the lairds engross for profit, rather than pleasure. The song condemns both kinds of enclosure and ends with curses of the enclosing lords and lairds. Such curses, found in some ballads and also in Wordsworth's 'Goody Blake and Harry Gill', may have to do with the peasant tradition of cursing enclosure described by Keith Thomas.[44]

Though engrossment was a process that had been in place for a long time, it was always seen as a 'new' evil in poetry, perhaps because it was so often shaped by local experience:

> When five acres they did rent, then money they could save,
> But now for to support their pride, five hundred they must have,
> If these great farms were taken and divided into three;
> That we might see as happy days, as ever we see.[45]

In a way this is the complaint against large farmers already familiar to us, but it is more specifically about large chunks of land being controlled by one person. The impetus behind adding more and more to one's holdings is said to be a sign of pride and greed, and the solutions to this lie in dividing the land into smaller holdings that can be shared by more farmers and benefit more people. It is curious that the writer of this song decided the 500 acres should be divided into three, thus suggesting that 160 acres is an acceptable size for a farm while 500 acres indicates greed. I suspect this was done more for the sake of the rhyme scheme than to suggest how large a farm could be without being a problem.

The social cost: the loss of community

Historians have demonstrated that access to land had a social and cultural significance, perhaps greater than its economic significance. The common and wasteland were part of a culture of gift-exchange and neighbourliness, shaping the life of the community in important ways.[46] Loss of custom could involve loss of a sense of self, community and history.[47] This is particularly salient in the work of John Clare. According to Johanne Clare, John Clare eschewed a focus on the economic loss caused by enclosure, because his relationship with the land transcended economic concerns. His criticism of the enclosing class was based on their obsession with economic gain, and he preferred to emphasise instead the loss of happiness and freedom.[48] Many other poetic endeavours showed that the idea of the land evoked a rich array of associations. Its loss could mean the loss of social mobility, of freedom, of a home, of a playground, of a place of beauty and of artistic inspiration for the poor.

The disappearance of small farms could have unfortunate consequences for the peasantry's social mobility.[49] The timing and the effects of the disappearance of smallholders is still debated among historians.[50] Contemporaries also disagreed about the effects of enclosure on small farmers, but many of them thought they were pernicious.[51] The victims of enclosure and engrossment in popular songs were often small farmers as well as landless or land-poor commoners, and the anger against new-fashioned farmers (see chapter 2) and engrossment (see above) in late eighteenth-century ballads certainly suggests small farms were on the wane.[52] When no small farms were available for purchase or rental, it meant a peasant or agricultural labourer had little chance of improving his lot. David Davies felt mobility was very important to the happiness of the peasantry, this most 'useful class of men'. He argued they should be encouraged to improve their social condition, and should have some land and hope to get more.[53] That the new pattern of land-ownership made this difficult was one of the worries of Robert Bloomfield:

> The hope of humble industry is o'er;
> The blameless hope, the cheering sweet presage
> Of future comforts for declining age.
> Can my sons share from this paternal hand
> The profit with the labours of the land?
> No, though indulgent Heaven its blessing deigns,
> Where's the small farm to suit my scanty means?[54]

The land could be a home both in a narrow sense and in the larger sense of a community to which one belonged. For Robert Bloomfield, the fields were a home while he was working as a farmer's boy. A loving attachment to the earth and its produce is expressed in the poem 'The Farmer's Boy'. The popularity of his poem shows that it resonated with a widespread view of the peasantry.

The farmer's boy, Giles, revels in the contact with the soil as he works with the harrow and then sits on the bank to rest:

> His heels deep sinking every step he goes,
> Till dirt adhesive loads his clouted shoes,
> Welcome green headland! Firm beneath his feet;
> Welcome the friendly bank's refreshing seat![55]

Giles is compelled to make a home in the field when he works as a bird scarer because of the cold. He makes a little hut for himself where he can light a fire and warm himself.

In the case of squatters the fields provided a home in a much more literal sense. Ballads about gypsies made this point: 'Let the lord boast his castle, the baron his hall; / But the home of the Gipsies is widest of all.'[56] The heroine of another popular ballad, the Gipsy Queen, speaks in similar terms:

> With my kingdom I'm well content,
> Though my realm's but the hawthorn glade;
> And my palace a tatter'd tent,
> Beneath the willow shade.
> Though my banquet I'm forced to make
> On haws and berries a store,
> And the game that by chance we take,
> From some neighbouring hind's barn door.
> Yet 'tis I am a gipsy Queen.[57]

The loss of community experienced after enclosure has been well documented. Contemporaries feared that the decline of small farmers would create a shortage of 'honest and industrious' farm servants who usually came from such families, and that poor parish children would have fewer employment opportunities (also provided largely by small farmers).[58] Further damage to rural communities would be caused by the loss of rural pleasures and sports. John Blackner's description of the enclosure of Shenton Common illustrates this grievance. Shenton Common was the spot where village entertainments and sports were held, and it was enclosed and ploughed up in 1797:

> This spot, so long sacred to rural amusements, on inclosing the lordship of Shenton, was ploughed up, on the 27th of February, 1797. A spot of earth, comprehending about 324 square yards, sanctified by the lapse of centuries, as a place of rustic sport … Here the youth of Nottingham were wont to give facility to the circulation of their blood, strength to their limbs, and elasticity to their joints, but callous hearted avarice has robbed them of the spot.[59]

Thomas Whitby's hero, James, experiences both, the loss of home and the loss of a communal pastime, when he is expelled from his cottage so that a mansion can be built in its place, its grounds also taking up the spot previously used for village sports.[60]

One of the most memorable tributes to a common used for sport and play was perhaps that by Nathaniel Bloomfield, brother of the famous Robert Bloomfield. His 'Elegy on the Enclosure of Honington Green' was less known and admired than Robert's work and even mocked by critics: Byron wrote a little verse making fun of Nathaniel's literary ambitions. Nevertheless, the poem is useful to the historian for its frank, guileless critique of enclosure. Though a tailor's apprentice and not a farmer's boy like Robert, Nathaniel had grown up next to Honington Green along with other villagers and knew its worth. The author of the Preface to Nathaniel's collection of poems, Cappel Lofft, admitted that he was no enemy to enclosure himself because 'if the Rights and Interests of the Poor, and of small Owners, be very carefully guarded, an Enclosure may be a common Benefit'. He allowed, however, that in too many cases the outcome was unfavourable. Furthermore, although Honington Green was only half an acre large, Lofft sympathised with Bloomfield because the green 'ornamented the village' and especially because Robert and Nathaniel were born next to it, and played their childhood games upon it: 'There grew the first Daisies which their feet press'd in childhood'. Lofft also agreed with Nathaniel that the green was too small to really bring a serious profit to the enclosers and could have been left open. He concluded that all who loved poetry, respected genius or 'were anxious to preserve the little innocent Gratifications of the Poor' would wish the green had not been enclosed. In the poem, Nathaniel Bloomfield's narrator speaks of how the loss of Honington Green has changed village life: old pastimes and pleasures are no more. A mother regrets the loss of the common because she can no longer leave her children to play on the green while she does her chores:

> O'er the Green, where so often she blest
> The return of a Husband or Son,
> Coming happily home to their rest,
> At night, when their labour was done:
> Where so oft in her earlier years,
> She, with transport maternal, has seen
> (While plying her housewifely cares)
> Her Children all safe on the Green.[61]

The dispute between the poet Ann Yearsley and Levi Eames, a Clifton lawyer who owned the piece of land used for play by her children, reflects the significance such a space could have for the poor. After Eames' footman had savagely beaten two of her sons for trespassing on the land, Yearsley tried to sue the footman but was unsuccessful, partly due to a lack of funds. Yearsley published *Stanzas of Woe*, which denounced Eames.[62] The poem invites Eames to remember his own childhood and compare it to that of Yearsely's children:

> Did'st thou then deem it guilt o'er hills to stray?
> Or bathe thy tender limbs in limpid streams?
> Or stretch thee careless *on the new-mown hay*,
> Warm'd and inpsir'd by Sol's effulgent beams?
> Ah, no! Thou then could'st prize those pleasures high,
> Nor was thy skin by cruel lashes torn,
> Nor did the big tear fill thy pleading eye
> At sense of anguish thou could'st ne'er return.
> Yet these are ills that on my children fall,
> And fall from *Thee*, thou *Draco*, of the age!
> Their feeble cries shall for my vengeance call,
> And fill my soul with wild, eternal rage.[63]

According to poets, enclosure could cause even greater damage to rural communities through the depopulation of villages. It is by no means certain that this was the effect of enclosure, and some contemporaries even argued that the population might increase as a result.[64] Historians have also argued that depopulation did not necessarily go hand in hand with enclosure in the eighteenth century but poets persisted in using depopulation to create an emotional effect:

> But now the sledge, the file, no more resounds;
> No more the ploughboy, from the neighb'ring grounds
> At evening, trudges with the blunted share,
> Or broken traces to receive repair.
> Poor, stumbling Ball (it) no more shall thither plod,
> And dozing wait, in patience, to be shod.
> In fertile lawn, of idly-pamper'd steeds,
> A useless race, for false ambition, breeds.
> The fallow lands, where cheerful peasants earn'd
> Their weekly bread, to proud plantations turn'd,
> Forget to yield their auburn crops of grain,
> That fill'd the petty farmers's early wain,
> When, on his ambling nag, he took his round,
> With flaggon to the tatter'd saddle bound,
> Replenish'd well with hearty home-brew'd ale,
> The toil-contending reapers to regale.[65]

So wrote the poet William Holloway. The peasants as well as the rural artisans are forced to leave their native land after the local landlord encloses the area for his own private amusements. The contrast between an idle gentry and an industrious peasantry is parallel to a contrast between hard-working horses like Ball and 'idly-pamper'd steeds', used only to serve pleasure and 'false ambition'. Holloway's use of the term 'useless race' could denote both the useless breed of horses and the idle ruling class. It is applied again later in the poem to the deer roaming the newly enclosed parks replacing the 'rich corn-fields'. The argument for enclosure as increasing productivity is undermined by this picture of productive fields and a happy, industrious peasantry before enclosure, followed by 'proud plantations' that yield no crop and sustain no small farmers. The loss of land access drives small farmers to the cities:

> Now into one a hundred fields are thrown,
> Their tenants banish'd, and their pleasure flown!
> To crowded towns, the poor mechanic strays,
> To spend the sickly evening of his days.[66]

Eviction is also described in the song 'When my Old Hat was New', discussed above. The earliest version of it I could find comes from 1820–24. The Lauriston Castle version, which is undated, contains the following lines:

> The cot-houses are all thrown down,
> The commons ta'n away,
> Their sheep and kine they must remove
> No longer there to stay.[67]

The loss of land did not always mean the loss of home, but it nearly always seems to have meant a loss of beauty to poets. For John Clare enclosure was destructive of natural beauty and harmony and he used the images of dying birds and starving animals to make his point.[68] The irregularity of the commons provided greater scope for the poetic imagination. Thus the nostalgia of John Blackner: '[the common] by the curiosity of its shape, and by the magic raptures which the sight of it awakened in our fancies of the existence of happier times' was for him a fond memory.[69] In Nathaniel Bloomfield's poem, through enclosure the aesthetic experience is transferred from the poor to the gentry, whose notions of refinement and taste lead them to create vast pleasure grounds. The poor labourer may no longer walk and sit on the green grass but must walk upon roads of gravel and stones whose monotony 'Fatigues both the eye and the feet'.[70] He may no longer enjoy the wild flowers (which he prefers to the genteel flowers of the enclosed fields).[71]

One's relationship with the land also had implications for one's relationship with one's nation. The belief that having a claim on some land made one a more patriotic citizen was reflected in the franchise and was often voiced by contemporaries:

it is plainly agreeable to sound policy that as many individuals as possible in a state should possess an interest in the soil; because this attaches them strongly to the country and its constitution, and makes them zealous and resolute in defending them.[72]

Although there were those who felt access to land had a negative impact on the morals of the poor, making them lazy and insolent,[73] others argued the beneficiaries of allotment schemes worked very hard on their land and tried to save for hard times. Crime in such parishes decreased significantly, illustrating the ennobling effect of cultivation. Ownership or at least some measure of control over land made men work harder and care for it more.[74] Giving the poor some freedom through land was the best way of ensuring success for charity: 'one of the best species of charity is that which enables the poor man to exert with effects, and with honest freedom, that strength, and those faculties, which Providence has blessed him with, for the benefit and support of his family'.[75]

Thus a close relationship with the land improved the national character. This idea allowed poets and song writers to argue that enclosure and the loss of custom represented a betrayal not only of the peasantry but of the values of the whole nation.[76] Andy Wood's argument that disputes over custom politicised the poor, and that the language of custom was used during plebeian protest after 1790, further suggests that claims to land had an ideological importance in popular culture.[77]

In this context it is significant that by far the most overwhelming non-economic argument against enclosure expressed in verse was the argument that the loss of access was the loss of liberty. Songs about gypsies associated life on the land with a romantic view of man's communion with nature and freedom. In the words of the Gipsy Queen:

And where is there a Queen like me,
That can revel upon the green,
In boundless liberty.[78]

Liberty is also the central theme of the extraordinary ballad 'The Lament of Nun's Green'. According to the collector who published the ballad, Nun's Green consisted of 50 acres and was used by the inhabitants of Derby who had right of common on it. Part of it was sold in 1768 and the rest in 1791 for the purpose of building houses for the city. This provoked a lot of protest in the form of petitions, pamphlets and ballads, but the enclosure could not be stopped. The introduction to the ballad says the following of Nun's Green:

Who after upwards of 460 years (being a great and good Gift, by John of Gaunt, Duke of Lancaster, and Earl of Leicester) was tried, cast and condemned, on the 14th of February, 1791, for being serviceable to the Poor People of this Town, as well as a Stranger, but a great Eye Sore to some particular Gentleman; but the Execution is left till the Pleasure of Parliament be known.

The ballad appeared as a broadside with a woodcut of a man being led to execution. It was written from the point of view of a piece of land, which is given a human voice. But the one condemned turns out to have a double identity: it is both the land and the goddess of liberty who stands for the land – Liberty and the land are one and the same as the words of Liberty are also the story of Nun's Green:[79]

> I have liv'd here, Four Hundred and Sixty Years;
> Was station'd here by Glorious John of Gaunt,
> Who never thought the poor should ever want…

The enclosers, identified as 'gentlemen', are called 'tyrants'. Liberty, or Nun's Green, expresses fear that

> My other Sisters soon, must fall a Prey
> To those who falsely take my Life away.

This suggests an awareness of the greater damage enclosure was doing to the nation and the poor, a fear that access to land might be thoroughly eradicated.

For Nathaniel Bloomfield the enclosure of Honington Green also meant a loss of freedom. It is not possible for villagers to enjoy enclosed grounds in the same way because one has always to be afraid that the 'owner's dread voice' would shout 'You've no business here':

> While the Green, tho' but Daisies it's boast,
> Was free as the Flow'rs to the Bee;
> In all seasons the Green we lov'd most,
> Because on the Green we were free;
> 'Twas the prospect that first met my eyes,
> And Memory still blesses the scene;
> For early my heart learnt to prize
> The Freedom of Honington Green.[80]

Bloomfield ends the poem by speculating that future generations would not miss the common because they would have never experienced it in the first place. But this did not mean that their quality of life would not be affected:

> The Youths of a more polish'd Age
> Shall not wish these rude Commons to see;
> To the Birds that's inur'd to the Cage,
> It would not be Bliss to be free.[81]

For William Holloway the problem was independence, but he emphasised not so much economic dependence as the loss of freedom. The purpose of his poem (as he states himself) is to show how the engrossing of small farms hurts the peasantry, how small occupiers are driven to desperate solutions such as embracing a military life or 'being reduced to the most abject state of dependence, and submitting to the galling hardship of becoming *servants* on the spot where they once had been masters'.[82] He deals with this issue through the story of the small farmer Reuben, who uses the commons to graze his 'two fair fac'd cows' and lives happily with his wife on what they produced. However, the wicked landlord encloses the land, forcing Reuben to live in servitude and breaking his independent spirit. Displaced from the life he loves, Reuben ends up joining the army.

Thus enclosers who deprived the peasantry of liberty were cast in the role of oppressors. In many songs and poems we hear the somewhat mysterious tidings that 'oppression' forced the peasant from his cot. We are not told whether this was due to enclosure or engrossment or whether some other reason was used to bring about an eviction, but a sense of injustice was emphatic. Thus in David Service's poem 'The Caledonian Herd-Boy', David's father is tricked out of his large property by 'fraud' and is reduced to a cot and a little farm, which results in David having to work as a herd-boy.[83] In 'The Beggar's Petition' we hear this familiar story:

A little farm was my paternal lot,
Then, like the lark, I sprightly hail'd the morn.
But ah! Oppression forc'd me from my cot,
My cattle dy'd, and blighted was my corn.[84]

A real-life version of the story can shed some light on this theme. In 1785, due to improvements in husbandry, small farms were engrossed, among them that of Mr Johnston. He was moved to a cottage with two acres owned by the landlord Erick, who had evicted him in the first place. In 1792 Erick evicted the family from the cottage but Mr Johnston refused to move, vowing to live and die there: 'He died on 22nd December, 1792, and found peace and shelter from lairds and greedy tackmen in the grave'. Meditating on his father's story, William Johnston reflected: '…we should not be oppressive to our poorer neighbours, nor use the power we have over them for their injury. Both rich and poor must leave all they have in this world, and be no more seen.'[85] The issue here was engrossment and eviction, rather than enclosure, but the end result of landlessness was seen as catastrophic for one who had lived off the land his whole life.

Songs' sympathy for law-breakers trespassing on enclosed land

The loss of customary rights received much criticism in some contemporary pamphlets. An anonymous pamphleteer of 1812 wrote angrily about the restriction of nutting rights, which he saw as another shameful step in depriving the poor of the use of the land. He also mentioned the forbidding of hunting and fishing.[86] Punishments for not observing the new rules could be harsh. Writer C. J. Ribton-Turner recorded a case of six women in Gloucestershire in 1800 being stripped to the waist and beaten till bloody at the whipping post in front of the Town Hall for 'hedge pulling'. This was part of a general trend to include gathering offences like the breaking of fences for fuel under vagrancy legislation.[87] The destitution of offenders, as well as the harshness of the punishments, could often gain a measure of support or sympathy for law-breakers among poets and song writers. The song 'Wandering Mary' describes a poor single mother who is driven to steal hawberries from hedges. 'No thief am I, as some allege' she insists, partly because she is driven to this act by want, but partly invoking the lost custom that allowed the poor to use what nature had to offer.[88]

Because fuel became so much more expensive for the poor, hedge-breaking in winter excited particular pity, and the young Wordsworth gave expression to it in his 'Goody Blake and Harry Gill'. Wordsworth employed the ballad form, as he did in so many of his early poems. He wrote the poem in 1798, the same year Nathaniel Blooomfield wrote 'The Enclosure of Honington Green'. The ballad is about a dispute between two neighbours concerning fuel. While in most of the ballads and poems we have seen villains were large landowners or landlords, here the offender who failed to share the land with his poor neighbours is an ordinary cattle dealer who also seems to own a farm. Goody Blake is very poor and Harry Gill appears to have a relatively comfortable lifestyle, but the two are not that far apart socially, except that he has access to the land (which he owns or rents) and she does not. The conflict between the two illustrates the kind of divisions that could happen within a community as a result of the loss of customary rights. The right to gather fuel is denied Goody Blake and she is compelled to pull sticks off Harry Gill's hedge to warm herself in winter. Harry Gill catches her in the act, angrily grabs her by the arms and shakes her violently. Goody's response to this assault is to curse Harry, asking God to ensure that he may never feel warm again. Goody's wish is granted and Harry shivers with cold, his teeth chattering for the rest of his days.

Wordsworth uses the youth of Harry, a 'lusty drover', and Goody's frail old age to underline the latter's helplessness and the former's insensitivity:

> Young Harry was a lusty drover,
> And who so stout of limb as he?
> His cheeks were red as ruddy clover;
> His voice was like the voice of three.
> Old Goody Blake was old and poor;
> Ill fed she was, and thinly clad;
> And any man who passed her door
> Might see how poor a hut she had.[89]

Despite her old age, Goody works hard: she spins all day and does some other unspecified work for three hours every night. Despite all her efforts her earnings are not enough to pay for candles or fuel in winter. (All alone, she appears to have had no kin or friend to help her.) Like many of Wordsworth's poor, she has a cheerful, blithe spirit and in the summer can often be heard singing. But in winter the burden is too much to bear, except in the rare moments when she can find fuel:

> O joy for her! Whene'er in winter
> The winds at night had made a rout;
> And scattered many a lusty splinter
> And many a rotten bough about,
> Yet never had she, well or sick,
> As every man who knew her says,
> A pile beforehand, turf or stick,
> Enough to warm her for three days.[90]

So Goody's stealing from the hedge is a natural consequence of her situation. Wordsworth's intention for the story to serve as a warning to all farmers who denied the poor access to the riches of the land is made explicit in the last two lines:

> Now think, ye farmers all, I pray,
> Of Goody Blake and Harry Gill![91]

The lack of land access that made the poor resort to stealing fuel could also make them resort to poaching, particularly during a time of high prices. I have not been able to find popular ballads that speak about fuel disputes, but there are a number of songs in praise of poaching, though dating is hard as usual. Although game was not as great a necessity as fuel, the reason why poaching was condoned by landless labourers (in contrast to how it was seen by the elite) was a feeling that they should have some right to the fields and woods and that the game laws were unfair. Many ballads about poachers appear to be from the late nineteenth century but there are a few from the early 1800s. The 'Bold Poacher' was printed in many versions under different names. The one used here is from the period 1780–1812. It tells the story of Lincolnshire poachers who catch a hare and sell it. Although the game keeper is aware of their trespass, he is too afraid to interfere.[92] In a version printed by Swindells, the game keeper is actually the one to buy the hare. The poachers and the game keeper collaborate against the landlord. The song ends with the lines

> Here's to every poacher that lives in Lincolnshire,
> And here's to every game-keeper that wants to buy a hare,
> But not to every keeper that wants to keep his deer.[93]

The trespasses of poachers were condoned by most peasants and agricultural labourers, as well as by those who supported them in the debate about custom. According to David Davies, 'To be a clever poacher is deemed a reputable accomplishment in the country; and therefore parents take care to instruct their children betimes in this art; which brings them on gradually to pilfering and stealing.'[94] Cobbett apparently invited labourers to steal fuel, to poach and to avoid excisemen.[95]

Songs were also written to commemorate the death of poachers during confrontations between game keepers. 'Bill Brown' tells the story of the death of a young poacher during one of his nightly adventures near the town of Thirberg in 1769.[96] Though the details surrounding his death are unclear, the ballad was reworked to commemorate the story of William Mays of Sudborough (Lincolnshire), who was killed during a fight between his poaching friends and a group of gamekeepers in 1837. Roy Palmer provides both the newspaper account and the ballad based on this event and it is noteworthy how the former was on the side of the keepers, referring to the poachers as 'ruffians'. According to the newspaper account, the poachers outnumbered the keepers by ten men and were the first to start the fight, commencing 'a ferocious attack on the keepers with bludgeons, long poles, and other weapons, beating them dreadfully'. The death of William Mays was described as an accident: 'the deceased died from over-exertion'; supposedly no wounds were found upon the body. The keepers were said to have 'used the greatest forbearance in this unequal conflict'.[97] The ballad, on the other hand, is completely on the side of the poachers: the fight is started by a keeper, John Millow, who shoots at the poachers from behind a tree. Mays is clearly killed by the keepers:

> Then to engage the poachers,
> The keepers they did start,
> And so with strife took poor May's life
> And stab'd him to the heart.

Mays is made more sympathetic by an allusion to his wife and children, who
have to live with his loss. His blood is said to cry for vengeance and he acquires
the status of a hero:

> Mourn all you gallant poachers, mourn
> Poor May's [sic.] is dead and gone,
> An hero brave laid in his grave,
> As ever the sun shine on.[98]

There may not have been as many poems and songs against enclosure as
there were about agricultural labour or social relations, but the ones that exist
were written with passion and conviction. By way of conclusion I would like
to look at a couple of passages written by supporters of enclosure and show
how they were pervaded by the language and ideas found in the writings
of poets who opposed enclosure. Although the speaker or writer intended a
pro-enclosure message, some of the language and imagery employed undermined the argument. Henry Brougham's speech to parliament is a good
example of this. The speech was given in 1816, just before rural disturbances
erupted in East Anglia in May of that year. Brougham admitted enclosure
had happened too fast in order to produce enough food during a time of
war. However, he felt it was an inevitable process and its overall effects were
beneficial. Yet the following quotation has the disturbing effect of suggesting
overuse and abuse of the land:

> not only have even the most inconsiderable commons, the very village greens,
> and the little stripes of sward by the way-side, been in many places subjected
> to division and exclusive ownership, and cut up into corn-fields in the rage for
> farming; not only have stubborn soils been forced to bear crops by mere weight
> of metal, by sinking money in the earth, as it has been called – but the land that
> formerly grew something has been fatigued with labour, and loaded with capital,
> until it yielded much more.[99]

Brougham believed this had made England the greatest agricultural state in the
world, but the language is one of violence and of rape and it ruins the author's
argument that enclosure is good for the country. A similar passage, describing
a place called Bromley Common and used to support the argument that the
commons were unproductive also deconstructs itself:

> Several cottages are scattered around the common, which have a pleasing effect
> in relieving the eye while contemplating this extensive waste. Here the botanist
> may find every species of heath which his kingdom produces; the gravelly nature
> of the soil scarcely admitting of the growth of any thing except this plant, a
> dwarf furze, and rushes. In the summer months, when the former of these are

in bloom, the appearance of the common is extremely beautiful; but it cannot fail of producing regret in the mind of the spectator, that so large a tract of land is unproductive.[100]

The irregularity of the common, which we saw praised in verse, the variety of species growing on it, and the beauty of the wild flowers do not sound like things that would produce 'regret' in the mind of the spectator. In fact 'regret' for the loss of common fields appears to be a feeling suppressed by these two authors who wanted to make enclosure look like a public good. Although they were on the losing side, the poems and songs against enclosure written in the eighteenth and nineteenth centuries made use of powerful imagery and rhetoric. They show a consciousness of being wronged on the part of writers and readers that may have been more widely shared than it would appear at first.

Notes

1 Raymond Williams, *The Country and the City* (New York: Oxford University Press, 1973), 46, 61–8.
2 'The Land', (n.p., n.d.), B.L., Shelfmark Hs 74 11250. There is a Catnach version, 1813–38.
3 Williams, *The Country and the City*, 74–8.
4 Ann Bermingham, *Landscape and Ideology: The English Rustic Tradition 1740–1860* (Berkeley, Los Angeles and London: University of California Press, 1986), 39–40.
5 See Bermingham, Landscape and Ideology, 40 and John Barrell, The Idea of Landscape and the Sense of Place 1730–*1840: An Approach to the Poetry of John Clare* (Cambridge: Cambridge University Press, 1972), 114–18; J. M. Neeson, *Commoners: Common Right, Enclosure and Social Change in England, 1700–1820* (Cambridge: Cambridge University Press, 1993), 284–5; Johanne Clare, *John Clare and the Bounds of Circumstance* (Kingston and Montreal: McGill-Queen's University Press, 1987), 36–7.
6 Ian Dyck argues persuasively that Robert Bloomfield was against enclosure, though strictly speaking in 'The Farmer's Boy' we see criticism of the new farmers and the loss of the chance to buy land rather than explicit reference to enclosure. Ian Dyck, *William Cobbett and Rural Popular Culture* (Cambridge: Cambridge University Press, 1992), 87. For John Clare and for Goldsmith see also Williams, *The Country and the City*, 136–7, 78.
7 J. L. Hammond and Barbara Hammond. *The Village Labourer, 1760–1832: A Study in the Government of England before the Reform Bill* (London: Longman's Green, 1980), 39. For the argument that commons and wastes only sustained unhealthy and weak animals see Andrew Pringle, *General View of the Agriculture of the County of Westmoreland* (Edinburgh, 1794), 16; Jacob Malcolm, *General View of the Agriculture of the County of Buckingham* (London, 1794), 36; and William Harris, *On the Present Distress of the Country and Suitable Remedies* (London, 1816), 110. Jacob

Malcolm argued that the right of commonage and herbage were not worth having and that no more than one in ten made use of the right, but he used ten times what he had a right to, thus injuring his neighbours. Enclosure would remove this injustice. William Harris agreed that those who had access to commons and wastes were poorer than those who lived in enclosed areas: 'It is a matter of universal experience, that the population in the neighbourhood of those wastes, is at once the most wretched and mischievous which the country any where exhibits. Even the cattle are a stunted and degenerate race.'

8 Barry Reay, *Popular Culture in England 1550–1750* (London and New York: Longman, 1998), 173. See also Neeson, *Commoners*, Chapter 6. Cobbett as cited in Dyck, *William Cobbett and Rural Popular Culture*, 109. Cobbett thought access to the land was of great necessity if one hoped to be self-sufficient and proposed allotment schemes for the poor.

9 Henry Quick, *The Life and Progress of Henry Quick, of Zennor, Written by Himself*, ed. P. A. S. Pool (1844).

10 Holloway, *The Peasant's Fate*, Part II (1802).

11 Nathaniel Dale, *The Eventful Life of Nathaniel Dale, with Recollections & Anecdotes Containing a Great Variety of Business Matters, &c., as Occurred in the Life of the Author* (n.p., printed for the author, n.d.), 11, 88. From the story it appears that Dale's life as farmer began around 1840. In the poem the farm girls are gathering wild strawberries on behalf of the whole farm rather than for themselves.

12 Holloway, *The Peasant's Fate*, Part I (1802).

13 See Jane Humphries, 'Enclosures, Common Rights, and Women: The Proletarianization of Families in the Late Eighteenth and Early Nineteenth Centuries', *Journal of Economic History* 50, no. 1 (1990): 35–41.

14 For a detailed discussion of the ideology of the picturesque see Bermingham, *Landscape and Ideology*, 63–85.

15 'Lillies and Roses. A Favourite Song' (London: J. Jennings, 1790–1840), Bodleian Library, Harding B25(1109) and 'Helen the Fair' (London: J. Pitts, 1819–44), Bodleian Library, Harding B11(237A).

16 'The Song of Phoebe' *Phoebe, the cottage maid* (London, 1811), B.L., Shelfmark Ch 810. See also 'Poor Kate, the Lavender Girl' (n.p., R. Morley, n.d.), B.L., Shelfmark 1161.eee.22.

17 Anna Adcock, 'The Nutting Girl', in her *Cottage Poems* (London, 1808). See also Mr Upton, 'The Ground Ivy Girl', *The British Minstrel*, B.L. 11622.a.46, where the poor orphan little Nell sells ground ivy in London.

18 Rev. W. Huntington, *The Sinner Jaded; Or Memoirs of the Life of the Rev. W. Huntington, The Coal Heaver, Late Minister of Providence Chapel* (London, n.d.), 16. Huntington was born in 1774. For the court decision against gleaning in 1788 see Peter King, 'The Origins of the Gleaning Judgement of 1788: A Case Study of Legal Change, Customary Right and Social Conflict in Late Eighteenth-Century England', *Law and History Review* 10, no. 1 (spring, 1992): 1.

19 Anon., *The Beggar's Complaint, against Rack-Rent Landlords, Corn Factors, Great Farmers, Monopolizers, Paper Money Makers, and War, and Many Other Oppressions. By One who Pities the Oppressed* (Sheffield, 1812), 22.

20 Pamphleteers who regretted the loss of gleaning rights also may have had a more strict interpretation of the law than songs. Despite the 1788 ruling, gleaners continued to glean in many areas. Peter King, 'The Origins of the Gleaning Judgement of 1788', 2–3.

21 'The Gleaners', *Beauties of Glasgow* (Glasgow, 1802), L.C. 2836.

22 'The Cottager's Daughter' (London: J. Catnach, 1814–42), B.L. rb.m.93.

23 Peter Sherston, Esq., *The Months, Commencing with Early Spring; A Poem Descriptive of Rural Scenes and Village Characters* (Bath, 1809).

24 D. Hurn, 'August', in *Rural Rhymes; Or, a Collection of Epistolary, Humorous, and Descriptive Pieces* (Spalding, 1813).

25 Robert Bloomfield, 'The Farmer's Boy', in *Poems* (London: John Van Voorst, 1845), 30.

26 David Davies, *The Case of Labourers in Husbandry* (1795, Reprinted Fairfield: Augustus M. Kelly, 1977), 103. This can also be seen as a statement about how engrossment impoverishes. Davies is speaking of engrossment here. For the contemporary debate about parliamentary enclosure see Neeson, *Commoners*, 18–52.

27 For loss of independence see also J. M. Neeson, 'English Enclosures and British Peasants: Current Debates about Rural Social Structure in Britain c. 1750–1870', *Jahrbuch fur Wirtschafts Geschichte* 22, no. 2 (2000), 26. Neeson argues that while an independent peasantry survived longer in pastoral areas, there was still a lot of enclosure in the north and west which had damaging consequences. See also her *Commoners*, 34–5, 39, 178, for commoners' independence before enclosure and loss of it after.

28 Davies, *The Case of Labourers in Husbandry* (1795), 35, 48–9. For engrossment's contribution to proletarianisation see Neeson, 'English Enclosures and British Peasants', 31.

29 Thomas Marsters, *A View of Agricultural Oppressions: And of their Effects upon Society*, 2nd edition (n.p., Regist, 1798), 20.

30 Economic independence was often deemed desirable to reduce poor relief expenditure rather than simply to better the quality of life of the poor. Still, access to land was frequently seen as a way to economic independence. Thomas Estcourt's proposal for helping the rural poor in the parish of Lord Newton involved giving each of them as much land as they could cultivate, and they all accepted the offer. He claims the scheme worked out very well and the only ones to continue drawing poor relief were four old or sick parishoners. Thomas Estcourt, Esq., MP, *An Account of the Result of an Effort to Better the Condition of the Poor in a Country Village and Some Regulations Suggested by Which the Same Might be Extended to Other Parishes of a Similar Description* (London, 1804), 3.

31 Roy Palmer, *The Sound of History: Songs and Social Comment* (Oxford and New York: Oxford University Press, 1988), 41. Palmer is only aware of one ballad specifically written against country enclosure, from a 1753 manuscript. There are several ballads opposing town enclosures as well as references to enclosure in ballads on other subjects. Most ballads in print on town enclosures seem to be from the early 1800s: Neeson, *Commoners*, 286. Also, commoners only resisted enclosure when

they thought they had a chance to succeed, which further complicates finding evidence of protest: Neeson, *Commoners*, 260. For the local nature of custom see Andy Wood, 'The Place of Custom in Plebeian Political Culture: England, 1550–1800', *Social History* 22, no. 1 (1997): 49.

32 Clare, *John Clare and the Bounds of Circumstance*, 36.

33 'The Pleasant History of Thomas Hic-ka-thrift', in Samuel Pepys, *Chapbooks, Penny Merriments*, vol. 1, no. 3. Cited in Reay, *Popular Culture in England*, 53.

34 'Come, buy this new Ballad, before you doe goe: If you raile at the Author, I know what I know. To the Tune of Ile tell you but so', *Roxburghe Ballads*, 157–60.

35 'The Cries of the Poor against the Oppression of the Rich', *Two Excellent old Songs. Entitled, I. The Humours of the Age, II. The Cries of the Poor against the Oppression of the Rich* (n.p., n.d.), B.L., 11621.b.7.

36 'A New Song on the Times' (London: J. Pitts, 1819–44) in Roy Palmer, *A Ballad History of England from 1588 to the Present Day* (London, 1979), 94.

37 'Luckidad's Garland', *Luckidad's Garland; or, When my Old Hat was New* (n.p., n.d.), L.C. 2846. Another version was printed in Liverpool by W. Armstrong, Bodleian Library, Harding B 28 (56).

38 James Templeman, 'Farmer Hobson, a rural poem', in his *Poems and Tales*, vol. 1 (London, 1809): 'And here, no little farmer needy stands, / Oblig'd to sell his corn from off his lands / But several farms that many serv'd before, / Now all in one, increase the rich man's store; / Who, with a moderate profit not content, / Keeps up the price, and makes the poor lament.'

39 Samuel Jackson Pratt, *Cottage-Pictures; Or, the Poor: A Poem*, Part I (London, 1803), 19.

40 For the argument that enclosure was in the national interest see Neeson, *Commoners*, 42–6.

41 The Roxburghe ballad discussed above (see note 34) clearly expressed scepticism that enclosure was done for the common good: 'Yet they'le make as though / 'Twere for common good, / But I know what I know.'

42 'The cries of the poor against the oppression of the rich &c' (n.p., n.d.).

43 For the conversion of arable to pasture in seventeenth-century enclosure see G. E. Mingay, *Enclosure and the Small Farmer in the Age of the Industrial Revolution* (London: Macmillan, 1968), 26.

44 See Neeson, 'English Enclosures and British Peasants', 20, on how large landowners provided the impetus to enclose. For the cursing of enclosers see Keith Thomas, *Religion and the Decline of Magic* (New York: Scribner, 1971), 570.

45 'Times Altered or, the Grumbling Farmers', (n.d., n.p.), B.L., HS 74 1250.

46 See Neeson, *Commoners*, 159–71, 179ff.

47 See Wood, 'The Place of Custom in Plebeian Political Culture', 51–2.

48 Clare, *John Clare and the Bounds of Circumstance*, 36–7.

49 Neeson argues enclosure ended upward mobility for small farmers and peasants by making land too expensive to buy: Neeson, 'English Enclosures and British Peasants', 21. Also J. V. Beckett, 'The Disappearance of the Cottager and the Squatter from the English Countryside: The Hammonds Revisited', in B. A. Holderness

and Michael Turner, eds, *Land, Labour and Agriculture, 1700–1920* (London: The Humbledon Press, 1991), 65–6.

50 Beckett argues enclosure caused the disappearance of smallholders: Beckett, 'The Disappearance of the Cottager and the Squatter', 64. Mick Reed thinks enclosure was bad for labour but not necessarily for small farmers: see Mick Reed, 'Class and Conflict in Rural England: Some Reflections on a Debate', in Mick Reed and Roger Wells, eds, *Class, Conflict and Protest in the English Countryside, 1700–1880* (London: Frank Cass, 1990), 6. Roger Wells disagrees, saying the size of farms in the main corn lands increased markedly in the eighteenth century. Roger Wells, 'The Development of the English Rural Proletariat, 1700–1850', in Wells and Reed, *Class, Conflict and Protest in the English Countryside*, 29–53. The material used in this chapter obviously lends support to Wells's position.

51 John Howlett, Appendix to *Dispersion of the Gloomy Apprehensions, of Late Repeatedly Suggested from the Decline of our Corn-Trade, &c.* (London, 1797). Howlett talked about high rents' negative effect on small farmers' ability to compete with large ones: they could not produce a large enough quantity to meet the growing expenses.

52 For a discussion of the historiographic debate surrounding this issue see Neeson, 'English Enclosures and British Peasants', 18–21. For the decline of the small subsistence farmer see also Neeson, *Commoners*, 223–54.

53 Thomas Marsters also argued that, because of engrossment, there would not be enough farms for everyone who wanted to buy them. It is important to remember that Marsters thought enclosure was good, as long as it ensured the prevalence of many small farms rather than few big ones. He saw engrossment as a separate process from enclosure that did not necessarily have to follow enclosure. Marsters, *A View of Agricultural Oppressions* (1798), 70.

54 Robert Bloomfield, 'The Farmer's Boy', 40.

55 Robert Bloomfield, 'The Farmer's Boy', 7.

56 'The Gipsy's Tent' (Durham: G. Walker, 1797–1834), Bodleian Library, Harding B 11(175).

57 'The Gipsy Queen' (London: J. Pitts, 1819–44), Bodleian Library, Harding B11(3990).

58 Mr Curwen, *Thoughts on the Present Depressed State of the Agricultural Interest of this Kingdom; and on the Rapid Increase of the Poor Rates* (London, 1817), 7.

59 John Blackner, *The History of Nottingham, Embracing its Antiquities, Trade and Manufactures, from the Earliest Authentic Records, to the Present Period* (Nottingham, 1815), 36.

60 Thomas Whitby, *Retrospection: a Rural Poem*, Canto II (London, 1820).

61 N. Bloomfield, 'Elegy on the Enclosure of Honington Green' in *Elegy on the Enclosure of Honington Green and other Poems* (London, 1798), verse 6ff, verse 13. For an account of the impact of enclosure on rural recreation see Robert W. Malcolmson, *Popular Recreations in English Society 1700–1850* (Cambridge: Cambridge University Press, 1973), 107–10. Malcolmson argues that 'By the middle of the nineteenth century any kind of open space for recreation was very much at a premium'.

62 Mary Waldron, *Lactilla, Milkwoman of Clifton: the Life and Writings of Ann Yearsley, 1753–1806* (Athens and London: The University of Georgia Press, 1996), 174.

63 Ann Yearsley, *Stanzas of Woe, Addressed from the Heart On a Bed of Illness, to Levi Eames, Late Mayor of the City of Bristol* (Cambridge: Chadwyck-Healey, 1992; first published London, 1790), ll. 21–32.

64 See Pringle, *General View of the Agriculture of the County of Westmoreland* (1794), 16. See also George Rennie, Robert Brown and John Shirreff, *General View of the Agriculture of the West Riding of Yorkshire* (Edinburgh, 1799), 19. These authors thought that the newly enclosed farms would require a lot of labour, which would increase the number of agricultural labourers in the area. See also Malcolm, *General View of the Agriculture of the County of Buckingham* (1794), 27. For the argument that enclosure caused an increase in the labour supply in agriculture see G. E. Mingay, *Parliamentary Enclosure in England: An Introduction to Its Causes, Incidence and Impact 1750–1850* (London and New York: Longman, 1997), 142; and J. D. Chambers, 'Enclosure and the Labour Supply in the Industrial Revolution', *Economic History Review* 5, no. 3 (1953): 323. For the opposite argument see N. F. R. Crafts, 'Enclosure and Labour Supply Revisited', *Explorations in Economic History* 15, no. 2 (1978): 182.

65 Holloway, *The Peasant's Fate* (1802), 32–3. For the debate about whether enclosure depopulated see Neeson, *Commoners*, 39.

66 Holloway, *The Peasant's Fate* (1802), 33.

67 'Luckidad's Garland', *Luckidad's Garland; or, When my Old Hat was New* (n.p., n.d.), L.C. 2846.

68 Clare, *John Clare and the Bounds of Circumstance*, 43.

69 Blackner, *The History of Nottingham* (1815), 36.

70 N. Bloomfield, 'Elegy on the Enclosure of Honington Green', verse 4.

71 N. Bloomfield, 'Elegy on the Enclosure of Honington Green', verse 14, verse 5.

72 Davies, *The Case of Labourers in Husbandry* (1795), 56.

73 One contemporary who argued in this vein was John Billingsley, quoted by the Hammonds, *The Village Labourer*, 37, as saying that common right made peasants too proud and gave them a sense of independence which made them indolent and scornful of day labour.

74 See, for example, Pringle, *General View of the Agriculture of the County of Westmoreland* (1794), 8. Arthur Young also proposed land allotments for the poor: Arthur Young, ed., *The Annals of Agriculture*, vol. 30 (London, 1770–1813), 52, cited in Bermingham, *Landscape and Ideology*, 76.

75 Estcourt, *An Account of the Result of an Effort to Better the Condition of the Poor* (1804), 3–7. Another allotment proposal came from William Clarkson, but his idea only extended so far as to provide the poor with a vegetable garden and the chance to keep a cow. William Clarkson, Esq., *An Inquiry into the Cause of the Increase of Pauperism and Poor Rates; with a Remedy for the Same* (London, 1815), 56.

76 Clare, *John Clare and the Bounds of Circumstance*, 39. The poet William Holloway saw enclosure as a betrayal of English values, maintaining that 'Albion mourns'

such venal behaviour as depriving the poor of their cot and rendering the peasant 'meanly dependent': Holloway, *The Peasant's Fate* (1802), 36.

77 Wood, 'The Place of Custom in Plebeian Political Culture', 58.

78 'The Gipsy Queen' (London: J. Pitts, 1819–44), Bodleian Library, Harding B11(3990).

79 This ballad is very similar to John Clare's 'The Lament of Swordy Well', where the land is also made to speak and its enclosure is seen as a loss of liberty for the poor: 'There was a time my bit of ground / Made freeman of the slave, / The ass no pounder'd dare to pound / When I his supper gave.' 'The Lament of Swordy Well', J. W. Tibble, ed., *The Poems of John Clare*, vol. 1 (London: J. M. Dent & Sons, 1935).

80 N. Bloomfield, 'Elegy on the Enclosure of Honington Green', verses 14 and 15.

81 N. Bloomfield, 'Elegy on the Enclosure of Honington Green', verse 22.

82 Holloway, Preface to *The Peasant's Fate* (1802).

83 David Service, *The Caledonian Herd-Boy; A Rural Poem* (Yarmouth, J. D. Downes, 1802), 3.

84 'The Beggar's Petition' (n.p., n.d.), B.L., Shelfmark 11621.c.10.

85 William Johnston, *The Life and Times of William Johnston, Horticultural Chemist, Gardener, and Cartwright*, ed. Reginald Alenarley, Esq. (Peterhead, 1859), 10.

86 Anon., *The Beggar's Complaint* (1812), 22.

87 C. J. Ribton-Turner, *A History of Vagrants and Vagrancy and Beggars and Begging* (London: Chapman and Hall, 1887), 205, 214.

88 'Wandering Mary', *The New Myrtle and Vine; or, Complete Vocal library* (London: Thomas Tegg, 1806). On hedge-breaking as a legal offence see Neeson, *Commoners*, 279–80.

89 William Wordsworth, 'Goody Blake and Harry Gill', in his *Complete Poetical Works*, ed. Ernest De Selincourt (Oxford and New York: Oxford University Press, 1936), ll. 17–24.

90 Wordsworth, 'Goody Blake and Harry Gill', ll. 49–56.

91 Wordsworth, 'Goody Blake and Harry Gill', ll. 127–8.

92 'The Poacher' (London: J. Evans, 1780–1812), Bodleian Library, Harding B25(1508).

93 'The Bold Poacher' (Manchester: Swindells, 1796–1853), Bodleian Library, Harding B16(29b).

94 Davies, *The Case of Labourers in Husbandry* (1795), 59–60. On the widespread support for poaching in the countryside, see Douglas Hay, 'Poaching and the Game Laws on Cannock Chase', in *Albion's Fatal Tree: Crime and Society in Eighteenth-Century England* (New York: Pantheon Books, 1975), 207–8.

95 William Cobbett, *Political Register* 22 (May, 1830), 667, quoted in Dyck, *William Cobbett and Rural Popular Culture*, 114.

96 'Bill Brown' (Coppergate, York: C. Croshaw, 1814–50), Bodleian Library, Harding B28(286).

97 The newspaper account is from the *Lincolnshire Chronicle*, quoted in the *Northampton Mercury*, 21 January, 1837. Cited in Palmer, *A Ballad History of England*, 112–13.

98 'Sudborough Heroes', in Palmer, *A Ballad History of England*, 112–13.
99 Speech of Henry Brougham, Esq. MP on Tuesday, the 9th of April, 1816; in the Committee of the Whole House, upon the State of the Agricultural Distresses (London, 1816), 15.
100 John Dunin, *Outlines of the History and Antiquities of Bromley, in Kent* (Bromley, 1815), 43.

4

'Though My Labour's Hard Still 'Tis Sweet': the celebration of the life of work

Popular ballads often celebrated agricultural occupations and the working life. Given the long working hours of agricultural labourers, we have to consider work as integral to rural labourers' identity. By 'rural identity' I mean here a shared, public rural identity that would have been recognised by people both in the country and the city. How was the role of agricultural work seen by the rest of society and to what extent may this public view of it have been shared by agricultural labourers? Under the category 'agricultural work' I include all work connected to agriculture, including that of small farmers, rather than hired labourers exclusively.

In previous chapters we saw songs making claims about the sexual prowess of labourers, about what constituted good social relations in the countryside, and about the ill effects of enclosure. These claims were made by appropriating discourses that already existed in the culture and taking them further or putting them to new uses. I have tried to show that songs give us a window into a rural labouring mentality that was often a challenge to dominant assumptions about labourers. Songs and poems also made claims about the importance of agricultural work. These songs are different from songs discussed in previous chapters in that their appeal to rural labourers is less evident. Indeed, some of them appear to have a rather conservative message about Britishness and domesticity that brings them closer to some of Hannah More's fake ballads discussed in the last chapter. Even when they were bought or enjoyed by agricultural labourers, these songs represented only one possible way of thinking about work, and may not have reflected all of the labourers' true feelings on the subject.

While they acknowledged that work was a hardship and that rural life was difficult, songs spoke of the many compensations enjoyed by workers, such as domesticity and good health, they celebrated the labourer's (or peasant's) pride in his or her occupation and country, and they described the pleasures associated with agricultural labour. It is significant that most of the material comes from the period 1800–15, when agriculture was particularly important to Britain as part of the war effort. While it is possible to see these songs and poems as an attempt to tone down the hardship faced by labourers and persuade them to be loyal to Church and King, they could also be read as a reassertion of the significance of agricultural workers and small farmers for the rest of Britain. They may have appealed to labourers themselves because of their need to see themselves as hard-working and skilled, in contrast to a growing perception of them as lazy and marginal.

This celebration of agricultural work in songs can also be explained in terms of a public need for idyllic representations of the countryside. The art historian Ann Bermingham has shown that in the early 1800s painters wanted to represent the countryside as innocent and ideal due to a sense of loss, caused by enclosure and destruction of the landscape.[1] The reasons for the appeal of such art could be similar to the reasons for the appeal of some of the agricultural labour songs. These different explanations show the diverse readings to which the songs lend themselves. They can be read as reaffirming labourers' pride and identity on the one hand, and as trying to manipulate labour for the good of the nation on the other hand. In the absence of evidence of how exactly people saw these songs, I will say a word or two about each possible reading.

An effort to recover a 'rural identity' is bound to encounter many obstacles, because 'the countryside' consisted of a variety of groups with separate and often conflicting interests. Even within the group of agricultural labourers there were divisions. Thompson identified four kinds of agricultural labourers: farm servants, hired by the year or the quarter; regular labourers, who worked all year round on large farms; casual labourers, paid by a day-rate or piece-rate; and skilled specialists, contracting for the job.[2] It stands to reason that live-in servants had a different life from day labourers.[3] Also, some of these categories could overlap: a small farmer could also work as a day-labourer, or people could belong to different categories at different stages in their life. Aside from their different contractual arrangements, age and gender, agricultural labourers were further divided according to where they lived. Alun Howkins stresses the importance of the local to the labourer's experience, arguing that 'What it meant to be a labourer in different areas of England was literally to live in different worlds.' To a large degree culture was shaped by the local landscape.[4]

Also, we have to consider differences between small farmers and landless labourers, who would have had different interests and different experience.[5] While the former worked for themselves, the latter worked for a master. I will

write about small farmers separately insofar as the sources allow. One of the problems is that ballads do not always reveal whether their characters held land or common rights. When the word 'farmer' is used and the farmer is said to work on his own land, I have assumed that we are dealing with a small farmer, though no information is provided as to how much land he may have farmed. Furthermore, the words 'ploughman' and 'the plough' could refer either to a hired labourer or to a small farmer.[6]

Attempts to distinguish between farmers and labourers have also been fraught with difficulty. Small farmers can fit under the term 'peasants' as defined by Mick Reed. For Reed, the peasant was a household producer who used the land and family labour and did not hire labour all the time but only occasionally. Peasants did not make huge profits; they made a living. Often they had other occupations in the trades, crafts or service. Thus they worked on the land and sometimes at a craft too, while also hiring labour.[7] Because this is a chapter about agricultural labour, I have used labour as the dividing line: if the farmer in the song or poem is described as working, I have included him as sharing this experience with the agricultural labourer. If the farmer is only shown as supervising the work of others, I have classified him as a 'large farmer' and assumed his world was too different from that of agricultural workers to be considered here. In popular songs about work, hired labourers and small farmers shared an experience of agricultural work and proximity to the land, which contained both pains and pleasures.

The contrast between the arable south and the pastoral north also needs to be considered. While labourers and small farmers experienced considerable hardship in the arable south around 1800, they were still doing relatively well in the pastoral north. Day labourers were more common in arable areas by 1800 but rare in pastoral farming.[8] This was in part because the growth of industrial towns in the north provided alternative employment opportunities for labourers, as did the greater prevalence of rural manufacturing, forcing farmers to provide annual contracts in order to safeguard a steady supply of labour.[9] Thus farm service disappeared faster and earlier in the south and east, where arable prevailed: it was nearly gone by the middle of the nineteenth century.[10] This view, argued eloquently by Ann Kussmaul, has come under criticism of late. For instance, A. J. Gritt has argued that the contrast between north and south has been exaggerated by historians and that there were fewer servants in husbandry in the north in 1800 than Kussmaul has claimed. However, he still concludes that the south and east contained fewer peasants, even though the difference was smaller than previously supposed.[11]

The north also had a greater number of small farms than the south.[12] Most historians agree that in the south the number of small landowners declined after parliamentary enclosure.[13] Popular ballads do not fall easily into local categories like north and south, but my general sense is that a greater number of ballads celebrating the work and the lifestyle of the labourer or small farmer were printed in the north and a greater number of ballads depicting working life as painful were printed in the south. However, there is an overlap; both kinds of ballads were printed in both places.

A further complication to the notion of a rural identity is the presence of rural industry in much of the eighteenth-century countryside. Some historians have criticised the 'plough and cow' definition of rural history, which equates rural history with agricultural history, advocating a broader definition of rural history that would include rural industry.[14] Rural industry was very important and, by 1800, very widespread. Agricultural labourers might often supplement their income by doing some spinning or weaving at home.[15] Occupations like stocking knitting and coal mining provided employment for the inhabitants of many villages in the north.[16] After the decline of spinning, lace and straw-plaiting became alternative industries for women in the south and east.[17] But although bi-employment was common, Mick Reed has pointed out that occupational divisions were not clear cut and it is unwise to assume that some forms of income were primary and others secondary: 'a blacksmith with land is not necessarily a blacksmith first and a farmer second, nor is a labourer with land necessarily a labourer first.'[18] Rural industrial work did not preclude the experience of agricultural work for labourers. In most places industrial work usually stopped for the harvest, even if workers were otherwise fully employed in manufacturing.[19]

This chapter will focus on agricultural labour rather than on rural industry, because occupational typology was very strong in popular ballads. Songs about weavers, miners, tailors or shoemakers often did place these trades in a rural setting, but they never showed them performing agricultural labour. Each of these trades had a different literary or artistic stereotype associated with it. Each of them has its own history, its own pattern of prosperity and depression, and its own historiography. For these reasons, it would be impossible to do justice to all of them in a single book.

Ballads that focus on agricultural work are different from the songs I have described up to this point in that they presented less of a challenge to elite art, and their appropriation of mainstream discourses was less subversive. Representations of the working life as painful agree with the work of many historians. But we need to explain the verses that celebrated the joys of work in ways similar to the pastoral and the georgic genre, which required labourers to be happy and content with their lot. Working-class autobiographies and the work of peasant poets described work in very similar terms. Even Steven

Duck, one of the earliest practitioners of the anti-pastoral genre, in later poems wrote that, though everyone feared poverty, in fact the poor man was happy in his labour. Furthermore, he argued, even if poverty were as fearsome as many supposed, peasants should not complain but 'cheerfully bear our fate'.[20]

What are we to make of representations of labour in the work of self-taught poets like Steven Duck? Is it more or less 'authentic' than songs? With songs we are not sure who wrote them but we know they had a working-class audience. We know more about the circumstances of production of peasant poetry, since the authors are known to us, but many of them may have written for an elite literary audience rather than for their peers. In her study of nineteenth-century working-class literature, Martha Vicinus is suspicious of the work of self-taught poets. She argues they had the ambition to rise above their class and often used poetry as an escape from the pains of work. Their musings on nature were shaped by their reading, which was heavily dominated by eighteenth-century pastoral poets (they were more readily and cheaply available than the Romantics). This tradition saw hardship and divisive issues as unpoetic, and Vicinus argues that self-taught poets did not really represent working-class life or their experience, but merely imitated other poets.[21] However, this is not true of all peasant poets. John Clare wrote poetry that was very critical of his superiors for bringing enclosure to his village. Other peasant poets were also capable of using poetry to make sense of their experience, and they did not always slavishly follow pastoral examples. It is worth comparing some of their work to popular songs, particularly when they dwelled on similar themes.

Historians tend to conclude that the literary/artistic celebrations of the supposed pleasures of manual work were false while accounts of pain were true.[22] Perhaps the celebration of labour common in songs and poems was a way to make labourers accept their lot and served to contribute to what Thompson called 'the fatalism of the cottager'.[23] There were ballads and poems that confirm these suspicions, particularly the ones that struggled to convey the message that the simple life was best. They argued the labourer was happy because he or she had fewer ambitions and fewer cares than the great: he or she did not care about expensive clothes or book learning, was 'plain dressing' and 'plain dealing', and, most ridiculous of all, had no worries except for love.[24] The message was that, to be happy, one needed to get rid of one's desires; if one desired nothing, one lacked nothing. The shepherd's content in 'The Contented Ruricolist', for instance, is based on the fact that he never thinks of honour, or riches, or high title; he just worries about earning his bread. The song assumes the worry about earning one's bread is much less taxing than the cares of honour and title.[25] Also, in 'The Pious Cottager' the narrator says he pines for no pleasures beyond what he has, but his sole hope is for the life to come.[26] But songs contained a variety of sentiments and carried many shades of meaning. Not all songs that celebrated labour had the simple function of teaching the working poor to accept their place in society.

John Archer points out that 'For the labourer's part, notions of self-respect and dignity could be kept up only through displays of deference on the one hand or through acts of protest on the other'.[27] But it is conceivable that notions of self-respect and dignity could also be supported by poetic celebrations of labour. Though it is inaccurate to describe them as radicals, labourers and peasants were not without pride.[28] Gary Harrison points out that because moralists and reformers kept talking about industriousness, the poor soon realised they could use their labour as a source of legitimacy.[29] This accounts in part for the celebration of work found in popular songs and poems. As the ruling class had to legitimise its position of power to the rest of society, so the peasants and farmers had to explain their way of life and articulate their importance to Britain. This was an integral part of the structuring of a rural identity.[30]

The tension between the hardships and pleasures of work

Keith Thomas defines work as 'arduous, involving effort and persistence beyond the point at which the task ceases to be wholly pleasurable'. It is both a blessing and a curse.[31] Thus pain and pleasure are part of the very definition of work. The views of work as pain and pleasure both existed in the eighteenth century. Classical economists defined work as a curse, and argued every man would be idle if he could. If it was not painful, it was not work. A system of punishments and rewards was necessary to make a person work.[32] John Locke believed that 'labour for labour's sake is against nature'.[33] On the other hand, writers like George Berkeley believed there could be no happiness without labour, either physical or mental.[34] This contradiction is also present in the life of John Clare, as his recent biographer, Jonathan Bate, makes clear. On the one hand, Clare was not cut out for manual work and had a difficult time finding an occupation he could tolerate. On the other hand, based on his own account, working as a casual farm labourer for Francis Gregory was some of the best time in his life, because his master was kind and he was not strictly supervised.[35]

Even factory workers came to represent work in terms of this tension between pain and pleasure, although we know that work in the early factories was of the most difficult and dehumanising kind. Initially workers wrote angry lyrics protesting against growing mechanisation and factory discipline, but Vicinus argues that after 1840 they grew more accustomed to the factory system and added more cheerful or humorous songs to the angry ones.[36]

An ambivalent attitude towards work is also evident in when and where working songs were sung. Roy Palmer argues that labourers did not sing songs about work while they worked, but rather songs which were escapist, dealing with any other subject but work. He cites a priest in eighteenth-century France who congratulated poor people on their fine singing, and they answered they sung at work not because they were happy, but to lessen their sorrow and pain.[37] This appears to be confirmed with respect to industrial workers but we know less about what field labourers sung at work. They were always represented as singing, both in ballads and pastoral verse. We know that singing accompanied the completion of different stages of agricultural work. For instance, in the early nineteenth century it was customary to dance and sing at the end of a day's planting along the Scottish border to the music supplied by an itinerant fiddler.[38] Harvest songs accompanied the celebrations after the harvest in both north and south. There is no evidence regarding what particular songs were performed at these times, but it is plausible that songs celebrating the joy of labour were usually sung during periods of leisure.

The essence of the pleasure/pain dichotomy is expressed in two lines from the song 'Thrasher': 'My labour's hard but still 'tis sweet / And easy to endure.'[39] There is a contradiction between hard and sweet, between ease and the difficulty suggested by the word 'endure'. Even George Crabbe, who thought he was providing an overdue corrective to the pastoral idealisation of rural life, had to grapple with this tension. On the one hand, he states firmly that there is no rural paradise, that there has been no golden age since the fall of man, that the peasant's life is hard, and labour is painful.[40] On the other hand, he depicts a happy, industrious swain, whose needs are amply satisfied by his little cot and his meagre possessions.[41]

Thus, while songs reflected the difficulties of the rural life, they also celebrated its pleasures. Historians sometimes tend to ignore these, because they study the material life of rural workers and smallholders rather than their artistic expression. John Archer, for example, sees the life of agricultural labourers solely as unhappy with no redeeming features. He describes children as young as 6 (though usually 9–10) having to take up their first farm jobs in stone-picking, crow-scaring, stock-keeping, weeding and dibbling (making holes in the soil for planting), which 'left permanent psychological scars' on the workers.[42] When we compare that to the recorded experience of peasant poets or working-class autobiographers we see a more nuanced picture.

That is not to say that while an agricultural labourer (or small farmer) was doing back-breaking work in the field, he or she felt pleasure. What I want to argue is that the celebration of work could have had a positive role to play in popular culture. To show that the sources I am using represent an aspect of workers' experience that may have appealed to workers themselves and need to be taken seriously, I will first examine their accounts of the pain of labour. Then I will show how the same sources constructed an apology for agricultural labour by outlining the compensations, the sources of pride, and in the end the very joy of work. I hope by the end it will become clear why these songs and poems insisted that being an agricultural labourer or small farmer had its good sides.

Since these ballads and songs were so eager to promote agricultural labour, one might expect to see a more direct association between pleasure and work itself. However, in the majority of cases, the pleasure came from an experience other than the work itself. It is rare to see unequivocal praise of work. Songs and poems that celebrated agricultural work usually claimed that it was a fine thing to be an agricultural labourer or small farmer, but when read carefully they reveal that this was due largely to the rural way of life.

Let us examine more closely ballads and poems that appear to praise work and see to what extent this is really so. In 'The Return of Spring' the labourers' joy at the return of spring is in part due to their joy at resuming work:

> The ploughman with speed, and sack full of feed
> The carter drives out with his team:
> The shepherd with crook, and the angler with hook,
> Repairs to the vallies and streams.
> The farmer with brake, and the gard'ner with rake,
> All chearfully work out the day:
> Some whistle, some sing, all welcome the Spring,
> Which drove the cold Winter away.[43]

The return to work is intimately connected to the return of spring, and arguably the cheerful tone of the verses had more to do with the change of seasons, signalled by increased activity, than with ploughing or planting. This kind of pleasure in the new season is also suggested by the following lines from the pen of a peasant poet:

> Rejoicing to my labour go with speed,
> Breaking the stubborn clods, then sow the seed,
> Yea, crop the ragged hedge-rows when they need.[44]

Many ballads showed agricultural labourers at work as cheerfully singing or whistling.[45] In one song a thresher is made to say "Tis for myself when all is said, / I work thus with such glee'.[46] The 'glee' in this case suggests the thresher is happy to be able to make a living, or perhaps he is a small farmer working on his own farm, thus the words 'for myself'. The good thing here is not the physical activity of threshing, but the employment. The following verse makes a similar claim for women's labour:

> So now to conclude and end my ditty,
> To all country lasses that are sweet and pretty,
> Never forsake your own country employment,
> No city can afford so sweet an enjoyment.[47]

Here the job is enjoyable because the worker is living in the country.

In most poems and songs the life of agricultural labourers was shown to be happy independently of the labour. When he or she was at rest, or when surrounded by friends and family, the labourer was happy and this compensated for the hardship of labour. Harvest songs were usually of this kind. The labourers rejoiced when the harvest was over – in other words, when work had ended:

> And their work being done
> They're the happiest people on earth.
> When harvest is done,
> With the former old song,
> The jolly farmer among the rest,
> We will dance, sing, and say,
> It is our holiday,
> We'l[l] have ale and good beer of the best.[48]

Most harvest songs celebrated the state of leisure and play that came with the end of work.[49] If the workers seem to be enjoying themselves during the harvest, often their happiness came from the surrounding environment: the pretty girls, the good liquor.[50] The completion of a task or a day's labour could bring about a sense of fulfilment, as in 'The Contented Ruricolist', where the labourer feels contented at the end of the day after his labour is done (but not during).[51] And of course, as in the pastoral tradition, there was love. In 'The Scotch Shepherd' the ploughman is happy in his humble life independently of his labour. It is not the work that makes him happy, but the carefree nature of his lifestyle and his love for his sweetheart.[52] The heroes of 'Clean Pease Strae' are also happy despite the poverty and hard work because they have their love.[53]

The memories of James Paterson confirmed the possibility of a pleasant life for agricultural labourers, apart from the difficult work. A few qualifications must be made. Paterson was writing about the north (Kilmarnock); he was not a labourer but the son of a farmer who employed labourers; and his parents were kind, old-fashioned masters who preserved the old paternalistic relationship with their employees:

> Much of the old-fashioned system prevailed at the Struthers. Both my father and mother were young; and there was a happy blending of pastime with labour. All sat at the same table, which, of course, was greatly extended in autumn, to accommodate so many reapers.[54]

Paterson described the agricultural labourer Henry, who boiled supper for the horses, swept the stables and the courtyard, acted as banister during harvest, raked and gathered hay, but was also literate and read *Aesop's Fables*: 'Although Henry's outward man was, in general, not worth a few shillings, still with all his appearance of poverty, he was comparatively rich. He seldom had less within his reach than a hundred guineas in gold.'[55] Leisure time was enjoyed to the full:

> The two packmen often led the chase in a game of hide-and-seek, and it was surprising to see how a band of hard-working men and women could enjoy themselves so much after the labours of the day were over, and how briskly they got up in the morning to renew their toil.[56]

Nostalgia for his childhood might explain Paterson's account and it is certainly an explanation for the celebration of the peasant's happy lot found in some late eighteenth- and early nineteenth-century songs. It may account for the peasant poet David Service's description of his 'carefree' life as a herd-boy and Robert Bloomfield's verses about the joys of working as a farm boy.[57] Samuel Catton's autobiography where he said of himself: 'in 1804 he went to live at a place called Tunstall, where he learnt to hold the plough, of which employment he was particularly fond' may have a similar explanation.[58] All of these accounts were written with hindsight, by mature men describing a happier youth in the country.

Nostalgia for home also played a role in some popular songs. Being away from one's home during a time of war must have made tasks like ploughing and threshing seem much more attractive. And, indeed, an anti-war feeling is suggested by the sense of loss found in many songs about ploughmen turned soldiers or sailors. In 'The Ploughboy Turned Soldier' the narrator reminisces about how he enjoyed working as a ploughman, sowing and harrowing while listening to the birds.[59] 'The Ploughman Turn'd Sailor' is about a ploughman whose friend, a ship's carpenter, persuades him to become a sailor. This is a grave mistake for him and he hates the battles and storms he has to face, dreaming about his wonderful life as ploughman. Finally he returns home to find his father has died and wife run away.

> Ah! Why did I roam
> When so happy at home,
> I could sow I could reap,
> Ere I left my poor plough to go ploughing the deep.

At first the ploughman/sailor is devastated but it turns out the news about his father and wife was a joke they played on him to teach him a lesson. He vows never to leave the plough again.[60]

Ballads and poems about the pleasures of rural life may have resonated with a rural labouring audience even in the south during the first half of the eighteenth century, when making ends meet as an agricultural labourer was relatively easier.[61] But such accounts continued to be produced after 1800 and we know that the audience for broadsides and chapbooks increased at this time. Nevertheless, most of them either recognised that work was a hardship or avoided the issue. However, in the next section I will discuss songs that more directly praised the experience of work and that tended to have a broader ideological agenda than the ones hitherto discussed.

Work as pain

In the middle of the eighteenth century the rural poets Steven Duck and Mary Collier described the hardship of agricultural work and the pains endured by labourers. The complaints of Steven Duck and Mary Collier found resonance in the poems of other peasant poets as well as in popular songs. When songs are read carefully, one can see that the way the work is described signifies that it was hard. 'Song of The Haymakers' is in many ways a typical harvest song, but the hay makers' work is clearly not a blissful state. They are hot, tired and dissatisfied: 'And hard is our work with the wain and the plough / Oh! But poor is our daily reward.'[62] 'The Painful Plough' through its title and refrain also suggests agricultural labour is difficult. In contrast to 'Song of the Haymakers', it speaks of the 'stormy winds and cold' that the ploughman must endure in winter.[63] Even Burns's 'The Cottager's Saturday Night', a ballad about domesticity, began with the following verse:

> November chill blows loud with angry brow,
> The short'ning Winter's day is near a close;
> The miry beasts retreat from the plough;
> The black'ning train of crows seek their repose

The toil-worn cottager from labour goes,
This night his weekly toil is at an end,
Collects his spades, his mattock, and his hoes,
Hoping the morn in ease and rest to spend,
And weary o'er the Moor his course does home-ward bend.[64]

The cold, the dark, the filth of the 'miry beasts' and the fatigue of the cottager paint a dark picture of his daily life. Also, his toil only comes to an end on a Saturday night and he gets only one day of rest. The wet and cold are also emphasised in 'The Goodman of Auchermouchtie; or, the Goodwife Turn'd Goodman', where the cold wind is said to 'slay' the ploughman. Both male and female agricultural labour is here described as painful: the ploughman finds his labour hard to bear, so he tries to exchange jobs with his wife, only to find that her labour is equally arduous.[65] 'The Jolly Thrasherman' speaks about 'hard labour', having to make a living by the sweat of one's brow, fatigue, 'yoke'. In addition, the labourer's rewards are poor in spite of all the effort: 'But still the times grow harder and I am very poor / We hardly know how to keep the wolf from the door.'[66]

Like songs, working-class autobiographies often spoke of hardship. Samuel Westcott Tilke, who worked on a farm as a ploughboy and looked after the team of horses, wrote: 'My sufferings, in the situation I filled, are not easily described.'[67] Reminiscent of John Archer's account of child labour, William Johnston described the suffering he endured when he was a 'herd laddie'. He was employed in the job by his aunt when he was 10 and though he only had to look after two cows, he found his duty quite onerous:

> Every one knows what a weary, monotonous life a 'herd laddie' has to endure. Exposed to all weathers, his only protection is a blanket; and with a 'run' as his ensign of office, he cowers beneath a hedge when it rains, or dances about when the sun shines, devours turnips, harries nests, or kindles a fire, at which he 'hunkers' down with his bosom crony.[68]

After 1800, due in part to the influence of George Crabbe, even pastoral poets became more sensitive to the difficulties of agricultural work. The anonymous *The Happy Shepherd* tells of 'the drudgery of rustic employments'.[69] The poet William Barre calls the fieldsman's work 'drudgery' and the poet D. Hurn uses the word 'pain' to describe the labour of the ploughman in the harsh Fen country.[70]

If life was difficult for the male agricultural labourer, it was even more so for rural women in the south and east. Historian K. D. M. Snell has shown that after 1750 there was a change in the pattern of agricultural work. Before most agricultural tasks were shared by both genders, whereas now there was a greater specialisation of work. Women had participated in reaping, loading and spreading dung, ploughing, threshing, thatching, following the harrow, sheep shearing, and in some places worked as shepherdesses, but in the nineteenth century their tasks became fewer and more limited.[71] Female wages in the south and east fell after 1760, with Norfolk and Suffolk being the most depressed. While men came to dominate arable agriculture, women found more employment in pastoral areas.[72] After the Napoleonic Wars home employments like weaving declined and the cheap labour of women as field labourers grew.[73] According to Alun Howkins, female field labourers were reviled in the nineteenth century because they were seen as the antithesis of the ideal of domesticity and femininity. Because of the expectation that women work indoors, women who did field labour came to be seen as suspect. Milkmaids fit the ideal well because dairying was usually done indoors.[74] Although the period studied by Howkins is later than the period we are dealing with, we already see in these songs more examples of women doing indoor work. Though there are songs like 'The Merry Reaper of the Moor', which celebrated women field labourers, the songs that made the most emphatic defence of women's work were about their work in the dairy or indoors.[75]

A wonderful song of this kind is 'Answer to Nae luck about the house. A favourite Scottish song'.[76] It tells the story of John, a husband compelled to do his wife's chores, such as minding the children and milking the cow, while she is away. Previously he had not appreciated Maggy's work, but now that he has to do it himself he sees how hard it is, makes lots of mistakes, and is grateful for her return. Again we see here a sensitivity to the fact that labour is a hardship itself, regardless of other difficulties one might face. A similar song is the classic 'The Churlish Farmer', which exists in numerous versions and was reprinted over and over again throughout the eighteenth and nineteenth centuries. A version of it was discussed above for what it had to say about sexuality, but it is also relevant here because of its exploration of the gendered division of farm labour. It echoes Mary Collier's 'The Woman's Labour' in highlighting contemporary understanding of the importance of female labour. As in 'Answer to Nae Luck about the House', the husband and wife exchange jobs. On a rainy day the farmer gets angry at his wife for enjoying the easy lot of working indoors, while he has to plough in the cold, and commands her to go to the field with his man John, while he stays at home. Soon the farmer finds that he does not have the skills to do his wife's labour and runs to the field to call her back, only to find that he has become a cuckold thanks to John.[77]

Aside from the hardship of work itself, songs often pointed out that the labourer faced economic hardship, usually due to high prices of provisions, unemployment and low wages. This was partly discussed in chapter 2 and it is an area on which a tremendous amount of historical research has concentrated. Some place the beginning of a rise in the cost of living in 1750, though most historians agree that the standard of living fell most sharply for agricultural labourers in the south after the Napoleonic wars.[78] Where service in husbandry survived, farm servants had a little more security as they were boarded and fed by the master, but they had little independence, low wages and long working hours, while hired labourers had to put up with poor food and housing and could be dismissed at any time.[79] After 1815 overpopulation and the return of soldiers created underemployment.[80] Since labourers after parliamentary enclosure were less likely to have land or common right and were more dependent on the wage, any fall in wages could have serious consequences.[81] In fact, wages were often too low to survive on, necessitating a parish subsidy.[82] If men's wages were low, women's wages had experienced an even greater fall because there was less work available for them and they had to rely on casual piece work or day labour. At the same time family size grew larger, so the overall family income was quite insufficient.[83]

The hardships endured by agricultural workers and small proprietors figured in diverse writings from the period. George Crabbe's description of the low standard of living of agricultural labourers and small farmers was echoed by the labourer Samuel Westcott Tilke:

> The poet, and persons possessed with all the imaginitiveness of romance are accustomed to delineate a rustic's life as one of bliss. Nothing can exceed the classic beauty of the Seasons, as depicted by the exquisite taste and genius of Thomson; nor can any thing be more artlessly and correctly portrayed than the experience of poor Giles, by Bloomfield, the Suffolk poet, in his lovely poem of 'The Farmer's Boy'. But there is much which the eye sees not, and many complainings and hardships which the peasantry have to endure, unobserved and unpitied by persons unaccustomed to rural life. Every situation has its peculiar trials, yet there is mercy in knowing that.[84]

Among the evils that plague the life of the agricultural labourer, the poet James Templeman listed low wages, high food prices, taxation and the tyranny of greedy farmers. He contrasted this to a time in the past, before taxes were raised, when the labourer could satisfy most of his wants with his wages and could even add roast or boiled meat, eggs, butter, cheese, live poultry and fresh fruit to his table.[85] He called those responsible for high taxes tyrants. This state of affairs led him to make the anti-patriotic statement:

> Boast then, no more, of England's favour'd isle,
> Perish the Muse that seeks us to beguile!
> Nor vainly speak of salutary laws,
> If men in power desert the suffrer's cause.[86]

This was his answer to the more patriotic pastorals and songs discussed below, which praised the wealth and fertility of rural England.[87] Templeman's nostalgia for a time of greater prosperity is shared by the song 'The Labouring Man', which contrasts the 'present time' with the good old days: in the past the labourer was cheerful, clean, neat and was paid 'a fair day's wages'; now he can barely make ends meet.[88]

The poverty of landless labourers was noticed by a number of other country poets. The poet William Nicholson describes Sandy the shepherd as too poor to get married. Giving up hope of finding a mate Sandy consoles himself with writing verse.[89] Ballads also acknowledged that the agricultural labourer could suffer want due to unemployment or old age. The hero in 'The Old Shepherd' is a poor and sorrowful old man, who has fallen on hard times after a life of work and is forced to beg.[90]

As we saw in chapter 2, the labourer's discomfort often came from having a bad master. Samuel Catton recalled working as a ploughboy in a village named Bramfield in Suffolk (a very depressed area), where his master and mistress were drunkards and their son deranged. He was very uncomfortable and badly treated.[91] The problems associated with a bad master were also described in the ballad 'Watty', whose hero became a live-in labourer for an unkind mistress. He was underfed and mistreated by the entire household.[92] The harsh master even invades the dreams of one poor labourer in James Templeman's 'Farmer Hobson': the tired James falls asleep and farmer Hobson appears in his dream, calling him an 'inattentive slave', giving him three blows, and telling him to confess that he has been sleeping all day instead of working.[93] Some contemporaries felt that agricultural labourers were more dependent on the whim of a master than industrial workers because while the latter worked by the piece, agricultural labourers worked by the day or week, and if the price of wheat fell the farmer could lay off half the hands and reduce the wages of the other half.[94]

It wasn't only agricultural labourers that spoke of hardship in songs and autobiographies. The work of farmers could also be hard. While celebrating the jolly life of the farmer, the poet William Barre describes the work as quite difficult: it takes place in the cold month of February. The farmer's work is compared to that of slaves.[95] The hard life of poor farmers is also described in the poem 'Pursuits of Agriculture':

Some difference there is, I ween,
Norfolk and Cumberland between
Where no fat farmer, but a boor,
Tills a few acres, lean and poor;
Where land is let so devilish dear,
The farmer must shave very near.
And he who pays such monstrous wages
To every bumpkin he engages,
Must practise every art and any
(Honest I mean) to save a penny.[96]

As we might expect, the small farmer is associated with Cumberland in this 1808 poem and the large farmer with Norfolk. As we can see, the lifestyle of the small Cumberland farmer is not that far removed from that of agricultural labourers.

In certain regions small farmers could be so poor as to evoke the pity of their betters. A contemporary recorded the miserable circumstances of a Welsh farmer:

> Descending from this station, I was requested by the gentleman who attended me, to examine the cottage of a small Welsh farmer in Cwm y Clo, as he said it was a tolerable specimen of this description of buildings in Caernarvonshire. I entered a small gate, and first observed a wretched hovel for his cattle: the hay-rick was formed by a large slate, placed near one side, with its edge on the ground: the room was so broken in and damaged, that only one corner afforded shelter to the miserable beasts from the fury of the mountain storms. I remarked, on the outside of this place, in an angle formed by the junction of two walls, a small slated roof, to protect from the rain the turf intended for fuel. A path between two rude stone walls, adorned with holly hedges, led me to the dwelling. The door was so low, that I was obliged to stoop considerably to enter; and coming out of a bright sun-shine, it was not till some time had elapsed that I was able to distinguish any thing in this hut, except the gleam of light that came down the chimney. This was at least equal to what the six small panes of glass in the window afforded. On the open hearth were a few peat-ashes, the remains of a fire with which the old man had a little while before cooked his dinner. The frame of the roof was formed by branches of trees fixed to larger timbers by straw or hay-bands. This frame was covered with sods, and the whole with slates, which, in the mountains, are obtained in great plenty. The furniture consisted of an old bed, an oak chest, a range of shelves for such poor eating utensils as were necessary in this lowly habitation, some old earthen vessels, some dingy pewter dishes, and a few other things, which, from the darkness of the place, were rendered indistinguishable to me.[97]

Such difficult circumstances often necessitated frugality and self-denial on the part of small farmers. A song that takes the form of a dialogue between a

Scottish farmer and a weaver makes this clear. When the weaver accuses the farmer of greed and luxury, the farmer explains how hard it is to pay the landlord, how unjust the rack rents are, and how he is compelled to be frugal and deny himself tasty food (which tradesmen could afford) in order to make ends meet. He points out his whole family has to work: his boys delve, thresh and plough, his girls milk the cow, spin and sew.[98]

The post-war agricultural depression caused many bankruptcies among smaller farmers (and even hurt larger agrarian capitalists).[99] In her autobiography, the farmer's daughter Rose Allen described some of the hardships that could befall a farmer after a failed harvest in 1824. Compelled to let go of two farm servants, her family was left with only one servant, which made it necessary for the rest of them to work harder. The cattle were dying and her father fell ill at the same time. They had to apprentice her brother, 15, to a farmer.[100]

Compensations for the pain of work

Despite all these hardships, ballads and poems claimed that there were delights, which compensated for whatever pain the labourer might endure. The notion that agricultural labour was much better than industrial labour was shared by Adam Smith, who thought the monotonous, mechanical nature of industrial labour and the repetitiveness of mechanised tasks made labourers stupid and unhappy, while agricultural labour allowed them to exercise considerable skill and creativity.[101] The songs of nineteenth-century factory workers sometimes expressed a certain envy of their agrarian counterparts. 'The Factory Bell', written in the 1830s from the point of view of a factory worker, points out the advantage of the more lax supervision and time organisation enjoyed by agricultural workers.[102] The work of small farmers could be even more favourably contrasted with industrial work.[103] Their relative independence from employers or patrons was often emphasised in popular songs.[104]

The stereotype of the healthy environment of the country was also used to make rural work seem preferable:

> We dwell in the meadows and toil in the sod,
> Far away from the city's dull gloom
> And more jolly are we, though in rags we may be,
> Than the pale faces over the loom.[105]

The health benefits of any kind of physical labour were discussed in a number of eighteenth-century texts. John Locke believed an idle lifestyle caused gout and spleen. He denigrated the leisured gentleman and scholar who becomes a useless member of the commonwealth in that mature age which should make him most serviceable, whilst the sober and working artisan and the frugal laborious countryman performs his part well and cheerfully goes on in his business to a vigorous old age...[106]

Edmund Burke argued that 'excessive rest and relaxation can be fatal producing melancholy, dejection, despair, and often self-murder' while labour, defined as the overcoming of difficulties, was 'necessary to health of body and mind'.[107]

Songs picked up on the idea that physical labour in the fresh air of the countryside made one healthier than one's urban or industrial counterparts. This relates to the chapter on sexuality, where we will see that songs about peasant sexuality also made the assumption of peasants being healthier and thus better lovers than those who lived in the city. We can see this theme in 'The Merry Reaper of the Moor':

> The miser views his splendid store,
> Yet full infirm his senses fail,
> He wastes his health in saving more;
> Unlike young Lubin of the vale.

> Those who till noon on pillows lie,
> In twelve months live but half a year,
> While they who would be truly wise,
> Who would both health and wealth secure;
> Like me, must with the sky-lark rise,
> The merry reaper of the moor.[108]

Industriousness is conducive to well-being, while sloth causes illness. Similarly, 'The Cumberland Farmer' contrasts the happy farmer who has his health with the unhappy squire who has gout. The squire would gladly exchange places with the farmer if he could get rid of his affliction.[109]

Songs and poems credited agricultural labourers and farmers with a poetic sensibility and an awareness of the beauty of nature, which could further ease the hardship of work.[110] In the 'Sheep Shearing' the narrator describes in detail the flowers and birds whose beauty makes the sheep shearers' labour more joyful.[111] Peasant poets too, whether because they were imitating conventional pastoral or because they genuinely valued the natural world, took pains to convey a sense of natural beauty. Loving descriptions of birds and green woods can be found in the work of the peasant poet Thomas Darby.[112]

David Service took this a step further, making a connection between his religion and his love of nature:

The great Creator's high and matchless power
Shines in each spire of grass, and simple flower.[113]

It is difficult to tell whether life influenced art or art influence life, but autobiographical writings by agricultural labourers and farmers expressed similar ideas.
In his autobiography William Johnston remembered fondly his years as a herd
laddie: 'Here my youthful mind first began to feel the influence of nature.
The singing of the lark, the habits of birds, and the ever changing seasons, all
impressed my young mind.'[114] This feeling was shared by one working-class
writer in her autobiography. Rose Allen, also discussed above, was a farmer's
daughter whose family was compelled to move to town, where she became a
servant, often thinking nostalgically of her rural home: 'As the [wagon] drove
up the avenue of Holly Grove, Mr Stanhope's place, a delicious fragrance filled
the air, of new-mown hay and flowers, and reminded me of past times, when
such delights were habitual.' In the end she returned to her native Hale, where
she and her sweetheart settled to a 'quiet cottage life'.[115]

Farmers were also associated with poetry and an aesthetic appreciation of
nature in some of these texts.[116] In the 'Dialogue between the farmer and
weaver', the farmer boasts of his poetic talent but the weaver finds his clumsy
pastoral verses a monstrosity. The farmer gives a list of the poets that have
influenced him:

Allan Ramsay's songs, Burns, and
Some English Poems too; but modern lays,
Of Southern kind, ne'er met my warmest praise;
Not but they're very fine, so critics mention,
What then? They're quite aboon my comprehension;
Save such as Bloomfield, sweetes singing souter,
Though his plain Muse, some snarling critics hoot her;
And such as Thomson, Pomfret, Pope, and Pyes,
Their stile's too dazzling for my vulgar eyes.

The weaver is appalled and calls him a vulgar bumpkin, pointing out that the
most refined modern poets write about more fanciful subjects, rather than
nature.[117] But as we will argue in the following section, farmers were depicted
as having a slightly different relationship to nature from agricultural labourers.
Their concern was more to control nature and make it yield abundance, while
the labourer was content to simply admire it.

By the end of the eighteenth century domesticity was increasingly seen as one
of the rewards of industry. According to Ann Kussmaul, live-in servants were
seen as part of the farmer's family. With the decline of service in husbandry,

the labourer's own immediate family gained a greater significance.[118] Paintings of rural life at the end of the eighteenth century often showed the peasant surrounded by wife and children.[119] The elite praised and encouraged domesticity among the peasantry, but the idea did not necessarily originate with the elite. Celebrations of domesticity were usually to be found in popular songs that otherwise portrayed rural labour as painful and difficult:

> With Phoebus the toil of the day we begin,
> I shepherd my flock, while she sits down to spin,
> Our cares thus domestic we'll arduous pursue,
> And ever will love, when we've nought else to do.[120]

In 'The Jolly Thrasherman' the agricultural labourer is rewarded by the squire for his love of his family. Having encountered the thresher on one of his walks along the highway, the squire asks him how he maintains his wife and children. The thresher lists the jobs he does – reaping, mowing, hedging, ditching, harrowing, ploughing. When the hard day's labour is done, he goes home and takes his youngest baby in his lap, feeling happy because he is surrounded by his loved ones. The squire is particularly pleased to hear of the thresher's fondness for his wife and rewards him with sixty acres of good land.[121]

Though describing a small farmer rather than a labourer, 'The Muirland Farmer' creates a similar picture of domestic bliss:

> I've a daintie wee wifie to daut when I please,
> Twa bairnies, twa callans, that skelp owere the leas,
> An' they'll soon can assist at the ploughin o't.[122]

It is natural that domesticity should be so important to small farmers because they usually relied on the labour of their whole family to run the farm. The hero of 'The Muirland Farmer' has hired two servants but he is eager for his two sons to come of age so they could do the ploughing.[123] 'The Cottager's Saturday Night', whose hero also appears to have been a small farmer rather than a hired labourer, depicts a happy rural household, where all the members contribute to the family economy. The older children work as farm servants ploughing, herding or doing errands. As usual, the wife is responsible for the dairy. They only have one cow, but it is enough to make some cheese, which the wife prefers to feed her husband instead of selling.[124]

The family's role in comforting the farmer and making him forget his toil is emphasised in another song:

> Now the dew-drop of eve is shed from the skies
> And the farmer his work has completed,

> Then home to his cottage he cheerfully hies,
> 'Mongst his neighbours and family seated.
> A jug of brown nappy – oblivion of toil,
> With a friend and his wife is quaff'd cheerly;
> He toasts his good landlord, he blesses the soil,
> And his dame and his offspring loves dearly.[125]

Rural poets from the same period shared this vision of domesticity.[126] As we saw in the song about the generous squire, domesticity was sanctioned by the elite, so in contrast to the songs in chapter 2, these songs portrayed social relations as amicable and harmonious. However, both the songs and the poems, by saying that domesticity was a relief from the pains of labour, made it clear that agricultural labour was a hardship.[127]

Pride in agricultural occupations

In songs and poetry the pride farmers and agricultural labourers took in their work had to do in part with skill and physical strength. They boasted both of their specialised skills and of the variety of tasks they could perform. It was the diversity of agricultural labour that made Adam Smith describe it as superior to mechanical or industrial labour and this quality was praised by ballad writers, resulting in a series of lists of different agricultural tasks. In the words of one peasant narrator, 'I can plough, sow, mow, sheer, thresh, dike, milk, kurn, muck byre, sing a psalm, mend a car-gear, ance a whornpeype, nick a naig's tail, hunt a brock, or feght iver ayen o'my weight in aw Croglin parish'.[128] The farmer-poet Nathaniel Dale made a similar list, describing the skills of female farm servants who strained the milk in the dairy, turned the cows to graze, swept the floors, made the beds, washed the dishes, cleaned the parlour chairs, brushed the floor cloths, hunted for eggs in the yard, cooked, spinned yarn, gathered wild strawberries, churned the cream, scoured the pails and the skimmer, fed the geese and chickens, and took care of any infants present in the household. The poem also praises farm servants' beauty but, unlike the milkmaid songs in chapter 5, it foregrounds the skills. Dale seems to have employed such female farm labourers as he describes. The emphasis on work rather than on sensuality may have to do with the change in taste, so aptly described by John Barrell, which required images of industrious rather than playful rural workers.[129]

Pride in physical strength in the form of competitions among field labourers to see who could work the fastest was common in poems and songs. Songs praised the peasant who was 'Whistling off toils, one half of which might make / The stoutest Atlas of a palace quake' and enduring heat, cold and exertion which might make more cowardly types faint. The peasant's endurance was exceptional: 'He bears, what we should think it death to bear.'[130] Physical prowess was not only associated with masculinity: women labourers also partook of this strength, carrying the heavy milking pails and enduring rough weather as part of working outdoors.[131]

One of the reasons songs celebrating agricultural labour could have been popular during the French wars is that agriculture was such an integral part of the war effort. With the foundation of the Board of Agriculture, some contemporaries felt that the significance of the farmer was finally being recognised.[132] The historian W. Freeman Galpin connected the rise of societies for advancement in agriculture in all parts of the country, the growing number of agricultural magazines, the numerous newspaper columns dedicated to agricultural matters, and the prizes offered by the Board of Agriculture for improved crops to the war.[133] This appreciation of agriculture extended to farmers and agricultural labourers. It is natural there should have been renewed appreciation for the people who were feeding Britain during that time. Jeanette Neeson has shown how the argument that wage labourers were more productive than peasants because their dependence made them work harder was used to justify enclosure during these years.[134] Reports to the Board of Agriculture which supported enclosure also connected labour to the national interest.[135] Perhaps the demand for fictional representations of farmers and agricultural labourers who argued their profession was the basis of national wealth in this period owed something to these developments.

As William Clarkson put it, agricultural labour was more central to the economy than any other because without food society could not exist.[136] The agricultural labourer was depicted as confident in the knowledge that his labour sustained the rest of the country.[137] Thus in 'The Husbandman and Servant Man' the husbandman could argue that if no one followed the plough neither lords nor kings, nor merchants or tradesmen would survive.[138] The same sentiment is expressed in 'The Painful Plough': 'Were it not for the plough men both rich and poor would rue / For they are all dependent upon the painful plough.' The song creates a fictional genealogy for ploughmen, tracing their history to the beginning of the human race: the first ploughman was Adam, followed by his son Cain. The great feats of ancient heroes and wise men such as Sampson, Solomon, Alexander and King David are only possible thanks to the work of the plough.[139] In another song this boast is attributed to a thresher, who argues that he is greater, kinder and better than kings because he gives the hungry food to eat and the thirsty liquor to drink, comforting both rich and poor.[140] 'The Farmer's Ingle' expresses a preference for the farmer's profession over the lot of kings, poets and priests, while 'A new song on the Farmer's Glory' extends the list to tradesmen, doctors, excisemen, parsons, maltmen, landladies and landlords.[141]

An association between agriculture and patriotism was made by many ballads celebrating agriculture. This was especially true in ballads about farmers or millers but occasionally happened in ballads about labourers too. 'The Miller's Song' praises the miller for his love of Britain and his loyalty to King George:

> He's a freeholder sufficient to give him a vote,
> At elections he scorns to accept of a groat,
> He hates your proud placemen and do what they will,
> They ne'er can seduce the staunch man of the mill.[142]

In one case what appears to be a harvest song ends abruptly with a message of loyalty to Pitt that almost seems like it was added as an afterthought and has little to do with the rest of the song. After describing the innocent joys of the harvest, the song suddenly concludes:

> Let the statesmen desire,
> What at court doth aspire,
> For his country's good let it be;
> True justice and Pitt,
> In the house always sit
> And time will mend sooner you'll find.[143]

As we see in 'The Joys of the Harvest', where the harvest workers drink to the health of the 'barley-mow' and to 'good George our King', thoughts of the harvest often seem to have inspired patriotic feelings in song writers.[144] In 'The Ploughboy Turned Soldier', a ploughboy misses his work and his home, but assures his beloved Polly that 'It's an honour and pleasure to be ploughing the deep' because he is fighting for 'sweet liberty'.[145] In another song a thresher professes he would happily work as a thresher for the rest of his days, unless his king calls on him to guard his native soil, in which case he would 'swing round the flail, / and thrash the proud foe, to secure mug-brown ale'.[146] Beer, one of the products of agricultural labour, was often celebrated as the true British beverage and contrasted with French wine:

> Content with the riches of Britain's fair isle,
> Let the subjects of Britain rejoice;
> May no foreign vintage our sense beguile,
> No stream of the grape have our voice.[147]

Patriotic ballads with a rural setting often celebrated Britain's wealth, commerce, religion, military strength and liberty.[148] In this popular ballads were very similar to patriotic pastoral poetry and loyalist songs, except that the latter put more emphasis on contrasting the supposedly happy lives of British peasants with the hard lives of foreign (particularly French) peasants.

An old and common literary stereotype of the agricultural labourer and farmer which was now revived was that they were less corrupt and more honest than anyone else. Many such songs used agricultural occupations as a metaphor for how the world operated, describing social relations in terms of a wagon, a mill or a dairy, and depicting all the professions, except for agrarian ones, as tainted by greed. These songs were both about the particular rural occupation and about social structure/social relations. The narrator of one such song, 'Young Ralph the Waggoner', thinks the world is like a waggon with the 'for-horse' pointing the way and the rest following behind. He then describes the corruption of the statesman, the lawyer, the doctor, using metaphors from his trade to explain each: the lawyer often 'drives his clients to the devil' as soon as he has been paid, and the doctor is happy to prescribe his patient 'a long journey' – in other words, will send him to his doom, as long as he receives a fee.[149] The milkmaid's work was used in a similar way. After avowing her pride in her occupation, a milkmaid contrasts her work with that of others:

The Statesman, the Doctor, the Lawyer in silk,
The Bishop in lawn – are but dealers in milk;
While one milks his patient, and drains him of health,
Another his client can milk of his wealth;
While one has the national dairy at call,
The church t'other milks – without preaching at all.
Thro' life then I'll merrily trudge to and fro,
And still cry my milk, any milk below![150]

The diet of agricultural labourers and farmers was an important part of songs and poems' construction of a rural identity. Diet was indicative not only of a rural but of a more regional northern or southern identity; celebrations of food were more likely to come from the north. If food was an issue in songs about southern labourers, it was usually in connection with domesticity – the wife kept the cheese for the husband's dinner – or a complaint that things which were affordable, like fruit and fish, were no longer so. This is an example of a social change making its way into an otherwise conventional genre. The diet of labourers in the south deteriorated after parliamentary enclosure because they no longer produced their own food and because prices increased. Earlier, milk, butter and other small articles could be bought from small farmers, but now big farmers had displaced them and took everything to town. Meat and cheese were now a rare part of the diet and even fruit, fish and milk were not common.[151] The elite tried to educate the poor to be frugal and adopt a northern diet of rye, barley and oatmeal but southern labourers continued to insist on wheat.[152] In the south the northern diet continued to be viewed with contempt. Thus rural poetry written in the south mocked the food of the north. For example, *Pursuits of Agriculture* tells readers that Cumberland farmers ate potatoes from 'potatoe-land' and that though these were readily available, cheap and easy to cook they are the food that 'others throw away'.[153]

Songs about farmers and rural poems from the south did praise the southern diet, perhaps because they were more likely to have an audience of farmers or urban middle-class readers than songs about labourers. But even poets recognised the deterioration of labourers' diets. From James Templeman we have a poetic celebration of Cheshire cheese, which he feels should form part of the diet of the labouring poor. Perhaps reacting to the widespread notion that finer food was dangerous to the morals of the poor, he argues the labourers deserved the best of food to help their strength and spirits, while 'idle drones' could have worse meat.[154] He is nostalgic about a past when roast meat, eggs, butter, cheese, live poultry and fresh fruit could form part of a labourer's diet. Now wages are too low for this.

Songs and poetry about agricultural labour from the north took pride in what their southern counterparts might detest. The peasant poet David Service has a long discussion of diet in his poem 'The Caledonian Herd-Boy'. The herd-boy's supper consists of thick and hot barley broth, two pounds of salted meat and 'green herbage', grey peas and horse beans. He admits this northern diet is coarser but more wholesome than in the south:

> Ye gentler mouths, whom Norfolk dumplings cheer,
> Who float your puddings down with ale, or beer:
> How would you raise your brows with anger great,
> Did your household afford no better meat.

Explaining that as different peoples have different customs so they enjoy different diets, he then suggests food is an integral part of a Scottish rural identity:

> Who hence infers that eating coarser food,
> Makes men less virtuous, active, wise, or good?
> The Caledonians have a keener air,
> A sky more calm, serene, and ever clear;
> Decocting food more coarse with mirth and joy,
> They'd live on that, would Englishmen destroy.[155]

In 'Dialogue between a Scottish farmer and a weaver', the poor weaver is advised to

> Contented be wi' fod o'Scotish growth
> Food you were us'd to in your early youth;
> At e'en and morn wi' parritch fill your wymes,
> Let tea and toast be only us'd at times;
> Nor chow your cude on puffy rows or bakes,
> But crumpt substantial new meal aiten cakes;
> At dinner-time potatoes, kail, and beef,
> Of luxuries let these be aye the chief.

The farmer advises him to only drink tea on the Sabbath or special occasions. The weaver complains he likes to have more meat and tea, but the farmer counters by referring to Scottish heroes like Wallace and arguing they did not chase the English on tea and cream, but on meal from oats.[156]

As labourers and farmers felt pride in their diet so they felt proud of their attire. The country girl in 'A Sweet Country Life' scorns urban fashions, professing a love for home-spun country clothing instead.[157] From a milkmaid we hear that she prefers her homely, wholesome and clean outfit consisting of a blue apron, plain russet gown and spotted silk handkerchief to the silks and satins of her betters.[158]

An important difference between labourers and small farmers was that farmers often boasted of plenty and abundance. 'The Farmer' is clearly a song about a small farmer who does a lot of his own labour, but he is still very proud of his possessions:

> By reaping and mowing,
> By ploughing and sowing,
> Dull nature supplies me with plenty;
> I've a plentiful board,
> And a cellar well stor'd,
> And my garden supplies me each dainty:
> I have land, I have bowers, I have fruits, I have flowers,
> And I am here as Justice of Quorum;
> In my cabin's far end
> I've a bed for a friend.
> With a clean fire side and a Jorum.[159]

Unlike the songs and poetry about labourers, this song does not credit the farmer with sensitivity to natural beauty: nature is 'dull', and it is only animated by his labour.[160] As usual, the hero in 'The Farmer' points out he does not envy the great and the rich because he has his own ham, chicken and lamb. Though he seems so well to do he also shears his own sheep and makes his own clothes. He appears to be a subsistence farmer who farms to make a living. The husbandman in 'The Husbandman and Servant Man' also appears to be a small farmer, whose sole delight is the produce of his farm, his fat oxen, and fine corn. Though the farmer takes pleasure in his work, his contentment comes from his comfortable lifestyle more than the skills he has. At the end the servantman, who appears to be a domestic servant rather than an agricultural labourer, is convinced and wishes he were a husbandman.[161]

Michael Pickering's careful analysis of this song also concludes that it is a celebration of rural identity and agricultural work. He illustrates that the song was still popular at the end of the nineteenth century despite the disappearance of small farmers ('husbandmen') from the countryside. According to Pickering, 'husbandman' came to stand for agricultural labourers. The song appealed to an old-fashioned moral economy at a time when agricultural labourers were increasingly underpaid and losing the respect of their superiors.[162]

The celebration of work as nationalist propaganda

The tone and sentiments in some of these songs bring them closer to Hannah More's tracts than any of the songs discussed in this book. 'The Happy Milk Maid', for instance, might have been ironic, but it could also be read as a reaffirmation of social hierarchy: 'Tell me not of bondage, 'tis all a mere joke, / I'm never more happy than under a yoke.'[163]

The patriotic element during the French wars is particularly striking. Robert Burns's 1786 version of the song 'The Cottager's Saturday Night', which expressed Scottish nationalist sentiments, was reworked and reprinted in the early 1800s as a song in praise of Church and King; the Scots dialect was eliminated, and references to 'Scotia' were replaced with 'Britain'. Its northern origins were still visible because the hero happily feasts on oatmeal porridge and milk, which would not have been the case in a song from the south.[164] Still, its most direct praise of Britain is not as extensive as that in songs we know to have been written as propaganda, and there is no explicit invitation to take up arms. Nationalism is only invoked in the last verse:

> O Britain! My most dear, my native soil!
> For whom my warmest wish to Heaven is sent!
> Long may thy hardy sons of rustic toil,
> Be blest with health, and peace and sweet content!

This is still not as didactic or war-like as the 'The Ploughman's Ditty', which was written for Hannah More's Cheap Repository Tracts (but not by her) and was intended as a method of persuasion to fight for Britain. The song aims to refute the argument that labourers have nothing to lose and have no reason to fight against France:

Because I'm but poor
And slender's my store,
That I've nothing to lose is the cry, Sir;
Let who will declare it,
I vow I can't bear it –
I give all such praters the lies, Sir.

The ploughman, argues the song, has very much to lose: he has a house, a garden, and an orchard. He has his wages, which the French would not pay him. He has a wife and child:

And 'twou'd make me run wild
To see my sweet child
With its head on the point of a pike, Sir.

He also has his Church and his king as well as liberty and the rule of law. If the squire should try to oppress him, the law would ensure he gets 'instant redress'. Therefore he is eager to fight the French 'like a lion' after having turned his ploughshare into a sword.[165]

In the absence of evidence it is difficult to know how the audience reacted to patriotism in songs. What makes the songs of this chapter different from the Cheap Repository Tracts is that they give us a glimpse into some of the hardships faced by agricultural labourers and small farmers, as well as the more positive stereotypes associated with rural life. It is possible that some degree of national pride was tolerated across class boundaries by both rural and urban audiences for popular ballads.

Conclusion

Representations of agricultural work in popular songs reflected the dialectic of work, which saw work as alternatively painful and pleasant. They shared this view of work with other texts, both fictional (rural poetry) and non-fictional (working-class autobiographies). The hardship faced by agricultural labourers and small farmers was associated with the physical difficulty of work, exhaustion, rough weather and bad masters. It was also associated with economic difficulties such as high prices and low wages. These pains were shared by both male and female agricultural workers and to a large extent also by small farmers as represented in songs. Nevertheless, songs also celebrated work. They spoke of compensations: agricultural work was better than industrial labour because it was healthier and because it allowed the cultivation of an aesthetic sensibility associated with the admiration of nature. Domesticity was another reward for the industrious labourer. Furthermore, positive representations of agricultural labour included sources of pride for the men and women involved. These included the possession of specialised skills, the ability to perform a wide diversity of tasks, physical strength and endurance, the knowledge that one's work was the basis of the nation's economy, patriotism, and a cultural stereotype associated with types of food and with an honest character. Songs about farmers added prosperity and independence to the list. In the section on the pleasure of work I raised the question of to what extent celebration of work can be directly connected to the actual performance of the various agricultural tasks, and I concluded that despite the apparent joy workers took in the work, the source of pleasure usually turned out to be something else, such as the return of spring or the completion of a task. Some expressions of love of work both in songs and in working-class autobiographies were refracted through feelings of nostalgia about being away from home or about one's youth. Thus the celebration of work referred primarily to the occupation and to the lifestyle. In the last section I asked how similar were the working songs we have been looking at to loyalist propaganda during the war years and concluded that while they shared the element of patriotism, the loyalist songs were more overtly didactic and more directly concerned with the war.

This chapter does not argue that songs reflected the reality of work. Rather it seeks to find out what historical conditions can explain their popularity in the period 1800–15. Thus, songs about agricultural labour can be read as a popular version of the rustic or as an encouragement to labour as part of the war effort. They can also be read as resonant with how agricultural labourers and farmers saw their role in society, or how they wanted to be seen. I hope the evidence in this chapter shows that these songs were more than simple pastorals and that they presented a more subtle depiction of work, which needs to be taken into account when trying to understand the place of labour in early nineteenth-century Britain.

Notes

1 Ann Bermingham, *Landscape and Ideology: The English Rustic Tradition 1740–1860* (Berkeley and Los Angeles: University of California Press, 1986), 11.

2 E. P. Thompson, *The Making of the English Working Class* (Harmondsworth: Penguin Books, 1980), 235.

3 See Ann Kussmaul, *Servants in Husbandry in Early Modern England* (Cambridge: Cambridge University Press, 1981), 3, 120ff. Kussmaul makes a good case for the different lifestyles of the two kinds of labourers and the negative economic and social changes associated with the decline of live-in service in the south and east at the end of the eighteenth century.

4 Alun Howkins, 'The English Farm Labourer in the Nineteenth Century: Farm, Family and Community', in Brian Short, ed., *The English Rural Community: Image and Analysis* (Cambridge: Cambridge University Press, 1992), 85–6.

5 Thompson, *The Making of the English Working Class*, 241. On the other hand, these two groups often had similar grievances: for example they both protested in the Swing riots. Mick Reed, 'The Peasantry in Nineteenth-Century England: A Neglected Class?' in Barry Stapleton, ed., *Conflict and Community in Southern England* (Stroud: Alan Sutton, 1992), 229.

6 For the divergence between farmers and labourers and for how the 'new farmer' came to embody luxury and refinement, see J. L. Hammond and Barbara Hammond, *The Village Labourer, 1760–1832: A Study in the Government of England before the Reform Bill* (London: Longman's, Green, 1980), 212.

7 Mick Reed, 'Class and Conflict in Rural England: Some Reflections on a Debate', in Mick Reed and Roger Wells, eds, *Class, Conflict and Protest in the English Countryside, 1700–1880* (London: Frank Glass, 1990), 9–13.

8 Ann Kussmaul, *A General View of the Rural Economy of England 1638–1840* (Cambridge: Cambridge University Press, 1990), 22, also her *Servants in Husbandry*, 104.

9 Kussmaul, *Servants in Husbandry*, 109, 121.

10 Kussmaul, *Servants in Husbandry*, 120. She lists the following counties as having experienced little decline in service: Northumberland, Rutland, Warwickshire, Westmorland, and the North and West Ridings of Yorkshire. In 1800: Cheshire, Cumberland, Durham, Huntingdonshire, Kent, Leicestershire, Lincolnshire, 29. For the difference in hiring practices between north and south, see also Howkins, 'The English Farm Labourer', 88ff.

11 A. J. Gritt, 'The Census and the Servant: A Reassessment of the Decline and Distribution of Farm Service in Early Nineteenth-Century England', *The Economic History Review* 53, no. 1 (2000): 105.

12 Kussmaul, *Servants in Husbandry*, 121.

13 For the argument that England had never had many small yeomen since the fifteenth century see Donald E. Ginter, 'Measuring the Decline of the Small Landowner', in B. A. Holderness and Michael Turner, eds, *Land, Labour and Agriculture, 1700–1920* (London: The Hambledon Press, 1991), 47. Given the fact

that the material used in this chapter frequently speaks about small farmers, this line of reasoning is less convincing than that of the Hammonds.

14 Mick Reed, 'Class and Conflict in Rural England', 1. John Archer also praises historians who have destroyed the rural idyll accepted by earlier rural history: 'Figuratively speaking, the 'ploughs and cows' economically oriented histories (the phrase is Snell's), were smashed or maimed by this younger generation of historians', *By a Flash and a Scare: Incendiarism, Animal Maiming, and Poaching in East Anglia, 1815–1870* (Oxford: Clarendon Press, 1990), 9.

15 Until the 1820s it was common for agricultural labourers in England to have looms in their homes. Archer, *By a Flash and a Scare*, 45.

16 Kussmaul, *A General View*, 27.

17 K. D. M. Snell, 'Agricultural Seasonal Unemployment, the Standard of Living, and Women's Work, 1690–1860', in Pamela Sharpe, ed., *Women's Work: The English Experience 1650–1914* (London: Arnold, 1998), 109.

18 Reed, 'The Peasantry of Nineteenth-Century England', 148–9.

19 Ann Kussmaul, *A General View*, 15.

20 Stephen Duck, 'On Poverty', in *Poems on Several Occasions* (1736; reprinted Menston Scolar Press, 1973), 7.

21 Martha Vicinus, *The Industrial Muse: A Study of Nineteenth-Century British Working-Class Literature* (London: Groom Helm, 1974), 142–4.

22 See for example Keith Thomas, Introduction to *The Oxford Book of Work* (Oxford: Oxford University Press, 1999), xx–xxi. Thomas makes a sharp distinction between 'realistic', 'unsentimental' accounts of work, such as that of Stephen Duck, and 'wildly sentimental' rural nostalgia.

23 Thompson, *The Making of the English Working Class*, 240.

24 'Farewell to Spring' (Glasgow, 1802), B.L., Shelfmark 11606.aa.23.

25 'The Contented Ruricolist' (Glasgow, 1802), B.L., Shelfmark 11605.aa.23.

26 James Lamb, 'The Pious Cottager', in *A Small Collection of Original Pieces in Verse, Consisting of Epistles, Songs, Rural Ballads, and Hymns* (1819).

27 John Archer, *Social Unrest and Popular Protest in England, 1780–1840* (Cambridge, Cambridge University Press, 2000), 9–10.

28 Thompson, *The Making of the English Working Class*, 249. Though they do not use the language of identity, the Hammonds think that common right was a crucial part of peasants' understanding of their place in the world and gave them a sense of pride and independence. Hammonds, *The Village Labourer*, 37.

29 Gary Harrison, *Wordsworth's Vagrant Muse: Poetry, Poverty, and Power* (Detroit, MI: Wayne State University Press, 1994), 36.

30 The connection between the rural and English national identity has been written about extensively. See for an example Stuart Laing, 'Images of the Rural in Popular Culture, 1750–1990', in Brian Short, ed., *The English Rural Community: Image and Analysis* (Cambridge: Cambridge University Press, 1992), 135.

31 Thomas, Introduction to *The Oxford Book of Work*, xiv, xvii.

32 Thomas, *The Oxford Book of Work*, xviii.

33 John Locke, *Of the Conduct of the Understanding* (1706), excerpted in Thomas, *The Oxford Book of Work*, 10.

34 George Berkeley, *A Word to the Wise* (1749) excerpted in Thomas, *The Oxford Book of Work*, 122.

35 Jonathan Bate, *John Clare: A Biography* (New York: Farrar, Straus and Giroux, 2003), 69–70.

36 Vicinus, *The Industrial Muse*, 47.

37 Roy Palmer, *The Sound of History: Songs and Social Comment* (Oxford and New York: Oxford University Press, 1988), 85.

38 Vicinus, *The Industrial Muse*, 148.

39 'Thrasher', *Batchelar's Rural Songster. An Excellent Collection of Popular Songs* (London: T. Batchelar, 1813–15), L.C. 3087.

40 George Crabbe, 'The Parish Register', in *The Complete Poetical Works*, Vol. 2 (Oxford: Clarendon Press and New York: Oxford University Press, 1988), ll. 25–6, l. 17.

41 Crabbe, 'The Parish Register', l. 40.

42 Archer, *By a Flash and a Scare*, 26–7.

43 'The Return of Spring' (Glasgow, 1801), B.L., Shelfmark 11606.aa.23.

44 Thomas Darby, 'Rural Life', in *Poems Descriptive of Rural Scenery* (Birmingham, 1815).

45 See 'The Ploughman', *Six Favourite Songs* (Falkirk: T. Johnston, c.1801), L.C. 2829. The hoppickers in 'Hoppicker's Song' (n.p., n.d.), B.L. Shelfmark 1876.d.41, sang that 'pleasure attends on the toils of the day , /And labour is crown'd with delight', thus making a more direct claim that labour brought pleasure. Also 'The Ploughman' (n.p., n.d.), B.L., Shelfmark 1876.d.41, expressed joy in the profession. For a singing ploughman see the work of the peasant poet Thomas Darby Jr, 'On Spring', in his *Poems Descriptive of Rural Scenery* (1815): 'The ploughboy with his rustic song / Hails the return of spring, / Or as he cheers the team along, / Makes woodland echoes ring.'

46 'Thrasher', *Batchelar's Rural Songster. An Excellent Collection of Popular Songs* (London: T. Batchelar, 1813–15), L.C. 3087. See also 'The Villager' (Salisbury: Fowler, 1770–1800), B.L., Shelfmark 11622.c7, 'Labour his business and his pleasure too'.

47 'A Sweet Country Life', *The True Hearted Maiden* (Glasgow, 1802), L.C. 2837.

48 'The Pleasures of a Country Life' (Glasgow, 1802), B.L., Shelfmark 11621.b.9.

49 See also 'Harvest Home', *The Lincolnshire Knight; Or, the Poor Rich Man* (Glasgow: The Robertsons, 1802).

50 'The Joys of the Harvest' (n.p., n.d.), L.C. 2846.

51 'The Contented Ruricolist' (Glasgow, 1802), B.L. Shelfmark 11606.aa.23. See also 'Rural life' (London: Thomas Evans, n.d.), B.L., Shelfmark 11606.aa.22 and 'The Sheep Shearers' (London: Toy and Marble, n.d.), B.L., Shelfmark HS 74 11250.

52 'The Scotch Shepherd', *When Late I Wandered* (Stirling: M. Randall, n.d.), L.C. 2870.

53 'Clean Pease Strae' (Glasgow, n.d.), L.C. 2845.

54 James Paterson, *Autobiographical Reminiscences: Including Recollections of the Radical Years, 1819–1820 in Kilmarnock* (Glasgow, 1871), 9.

55 Paterson, *Autobiographical Reminiscences*, 5–6.

56 Paterson, *Autobiographical Reminiscences*, 9.

57 Service, *The Caledonian Herd-Boy* (1802), 4ff.

58 Catton, *A Short Sketch of a Long Life* (1863), 2–3. Of course later he ended up with a cruel master and he no longer enjoyed the work.

59 'The Ploughboy Turned Soldier' (n.p., 1801?), B.L., Shelfmark 11606.aa.23. Though it idealised the ploughman's work, the overall message of this song was patriotic.

60 'The Ploughman Turn'd Sailor', L.C. 2808. Sometimes ballads spoke of fear of the press gang. 'A Dialogue between Will and Jack' (Newcastle, 1780) described the widespread fear of a French invasion and listed farmers and millers among the many professions terrified of the press gangs. The narrator ridiculed their fear because only the poor were at risk: the poor pedlar must turn ploughman to save himself, since ploughmen were exempt, while pedlars were treated like vagrants and often impressed.

61 Kussmaul, *Servants in Husbandry*,113. Real wages rose, allowing youths to stay home rather than become servants and set up separate households earlier.

62 'Song of the Haymakers' (n.p., Hodges, n.d.), B.L., Shelfmark 11621.k.4 vol. 2. Of course, the next few lines, which I have quoted on p. 124, said that rural life was much happier than life in the city and this made up for the difficulty.

63 'Painful Plough' (Manchester: Bebbington, n.d.), B.L., Shelfmark 1876.l.41. Another version of it is entitled 'An excellent new song; entitled the farmer's glory' (n.p., n.d.), L.C. 2846.

64 'The Cottager's Saturday Night: a Poem' (London, J. Evans & Son, 1813–20), L.C. 2729.

65 'The Goodman of Auchermouchtie; or, the Goodwife Turn'd Goodman' (Glasgow: J. and M. Robertson, 1802), L.C. 2837. See also 'The Poor Man's Labour's Never Done', *The Poor Man's Labour Never Done or, the Mother's Advice* (Glasgow, 1802), L.C. 2837, where the labourer speaks of being cold, wet and tired at the end of a working day.

66 'The Jolly Thrasherman' (n.p., n.d.) B.L., Shelfmark HS.74.11250.

67 Samuel Westcott Tilke, Chapter 4, *An Autobiographical Memoir* (London: Printed for and sold by the author, 1840).

68 He also said that these hard-working lads often prospered later in life, which compensated for their hard work. William Johnston, *The Life and Times of William Johnston, Horitcultural Chemist, Gardener, and Cartwright*, ed., Reginald Alenarley, Esq. (Peterhead, 1859), 10. For John Clare, field labour was also very hard. John Clare, *Sketches in the Life of John Clare* (1821) excerpted in Thomas, *The Oxford Book of Work*, 125.

69 Anon., *The Happy Shepherd: Or, Rural Retirement; A Moral Tale* (Gainsborough, 1806), 9.

70 William Barre, 'September', *The Months: A Rural Poem; And Other Pieces* (London, 1813). D. Hurn, 'On the Fens, addressed to T. F. Esq', in his *Rural Rhymes; Or, A Collection of Epistolary, Humorous, and Descriptive Pieces* (Spalding, 1813).

71 Snell, 'Agricultural Seasonal Unemployment', 78, 102. Howkins agrees that in the south and east female labour became more and more casual in the nineteenth century, 'The English Farm Labourer', 99.

72 Snell, 'Agricultural Seasonal Unemployment', 87, 92, 99–100.

73 Thompson, *The Making of the English Working Class*, 244–5.

74 Howkins, 'The English Farm Labourer', 100–1.

75 'The Merry Reaper of the Moor' (n.p., n.d.), B.L., Shelfmark 1077.g.47. The song offers a rare glimpse of bi-employment as its heroine works as a reaper during the day and tells fortunes in the evenings or her spare time. For wives doing the dairy, see 'The Cottager's Saturday Night; a Poem' (London, J. Evans & Sons, 1813–20), L.C. 2729 and James Templeman, 'Farmer Hobson, a Rural Poem', Book I in *Poems and Tales*, vol. 1 (London, 1809).

76 'Answer to Nae Luck about the House. A Favourite Scottish Song' (Salisbury, 1785), B.L., Shelfmark HS 74 1250.

77 'The Churlish Farmer', (n.p., n.d.), B.L., Shelfmark 1161.a.5.

78 For a discussion of trends in the standard of living after 1750 see Ann Kussmaul, *Servants in Husbandry*, 101. The rise in the cost of living was aggravated by a rise in population. Kussmaul, 120. For the late eighteenth century see Thompson, *The Making of the English Working Class*, 234.

79 Thompson, *The Making of the English Working Class*, 236.

80 Thompson, *The Making of the English Working Class*, 244–5. Thompson provided plentiful evidence that in the south and east agricultural labourers suffered a lot after the war and expressed their frustration through riots and threatening letters as well as covert forms of protest. Ann Kussmaul also argues that a decline of service in husbandry made life more difficult for labourers in the south because they were at the mercy of fluctuating prices of food, which would have previously been paid by the master (Kussmaul, *Servants in Husbandry*, 124). However, other historians point out that the decline of live-in service gave agricultural labourers greater independence. The Hammonds have also argued that the post-enclosed villages of the nineteenth century allowed fewer opportunities for social advancement to labourers. Hammonds, *The Village Labourer*, 33.

81 Hammonds, *The Village Labourer*, 32, 106.

82 Hammonds, *The Village Labourer*, 167.

83 Hammonds, *The Village Labourer*, 104–5.

84 Tilke, Chapter 4, *An Autobiographical Memoir* (1840).

85 According to historians like Ann Kussmaul it was reasonable for labourers in the nineteenth century to see the inflationary period before 1790 as a Golden Age of the consumer. Kussmaul, *Servants in Husbandry*, 121.

86 Templeman, 'Farmer Hobson, A Rural Poem', Book II in his *Poems and Tales*, vol. 1 (1809).

87 On high prices of provisions see also 'Bacchus's Calendar', *The Cabin Boy; Or, the First Step to Fame, a New Song Book. Wherein are All the New Songs Sung in Harlequin and Mother Goose, Arbitration, Tekeli, &c.* (London, 1807), B.L., Shelfmark 11602.e.28.

88 'The Labouring Man' (n.p., Ryle, n.d.), B.L., Shelfmark HS. 74.11250. The

allusion to cleanliness may have to do with what the Hammonds have identi-
fied as a tendency to dress in rags in the nineteenth century, even if one had
decent clothes, in order to persuade parish authorities that one was worthy of poor
relief. See Hammonds, *The Village Labourer*, 226. On wages, see T. L. Richardson,
'Agricultural Labourers' Wages and the Cost of Living in Essex, 1790–1840: A
Contribution to the Standard of Living Debate', in B. A. Holderness and Michael
Turner, eds, *Land, Labour and Agriculture, 1700–1920* (London: The Humbledon
Press, 1991), 89. Richardson argues that for the poor in Essex wages stayed the
same, while prices of provisions rose, which lowered the standard of living.

89 William Nicholson, 'The Country Lass', Part IV in *Tales in Verse, and Miscellaneous
Poems: Descriptive of Rural life and Manners* (Edinburgh, 1814). On the poverty of
agricultural labourers see also Hurn, 'December', in *Rural Rhymes* (1813).

90 Nicholson, 'The Old Shepherd', *Tales in Verse* (1814).

91 Samuel Catton, *A Short Sketch of a Long Life of Samuel Catton, Once a Suffolk
Ploughboy* (London and Ipswich, 1863), 3.

92 R. Anderson, 'Watty', *Ballads in the Cumberland Dialect* (Carlisle, 1805), B.L.,
Shelfmark 74/lr 301 h 3.

93 Templeman, 'Farmer Hobson, a Rural Poem', Book II in his *Poems and Tales*, vol.
1 (1809).

94 Anon., *A Defence of the Land-Owners and Farmers of Great Britain; And an Exposition of the Heavy Parliamentary and Parochial Taxation Under Which they Labour*
(London, 1814), xii–xiii.

95 Barre, 'February', *The Months* (1813).

96 Anon., *Pursuits of Agriculture; A Satirical Poem, in Three Cantos* (London, 1808),
117. In a footnote the author points out that despite the prevalent opinion about
Cumberland's poverty, there were a number of substantial and enlightened yeomen
in the area.

97 Rev. W. Bingley, *North Wales; Including the Scenery, Antiquities, Customs, and
Some Sketches of Natural History* (London, 1804), 219. But despite this picture
of poverty, Bingley's conclusion was to quote Goldsmith's observation that man
needs very little to keep him cheerful and happy and that he could feel like a
monarch in his little shed.

98 'Popular Opinions, Or a Picture of Real Life, Exhibited in a Dialogue Between
a Scottish Farmer and a Weaver' (Glasgow, 1812). Nevertheless the farmer is
described as fat, affluent and well-to-do while the weaver is thin, pale and poor.

99 Roger Wells, 'Popular Protest and Social Crime: The Evidence of Criminal Gangs
in Rural Southern England 1790–1860', in Barry Stapleton, ed., *Conflict and
Community in Southern England* (Stroud: Alan Sutton, 1992), 135. Wells shows
that in the nineteenth century small farmers were numerous and economically
significant in the south and east. Also see Hammonds, *The Village Labourer*, 175.

100 Nevertheless, she loves her home and prefers it to life in the city. Rose Allen, *The
Autobiography of Rose Allen* (London, 1847), 54–5.

101 Gertrude Himmelfarb, *The Idea of Poverty: England in the Early Industrial Age*
(New York: Knoph, 1983), 55. The Hammonds also suggested that field labourers

were softened by the influence of nature compared to urban workers. Hammonds, *The Village Labourer*, 238.

102 Vicinus, *The Industrial Muse*, 47.

103 See for example 'Popular Opinions, or a Picture of Real Life, Exhibited in a Dialogue between a Scottish Farmer and a Weaver' (Glasgow, 1812). The farmer argues his life is much better than the weaver's. At the same time the weaver is more radical and critical of society, while the farmer is conservative and content with his lot.

104 See for instance 'The King and the Miller' (n.p., n.d.), L.C. 2837, where the miller was proud of his economic and social independence, which he contrasted to the misery of trying to obtain favours at court. The miller was also said to be more honest than courtiers, in spite of the fact that he stole from other people's flour to make his own pudding. Another version is 'If so Happy a Miller, then Who'd be King' (n.p., Dodsley, n.d.), B.L., Shelfmark 11661.eee.22.

105 'Song of the Haymakers' (n.p., Hodges, n.d.), B.L., Shelfmark 11621.k.4 vol.2.

106 John Locke, 'Labour' (1693) excerpted in Thomas, *The Oxford Book of Work*, 125.

107 Edmund Burke, *A Philosophical Enquiry into the Origin of Our Ideas of the Sublime and Beautiful* (1757) excerpted in Thomas, *The Oxford Book of Work*, 123.

108 'The Merry Reaper of the Moor' (n.p., n.d.), B.L., Shelfmark 1077.g.47.

109 Anderson, 'The Cumberland Farmer', *Ballads in the Cumberland Dialect* (1805). See also 'The Ploughman', *Six Favourite Songs* (Falkirk, T. Johnston, c. 1801), L.C. 2829, which alludes to the ploughman's good health.

110 Admiration for nature could be voiced by either a male or female narrator. In 'The True Hearted Maiden' a country girl compared man-made music to the music of nature: 'No fiddle nor flute, no hautboy, or spinnet, / Can ever compare with the lark and the linnet, / Down as I lay among the green bushes, / I was charmed by the notes of the blackbirds and thrushes.' 'The True Hearted Maiden' (Glasgow, 1802), L.C. 2837.

111 'Sheep Shearing', *Batchelar's Rural Songster. An Excellent Collection of Popular Songs* (London, T. Batchelar, 1813–15), L.C. 3087.

112 Darby , 'On Spring', *Poems Descriptive of Rural Scenery*.

113 David Service, *The Caledonian Herd-Boy; A Rural Poem* (Yarmouth: J. D. Downes, 1802), 3.

114 Johnston, *The Life and Times of William Johnston* (1859), 10. See also Anon., *The Happy Shepherd* (1806) where the little shepherd's favourite study in school was poetry, 9.

115 Allen, *The Autobiography of Rose Allen* (1847), 55. The country girl in 'A Sweet Country Life' also advised her friends: 'Never forsake your own country employ-ment, / No city can afford so sweet an enjoyment', 'A Sweet Country Life', *The True Hearted Maiden* (Glasgow, 1802), L.C. 2837.

116 One example is the farmer–poet D. Hurn who wrote 'On the Fens', a long poem about his native land. See Hurn, *Rural Rhymes* (1813).

117 'Popular Opinions, or a Picture of Real Life, Exhibited in a Dialogue between a Scotish Farmer and a Weaver' (Glasgow, 1812).

118 Kussmaul, *Servants in Husbandry*, 128.

119 John Barrell, 'Sportive Labour: The Farm Worker in Eighteenth-Century Poetry and Painting', in Brian Short, ed., *The English Rural Community: Image and Analysis* (Cambridge: Cambridge University Press, 1992), 124.

120 'The Summer was Over' (Glasgow, 1801), B.L., Shelfmark 11606.aa.23.

121 'The Jolly Thrasherman' (n.p., n.d.), B.L., Shelfmark HS. 74.11250.

122 'The Muirland Farmer' (Stirling: J. Fraser & Co., c.1798–1827) B.L., Shelfmark rb.s.910. Another allusion to children's work in farming is to be found in 'Pastorella', where children look after the cows and sheep. George Smith, 'Pastorella', in *Pastorals*, 2nd edition (London: Whittingham and Rowland, 1811).

123 'The Muirland Farmer' (Stirling: J. Fraser & Co., c.1798–1827).

124 'The Cottager's Saturday Night: A Poem' (London: J. Evans & Son, 1813–20), L.C. 2728.

125 'The Farmer's Treasure', *The Farmer's Treasure* (Greenock: W. Scott, c.1815), B.L., Shelfmark rb.s.1955.

126 See also Hurn, 'On the Fens', *Rural Rhymes* (1813), where happiness is also associated with domesticity: 'A chaste and prudent, neat and homely wife, / Enhances ev'ry bliss of rural life. / At eve, when weary he returns from toil, / She fills his glass and cheers him with a smile: / And while his children tell their joy or grief, / Content he chats and picks his bone of beef.' The exact same sentiments are to be found in James Lamb, 'The Pious Cottager' (1819).

127 Again, many of these themes were shared by the songs of industrial workers. Vicinus cites a number of miners' songs that talk about domesticity and patriotism: *The Industrial Muse*, 69ff. See also 'The Farmer's Treasure' (Greenock: W. Scott, c.1801). Other kinds of work farmers are represented as doing are planting, pruning, threshing, ditching, mowing and diking.

128 Anderson, 'Watty', *Ballads in the Cumberland Dialect* (1805).

129 Nathaniel Dale, 'My Favourite Girls', *The Eventful Life of Nathaniel Dale, with Recollections & Anecdotes Containing A Great Variety of Business Matters, &c., As Occurred in the Life of the Author* (n.p., printed by the author, n.d.), 88. Some songs about female labour were unfair to women. For instance, 'The Poor Man's Labour Never Done' described a lazy wife who caused her husband's labour to be doubled. It generalised that all women preferred pleasure to work and made life hard for their husbands. 'The Poor Man's Labour's Never Done or, the Mother's Advice' (Glasgow, 1802), L.C. 2837.

130 'The Villager' (Salisbury: Fowler, 1770–1800), B.L., Shelfmark 11622.c.7. See also 'Honest Bob of the Mill', whose protagonist was proud of his honesty and physical strength. 'Honest Bob of the Mill', *The Ladies' Evening Companion. Being and entire new and choice collection of the most admired songs* (London: T. Evans, n.d.), B.L., Shelfmark 1077.g.47.

131 'The Milk-Maid's Life', cited in the Introduction to the *Roxburghe Ballads*.

132 Anon., 'A Defence, &c.', 16 May 1814, p. 15. B.L. pamphlets: 'for I contend, without fear of contradiction, that until the establishment of the Board of Agriculture, and the emulation which it excited, had roused the Farmer from the lethargy

of despondency into which he had sunk, and taught him to feel that he was not in reality the contemptible, the degraded, the insulted and despised 'Bunch Clod', which upon the Stage, and by all descriptions of trades-people, he was uniformly represented and considered to be, and even looked down upon as being of an inferior order and description from themselves…'

133 W. Freeman Galpin, *The Grain Supply of England during the Napoleonic Period. A Thesis* (New York: The Macmillan Company, 1925), 196–7.

134 J. M. Neeson, *Commoners: Common Right, Enclosure and Social Change in England, 1700–1820*, 42–6. On the importance of cultivating waste see also Michael Turner, *English Parliamentary Enclosure: Its Historical Geography And Economic History* (Dawson: Archon Books, 1980), 88.

135 See for example George Rennie, Robert Brown and John Shireff, *General View of the Agriculture of the West Riding of Yorkshire* (Edinburgh, 1799), 18–19. The writers argued that large farms bring about an increase in the number of agricultural labourers and a decrease in the number of peasants, which was good for agriculture.

136 He used this to argue labourers should be well paid: Clarkson, *An Inquiry into the Cause of the Increase of Pauperism and Poor Rates* (1815), 17.

137 This was more common in rural songs because it was easier to make the case that society could not function without food, but it was a theme occasionally taken up by industrial labour songs as well. Vicinus found eighteenth-century weaver songs that presented weaving as the backbone of the economy: *The Industrial Muse*, 39.

138 'The Husbandman and Servant Man' (London: J. Catnach, 1803–38), B.L., Shelfmark 1876.l.41.

139 'Painful Plough' (Manchester: Bebbington, n.d.), B.L., Shelfmark 1876.l.41. See also 'A New Song on the Farmer's Glory', *Bonny Jockey's Garland, Beautified with Several Merry New Song* (Newcastle: Angus, 1774–1825), L.C. 2751, where the whole nation was said to depend on the plough, but the 'plough' here meant the work of farmers rather than specifically agricultural labourers. A poem that made the same argument was Hurn, 'Ploughing', in his *Rural Rhymes* (1813). Hurn extended the role of the ploughman beyond the human realm: he maintained that the plough supplied food for man, bird and beast.

140 'Thrasher', *Batchelar's Rural Songster. An Excellent Collection of Popular Songs* (London: T. Batchelar, 1813–15), L.C. 3087.

141 'The Farmers Ingle' (n.p., n.d.), B.L., Shelfmark 1078.m.24. See also 'A new song on the Farmer's Glory', *Bonny Jockey's Garland, Beautified with Several Merry New Songs* (Newcastle, Angus, 1774–1825), L.C. 2751. A version of one of the songs above, 'The Jolly Farmer; or, All Trades beholden to the Plow', also put forth the idea that farming, which was seen as interchangeable with ploughing, was the foundation of society. 'The Jolly Farmer; or, All Trades Beholden to the Plow', *The Jolly Farmer's Garland Containing Five Excellent New Songs* (1750), B.L., Shelfmark c. 116.bb.11.

142 'The Miller's Song', *The Wood-lark; a Choice Collection of New Songs* (Tewkesbury, 1790).

143 'The Pleasures of a country Life' (Glasgow, 1802), B.L., Shelfmark 11621.b.9.

144 'The Joys of the Harvest' (n.p., n.d.), L.C. 2846.

145 'The Ploughboy Turned Soldier' (n.p., 1801?), B.L., Shelfmark 11606.aa.23.

146 'Thrasher', *Batchelar's Rural Songster. An Excellent Collection of Popular Songs* (London: T. Batchelar, 1813–15), L.C. 3087.

147 'Hoppicker's Song' (n.p., n.d.), B.L., Shelfmark 1876.d.41. See also 'Honest Will, the Farmer' (n.p., n.d.), B.L., Shelfmark 1876.l.41, though it is a bit later than our period, since it invited the listeners to drink to Queen Victoria. See also 'The Cottager's Saturday Night', where the hard-working peasant had no desires for wealth and luxury but loved his dear country and prayed that God would preserve it. 'The Cottager's Saturday Night; a Poem' (London, J. Evans & Son, 1813–20), L.C. 2729. See also 'Popular Opinions, or, a Picture of Real Life, Exhibited in a Dialogue between a Scottish Farmer and a Weaver' (Glasgow, 1812), which depicted the farmer as conservative, deferential and patriotic and the weaver as radical. B.L., Shelfmark 04422.aa.15.

148 'The Happy Farmer' (Salisbury: Fowler, 1770–1800), B.L., Shelfmark 11622.c.7.

149 'Young Ralph the Waggoner' (n.p., n.d.), B.L., Shelfmark 1077.g.47.

150 'The Happy Milk Maid' (n.p., n.d.), B.L., Shelfmark 11622.a.46. See also 'The Miller's song', *The Wood-lark; a Choice Collection of New Songs* (Tewksbury, 1790). The miller prided himself in his honesty and clear conscience. He did not envy those who made ten thousand a year because it was enough for him that he was a freeholder who could vote. He refused to be bribed at elections and was loyal to King George.

151 Hammonds, *The Village Labourer*, 110–11, 126. The role of enclosure in making food more expensive has been disputed by Leigh Shaw-Taylor. Shaw-Taylor argues that by 1800 agricultural labourers in the south-east Midlands had long been without access to commons or cows and that they could not have been further hurt by enclosure. Assuming his figures are accurate, the rise in prices during the war would still have affected agricultural labourers. See Leigh Shaw-Taylor, 'Labourers, Cows, Common Right and Parliamentary Enclosure: The Evidence of Contemporary Comment c.1760–1810', *Past & Present* 171, no. 2 (2001): 125–6. According to Shaw-Taylor, agricultural labourers did not keep cows.

152 Hammonds, *The Village Labourer*, 123–4. They also discussed the real difficulties southern labourers faced if trying to adopt the northern diet.

153 Anon., *Pursuits of Agriculture* (1808), 117.

154 Templeman, 'Farmer Hobson, a Rural Poem', Book I in *Poems and Tales*, vol. 1 (1809). The elite's worry about the poor eating too well is described in the Hammonds, *The Village Labourer*, 38.

155 Service, *The Caledonian Herd-Boy* (1802), 5.

156 'Popular Opinions' (Glasgow, 1812).

157 'A Sweet Country Life', *The True Hearted Maiden* (Glasgow, 1802), L.C. 2837.

158 'The Happy Milk Maid' (n.p., n.d.), B.L. Shelfmark 11622.a.46. See 'The Muirland Farmer' (Stirling: J. Fraser & Co, c.1798–1827), B.L., Shelfmark rb.s.910, where the farmer was delighted by his new boots and spurs which he was able to afford after many years of hard work.

159 'The Farmer', *A Garland of New Songs, Containing How Stands the Glass. The Cobbler, No Rest in the Grave. The Farmer* (n.p., n.d.), B.L., Shelfmark 11606. aa.22.

160 The poet William Nicholson picked up on this idea that farmers' prosperity might make them insensitive to natural beauty and depicted a greedy farmer who was blind to beauty in contrast to Sandy, the shepherd, who was poor but was literate and intelligent and wrote verses. Nicholson, 'The Country Lass', Part II *Tales in Verse* (1814).

161 'The Husbandman and Servantman' (London: J. Catnach, 1803–38), B.L., Shelfmark 1876.l.41. Farmer Will's pride in his station came from his honesty and independence (expressed in his ability to promptly pay his landlord), his generosity (he was kind to the poor, relieving their distress and condemning those who refused to do so) and his patriotism. He was also a small farmer who worked. See also Anderson, 'The Cumberland Farmer', *Ballads in the Cumberland Dialect* (1805). The Cumberland farmer said he was poor compared to 'gentlefolk', but it seemed he still had plenty of meat and drink. He also did his own ploughing and, like the agricultural labourers above, one of the things that made him happier than the rich was his good health.

162 Michael Pickering, 'The Past as a Source of Aspiration: Popular Songs and Social Change', in Michael Pickering and Tony Green, eds, *Everyday Culture: Popular Songs and the Vernacular Milieu* (Milton Keynes, Philadelphia, PA: Open University Press, 1987), 39, 57–60, 64.

163 'The Happy Milk Maid' (n.p., n.d.), B.L., Shelfmark 11622.a.46. See also 'The Sheep Shearers' (London: Toy and Marble, n.d.), B.L., Shelfmark HS 74 1250, and David Carey, *The Pleasures of Nature; Or, the Charms of Rural Life. With Other Poems* (London, 1803). Here it appears the ploughboy was happy during work: he was 'gay'; he sang to his team.

164 'The Cottager's Saturday Night', *The Cottager's Saturday Night; A Poem* (London: J. Evans & Son, 1813–20), L.C. 2729.

165 'The Ploughman's Ditty' (London: J. Hatchard, 1803). Curzon b.10(132).

5

Milkmaids and ploughmen: the celebration of rural labourers' sexuality

'John and Nell'
As Nell sat underneath her cow,
Upon a cock of hay,
Brisk John was coming from the plough,
And chanc'd to pass that way:
Like lightning to the maid he flew,
And by the hand he squeez'd her;
Pray John, she cry'd, be quiet do,
And frown'd – because he teaz'd her.

Young Cupid from his mother's knee,
Observ'd her female pride,
Go on and prosper, John, says he,
And I will be your guide.
Then arm'd at Nelly's breast a dart,
From pride it soon releas'd her,
She faintly cry'd I feel love's smart,
And sigh'd – because it eas'd her.[1]

This is a nineteenth-century popular song from a chapbook printed by W. Scott in Greenock. The imagery is very bawdy – the *double entendre* of Nell's sitting on a 'cock' of hay would not have been missed by contemporary readers. Nell's sighing at the end of the poem and the ease she feels afterwards also carry a reference to the act of lovemaking. The occupations of the two protagonists, a milkmaid and a ploughman, would have immediately led the audience to expect a story about sex. The bawdy song, involving rural characters engaging in erotic play, is a sub-genre of the popular ballad that would have been recognised by audiences in both the eighteenth and the nineteenth centuries.

There were hundreds of such songs circulating in Britain in the eighteenth and nineteenth centuries as printed broadsides and chapbooks. Some of them were tragic love songs; some were humorous bawdy ones. Here I will focus on the comic trope, though I will mention the sad laments for purposes of comparison. Historians have shown that although society in the eighteenth century was highly stratified and hierarchical, plebeians in both town and country could challenge the role of authority and elite culture through crowd action. This chapter will add to this understanding of popular culture, by showing that there existed an ideal of peasant beauty and sexual attractiveness that was defined against a stereotype of an impotent nobility and that found expression in popular songs. In the first half of the eighteenth century this ideal found support in a number of texts that would have been read by the elite. Medical writings associated peasant sexuality with nature, and deemed it to be healthier and more vigorous than the sexuality of the elite. Writers who felt England's population needed a boost also argued the peasantry were having more children than their social superiors. This was in part related to the notion that the aristocracy were replacing sexuality with luxury and consumerism. The figures of the milkmaid and the ploughman were depicted in elite art in the eighteenth century but they carried different connotations from their popular counterparts: milkmaids were ideals of feminine beauty, while ploughmen were representative of 'industriousness'.

At the same time, the other side of the argument thought the sexuality of the poor was evidence of their lax morals, imprudence and lack of intelligence. This view found artistic expression in satires of the countryside such as Gay's *Shepherd's Week*. Although these contrasting viewpoints suggest a debate about peasant sexuality, there is an overlap between elite culture and popular culture in the period 1700–70 on the issue of the sexual vigour of the peasantry. The end of the eighteenth century witnessed changing perceptions of working-class sexuality. In his *History of Sexuality* Foucault suggested that contrary to the notions prevailing in the 1970s sex was not repressed by the Victorians but manifested itself in a growing number of discourses. He called this a discursive explosion: 'There was installed rather an apparatus for producing an ever greater quantity of discourse about sex, capable of functioning and taking effect in its very economy.'[2] Foucault argued the discourse's effect was to create new sexual identities, but they were there for the purpose of control and they often distorted rather than revealed the truth about sexuality. He did not associate them with any class, gender or other interest. He placed the beginnings of this development in the seventeenth century and saw it as gaining momentum in 1800. Part of Foucault's model can be used to explain the evidence gathered in this chapter. We certainly see a proliferation of printed discussions about

No 14.

The MILKMAID.

'Twas at the cool and fragrant hour,
When ev'ning steals upon the sky,
That Lucy sought a woodbine grove,
And Colin taught the grove to sigh;
The sweetest damsel she, on all the plains;
The softest lover he, of all the swains.

He took her by the lily hand,
Which oft had made the milk look pale;
Her cheeks with modest roses glow'd,
As thus he breath'd his tender tale:
The list'ning streams a while forgot to flow,
The doves to murmur, and the breeze to blow.

'O smile, my love! thy dimply smiles
Shall lengthen on the setting ray:
Thus let us melt the hours of bliss,
Thus sweetly languish life away:
Thus sigh our souls into each other's breast,
As true as turtles, and as turtles blest!

So may thy cows for ever crown
With floods of milk thy brimming pail;
So may thy cheese all cheese surpass;
So may the butter never fail;
So may each village round this truth declare,
That Lucy is the fairest of the fair.

Thy lips with streams of honey flow,
And pouting swell with healing dews:
More sweets are blended in thy breath
Than all thy father's fields diffuse,
Though thousand flow'rs adorn each blooming field,
Thy lovely cheeks more blooming beauties yield.

Too long my erring eyes had rov'd
On city dames, in scarlet drest,
And scorn'd the charmful village maid,
With innocence and grogram blest:
Since Lucy's native graces fill'd my sight,
The painted city dames no more delight.

The speaking purple, when you blush,
Out-glows the scarlet's deepest dye;
No di'monds tremble on thy hair,
But brighter spangle in thine eye.
Trust me, the smiling apples of thine eyes
Are tempting as were those in paradise.

The tuneful linnet's warbling notes
Are grateful to the shepherd swain;
To drooping plants and thirsty fields,
The silver droops of kindly rain.
To blossoms dews, as blossoms to the bee,
So thou, my Lucy! only art to me.

But mark, my love, yon western clouds;
With liquid gold they seem to burn:
The ev'ning star will soon appear,
And overflow his silver urn.
Soft stillness now, and falling dews invite
To taste the balmy blessings of the night.

Yet, ere we part, one boon I crave,
One tender boon—nor this deny—
O promise that you still will love,
O promise this! or else I die:
Death else my only remedy must prove:
I'll cease to live whene'er you cease to love.'

She sigh'd and blush'd a sweet consent;
Joyous he thank'd her on his knee,
And warmly press'd her virgin lip,
Was ever youth so blest as he!
The moon to light the lovers homeward rose,
And Philomela lull'd them to repose.

4   'The milkmaid' (date unknown)

human sexuality at the end of the eighteenth century, but only some of these discussions served to create new and diverse sexual identities. At the same time in the late eighteenth century we can isolate a repressive discourse calling for abstinence and reform, and this can be very clearly associated with middle-class Evangelical reformers as well as new concerns about overpopulation. Vic Gammon, working with popular songs from the period 1600 to 1850, suggests that there is not much change in the songs themselves and that plebeian social norms, if anything, became more tolerant. While this chapter does not aim to show that songs reflected reality (Gammon rightly cautions against this approach), it suggests that songs also changed, and that it is worth considering songs side by side with the social evidence for both plebeian sexuality and elite moral attitudes.[3]

The growing concern about labourers' sexuality in elite discourse did not find sympathy in popular songs. On the contrary: the more reformers wanted to control the sexuality of the poor, the more popular bawdy songs became. With the growth of the printing trade after 1800, representations of peasant sexuality in popular songs also diversified and increased in number. Their celebration of agricultural labourers' sexual prowess suggests that their continued popularity may have been due in part to a strong sense of pride in their identity among the rural poor. It is difficult to see how they could have 'controlled' actual sexual behaviour, except insofar as they are silent on the subject of homosexuality. The actual experience of the poor in 1800, the pressures of a changing labour market and the need to move in search of work, made necessary greater tolerance for pre-marital sex. Thus popular and elite perceptions of sexuality diverged more after 1800.

A very large proportion of songs about love and courtship dealt with the issue of social rank: the hero and heroine were of different social standing, or suitors of different classes competed for the hand of the same woman. While the sexuality of the hired man was always contrasted to the master's sexuality, and the sexuality of milkmaids to that of rich ladies, we see more songs pitting farmers against hired ploughmen after 1800, suggesting a growing rivalry between these two groups.

Songs also allowed their female characters considerable agency. Some historians have argued that songs controlled female sexuality by depicting women as too easily acquiescing to male sexual demands. In fact, the heroines of songs were allowed a range of responses to demands for sex and this gave them considerable freedom by the standards of the time. The sexuality of both labouring men and labouring women was celebrated by popular ballads.

Arguments in favour of peasant sexuality in medical writing, population treatises and painting

In the eighteenth century sexuality gained a new prominence in the writings of doctors, social reformers and philosophers, as well as in popular literature. Historians speak of a new heterosexuality emerging at this time. According to Lawrence Stone the new ideal included sensual pleasure, and spread from the city to the countryside. He thought that plebeian attitudes to sex also became more lax during this period, though he admitted the evidence was hard to come by.[4] In the eighteenth century there were three kinds of discourse which supported the notion that peasant sexuality was in some ways superior to the sexuality of the elite: medical writing, which associated sex with health and nature; concern about depopulation; and concern about the growing tendency of the upper class to replace sex with luxury.

Sex was viewed as natural by much medical opinion. The well-known doctor Venette, who enjoyed a wide readership, praised and admired the genitalia, saying they were created by God and ought to be celebrated.[5] In fact, he argued, sex was more natural to man than to other animals: man was the most lascivious of creatures 'because he is disposed for the delights of Love at every hour and in every season; whereas most other creatures wait for certain Periods of Time in order to Copulate'.[6] He warned against asceticism and mortification of the flesh because this might make the genitals unhealthy and unfit for sex.[7] The doctor James Graham also supported a more permissive attitude to sex and spoke against legislators and divines who followed 'ridiculous customs' instead of following nature.

Sexual permissiveness in eighteenth-century writing went so far that medical writers entertained the idea of pre-marital sex. According to Venette, in some ancient cultures women were allowed to have intercourse before marriage so that they could find a man whose parts were compatible with their own. The worst thing possible was to marry a woman unused to or afraid of sex; this caused marriages to fall apart. For this reason, Venette argued, it would be well if couples examined each other naked or appointed persons for that purpose to make sure there were no impediments to reproduction before they marry. When a locksmith makes a new lock, Venette pointed out, we want to test it first and loosen the springs so as to avoid the trouble we may meet at first usage.[8] This last comment suggests sex prior to marriage was possible provided the couple were to marry afterwards and reminds us of the practice of bundling (sleeping together, after becoming formally engaged) common among the poor in some areas. Venette even went so far as to advocate the use of erotica to stimulate the senses, suggesting that languid, old or 'cold' men stimulate their minds and rouse their passions 'by the sight of rich, warm or of what are called lascivious prints, paintings, and statues; by amorous stories and dalliances…'.[9]

The idea that rural labourers were more beautiful than city people because they were exposed to fresh air and physical exercise was familiar to medical writers in 1700 and probably earlier. Eighteenth-century medical treatises believed the key to a good sex life was health, and prescribed exercise, a good diet and cheerfulness as cures for impotence.[10] Hard beds and fresh air were also good. James Graham argued that while a moderate amount of meat was healthy, vegetarians who fed on raw salads, succulent vegetables, ripe sugary fruits, mild farinaceous grain, cold water or 'rich balmy milk', made the best lovers:[11] 'What is it that makes the Irish ladies … Such excellent companions in bed? They run in the open air, and eat of good mealy potatoes, broken down in milk.'[12]

This idea seems to have had a long life. In 1805, Newenham also wrote about the nutritious make-up of potatoes and milk. Because of this excellent diet the Irish had 'in spite of political oppression', many people 'with well-formed vigorous bodies, and their cottages were *swarming with children*'. Their men were athletic and their women beautiful.[13] Apparently Scottish ladies also enjoyed such gifts of nature unlike their more urban English cousins:

> It is well known that the servant maids and common women of Scotland, who go continually summer and winter, wet and dry in frost and in snow, with their feet and legs, naked and bare – are the strongest – the rosiest and the healthiest women in the world. Their legs are as strong as pillars of iron, as thick as the waist of the southern fine lady, and as red as their cheeks…[14]

The urban/rural component to this contrast between sexualities is obvious. If luxury was considered bad for sex so was London. There was something about London that was not conductive to healthy reproduction. As youths moved to the city expecting a better life,

> they live[d] so poorly, and in want of all that is wholesome for life, live[d] in Cellars, [suffering] bad Diet, close packed, Want of Exercise, and, which is worse than all, the Reward of unlawful Lust, which, with such People, is promiscuous, and, having no fitting Expedients, as the Rich have, sweep whole shoals away, especially Children, of whom London is a Sepulchre.[15]

Healthy sexuality was seen to belong to the countryside. Every aspect of city life was bad for one's sex drive. Feather pillows and soft blankets were bad for the health and women who were spoilt in this way would not bear healthy children.[16] Urban fashions, such as high-heel shoes, did not allow women to run for exercise.[17]

When their masculinity was in question, aristocrats sought the aid of irresistible country girls. When Lady Saville discovered her son, Sir George, was a homosexual, she thought milkmaids might be able to cure him from it:

> Lady Saville had taken her young twig of Sodom into the country and, by way of weaning him from that unnatural vice, takes great pains to cocker him with every Abigail in her house and all the milk maid cunts in the neighbourhood.[18]

When the Bickerstaff family realised that, despite their use of breeding techniques to ensure a whiter skin and a greater height, there still remained some 'capital defects in the constitution of the family' they remedied the situation by 'that very judicious cross with Maud, the milk-maid'.[19]

A second argument for sexual permissiveness made in the eighteenth century was that, in contrast to the Malthusian concern over unchecked population growth, many eighteenth-century writers worried that England was becoming depopulated. The historian Donna Andrew discusses this in some detail in her study of philanthropy in eighteenth-century London. She argues that due to concerns about manning the army, in the 1740s and 1750s benevolent Londoners turned to charity because they thought it would increase the population.[20] In the 1770s and 1780s a large population continued to be seen as a sign of a healthy economy, although it was no longer believed to be the cause of it. There were early writers, like Richard Foster, who thought a large population might be a burden but they were a minority.[21]

Thus for most of the eighteenth century there were widespread fears that the English were not producing enough healthy children, which was quite worrisome for a society which held that its strength and wealth could be measured by the size of its population.[22] The constant need for more healthy children to fight wars and feed the rest of the country was part of the reason why working-class sexuality was seen as a positive thing. Roger North expressed eloquently these concerns in 1753, describing deserted fields and villages in the countryside, and even towns populated by a single shepherd or farmer. This lack of inhabitants devalued the land. Farmers were losing money because there were not enough people to eat the corn. Landlords also suffered because they did not have enough tenants to pay rents. North blamed this in part on the settlement laws which tied people to the parish where they were born.[23] While he was no friend of the poor, North realised their importance to the rest of society:

We love Depopulation while it is called easing us of the poor, that are, for the
most part, a Burthen, as also thievish and troublesome, until Want of Men,
Women and children, to plow, sow, weed, make Hay, carry thresh, spin & c.
makes a general Scarcity and Deerness of Manufactures, and consequently a
fastidious Plenty of some sorts of Products, as Wool, Cattle, &c. and also of
Corn, Hay, &c. but surcharged with vast Wages: and then we cry out, O the
Want of People![24]

Roger North also blamed parishes for discouraging marriage in order to save
on poor relief, because this led able young men to run away and poor women
who got pregnant to kill the child or become prostitutes.[25] Aside from the need
for labour, North recognised the importance of consumption:

It is strange Blindness to esteem Numbers of People a Burthen, when so much
good comes from them; their very Eating and Drinking is a Profitable Consumption of our Country's Product, and the Labour is sowing Riches for the Public
to Reap…[26]

After 1770 the concern about overpopulation and having too many mouths to
feed began to present a serious challenge to pro-population enthusiasts, though
it did not come to dominate until after the census of 1801. As late as 1805
there were writers concerned about depopulation. A minority of commentators continued to worry that England was not producing enough children,
although now they often blamed it on infrequent marriages and sex outside
of wedlock, which they claimed produced feeble children, who died before
reaching maturity.[27] Population growth was seen as so essential that it was even
used to defend enclosure and engrossment: according to John Howlett, enclosure and engrossment actually increased population in the countryside.[28]

It is crucial to our understanding of representations of sexuality to touch
on ideas of luxury in the eighteenth century. This is the third reason why
the sexuality of the labouring class was condoned. Most of the above writers
blamed depopulation on luxury, which they associated with the upper classes,
and, as we shall see later, this was a common theme in popular songs as well.
In the opinion of James Graham, high society was bad for wholesome sex
because other appetites – that is, luxuries – were replacing the need for sexual
pleasure.[29] The new love of luxury and 'dissipation' destroyed virility and
strength.[30] Thomas Newenham, comparing England and Ireland, agreed:

The greatest enemies to population are the artificial wants, the accumulation of
property, and the luxury and vices which are the constant attendants of opulence,
and which prevent a regular and early union between the sexes. The inhabitants of poor countries are more simple, more healthy, and more virtuous; and,

wanting little besides food, families are no burdens, and the prolific powers of nature have free scope to display themselves.[31]

John Howlett described the middle and higher ranks thus:

These latter have a certain pride of station; a shame and fear of descending beneath it a superior, perhaps, a false, refinement of thought a luxury and delicacy of habit; a tenderness of body and mind, which rendering formidable the prospect of poverty, and thereby checking the impulses of nature, frequently prevent matrimonial connections.[32]

Thus prior to the 1790s many writers seem to have agreed that

The labouring poor, who, in some sense, are forced to be temperate and active, are seldom without numerous and healthy issue, whilst the rich – those persons I mean whose time is spent in frivolous pursuits, in the gratification of every appetite, and in racketing about, turning day into night, and night into day, have generally a scantily puny offspring, and often none at all.[33]

The equation of sexuality with nature, the need for population growth, and the condemnation of luxury and city life led to the idea that peasants were more sexually adept than their social superiors, whose lives were more artificial. Although in these writings sex was not encouraged only for pleasure, but was seen to come out of a need for procreation and a desire to propagate the species, there was a freely voiced argument in support of it. Peasants or agricultural labourers were naturally associated with fertility because of their proximity to the land.

Painters often painted rich ladies in the garb of working women: Gains borough's painting of his wife as gleaner, and 'Mrs Graham as Housemaid' are examples.[34] The ideal of peasant beauty in art and in some literature was most commonly associated with milkmaids.

The idealisation of the milkmaid is familiar to anyone that has come in contact with eighteenth-century art. An example is Gainsborough's 'Landscape with a Woodcutter Courting a Milkmaid' of 1766, where a beautiful milkmaid is admired by a young man. John Barrell has noted that the pastoral figure of the shepherdess lost popularity, while the milkmaid resurfaced after 1700 and gained even greater popularity in the second half of the eighteenth century. Her origins in folklore made her seem a more realistic depiction of the peasantry, catering to new standards of taste. Barrell thinks a polite audience could identify with the milkmaid because her identity hovered between a rustic and a courtly one.[35] Ladies' fascination with dairying is well known and documented, as Emily Brooks points out in an article in *The National Trust*

Magazine. Lady Penrhyn (1745–1816) had a dairy with ornamental gardens approached by a path dotted with artificial mushrooms, some of them so large that one could sit on them. Most estates had a dairy, and these became more and more ornamented as the century progressed. According to Brooks, to aristocrats, dairymaids were the sexiest thing on earth.[36] The upper class's fascination with milkmaids even came to be noted in a popular song: 'The Praise of the Dairy-Maid' depicts the queen celebrating May Day by sporting with her many fair 'dairy-maids'.[37]

So far most of the evidence we have discussed has dealt with notions of female beauty in the eighteenth century. We will now turn to representations of male beauty and sexuality. Curiously, both ploughmen and aristocratic rakes defined their masculinity through sexual exploits, though each felt the other to be inferior in beauty and virility. Men would boast to each other about their sexual conquests.[38] In his discussion of the masculinity of the gentry, Anthony Fletcher cites an uncle giving advice to his nephew, saying it did not matter for a young man if a woman was ugly or beautiful, so long as he made love as often as possible.[39] But in popular song no male protagonist could match the alluring figure of the ploughman. Here we encounter a significant difference in high and low representation. John Barrell has shown that in high art the ploughman was the symbol of country labour, and for this reason could never be represented as idle.[40] Thus in Gainsborough's 'Landscape with a Woodcutter Courting a Milkmaid' the ploughman's figure in the background is the dark side of the landscape, contrasting with the milkmaid who represents courtly leisure.[41] This was not true in more popular texts, where ploughmen might be shown at play.

Negative images of peasant sexuality in satire and growing concerns about promiscuity

In contrast, there were voices raised in opposition to peasant sexuality in the early eighteenth century. Three main objections were made against it: that of immorality, that of lack of prudence or restraint, and that of lack of decorum.

There were occasional state prosecutions for obscenity, together with the more numerous cases processed by the ecclesiastical courts.[42] One such case is that of James Read and Angella Carter, who were charged with publishing 'The Fifteen Plagues of a Maidenhead' in 1706 and 1707 together with other similar poems in the form of half-sheet octavo pamphlets similar to chapbooks. The verse was also similar to seventeenth-century bawdy ballads. Read was found guilty but the case was then adjourned.[43] John Cleland himself was prosecuted for writing *Fanny Hill*.

A tension exists in some of the texts analysed thus far. Some writers on the subject both feared and admired the sexuality of the labouring class. First of all, virility was not an unmixed blessing. While a large penis was an important symbol of manhood and physical strength, it could also be linked to stupidity. Venette tells of the ancient general Heliogabulus, who recruited men with big noses (denoting big penises) because one could defeat the enemy with only a handful of these great warriors. However, Heliogabulus failed to realise that 'well hung Men are the greatest Blockheads, and the most stupid of Mankind'.[44]

In the works of Howlett, for instance, there are two ways of seeing peasant sexuality: in terms of libido and in terms of imprudence. To the mind of some of their social superiors, peasants were promiscuous or too foolish to restrain their sexuality. John Howlett lamented that the middle and higher ranks were much more likely to remain maids and bachelors than the labouring class: 'the marriages among the lower classes of society are to those among the middle and higher orders, in the proportion of nearly nine to one.'[45] Part of the reason for this was that those who had some wealth were afraid to lose it or to jeopardise the lifestyle they enjoyed for the sake of a wife and a family, while the working poor

> readily obey[ed] the suggestions of natural constitution, and embrace[d] the first opportunity of an inseparable union with some one of the other sex. They [were] perfectly regardless of what they may meet with in their passage thorough their humble walk of life.

While Howlett allowed this propensity to reproduce to be good for the country, he seems to have been rather scornful of it: that which was acceptable for peasants could not be expected of their betters, who had a greater variety of interests, as well as the ability to plan for the future. This line of thought led Howlett to conclude that an impoverished peasantry served the national interest, as it ensured a high population.[46]

A similar tension between an admiration for the poor's sexuality and a condemnation of their sexual imprudence could be found in an early eighteenth-century song, 'Kick Him Jenny. A Tale'. The characters are a squire, his lady, Jenny (a country maid), and Roger (her sweetheart). As Jenny and Roger make love, the squire and his lady observe them through a peephole. The lady shouts to Jenny to protect herself against an unwanted pregnancy, but the squire is on Roger's side and eggs him on.[47] Though the story is narrated in the third person, it is told from the point of view of the lord and his lady, who observe the sex and to whom Jenny and Roger seem ignorant and uncouth; the servants are lewd and incapable of self-restraint. At the same time there is a suggestion that the polite couple is somehow inadequate: as voyeurs they do not engage in the pleasures of love as fully. At the end it seems the narrator dissolves the ambiguity by saying ladies like to make love as much as servants but know better how to avoid pregnancy. Again, there is an implicit condescension toward working people: they simply do not know any better.

A degree of scorn for peasant sexuality was also present in satires of the countryside. This genre belonged to what Barrell and Bull have called 'anti-pastoral'.[48] It was not concerned with imprudence, but with peasants' inability to express love in the refined, courtly manner of their betters. Stories or poems of this kind were usually told from the point of view of a Londoner. John Gay was among the first to write an anti-pastoral, 'The Shepherd's Week', where he claims to be describing reality rather than Arcadia, depicting ploughmen and girls milking cows, rather than the traditional idle shepherds associated with the pastoral genre. Gay mocks these bumpkins for their amorous exchanges, giving them names like 'Buxoma' and 'Lobbin Clout'.[49] According to John Barrell, Gay wanted to show that a 'realistic' portrayal of the peasantry was incommensurable with writing love pastoral.[50] Within this comic genre, rustics were seen to be incapable of love, or their love was based on animal instincts and did not interfere with the low tasks they had to perform.[51]

Some bawdy songs prior to 1750 made fun of rural folk in a much less gentle manner than Gay. However, these usually came from songsters (i.e. books), which would have been more expensive and would have had a more polite audience because rural labourers at this time were very unlikely to own books. Here the portrayal of rural sexuality was not very sympathetic. While rural labourers were seen as sexually promiscuous, they were shown to be inferior to city people because of their gross manners. In an untitled song from a 1750 songster, Ursula – a fat, greasy farm servant – is the object of Roger the Plowman's clumsy love. Their rough lovemaking includes blows and kicks, and the resulting noise awakes the master who kicks them out to finish their amorous encounter in the hog-sty.[52] In addition to having a smaller audience, songsters were different from broadside ballads in that they were not reprinted as often. While the best-loved broadside ballads of the early eighteenth century continued to be printed and retained their popularity throughout the period, verse from songsters like the *Aviary* seldom made it to broadsides and chapbooks, and seems to have passed away with its time.

In addition to satire, there was a growing concern among some contemporaries that the common people were too promiscuous. The great enemy of sexual permissiveness in the eighteenth century has been associated by historians with the middle class.[53] Their fear of impropriety has been particularly well documented when it was directed at the aristocracy, as with the Mohawk scare in the 1700s.[54] The fear was manifested early on with the establishment of the Society for the Reformation of Manners, which was active from 1700 to around 1720. Despite the decline of the Society for the Reformation of Manners, throughout the eighteenth century voices of concern about public morality were raised every now and then. For instance, the 1749 edition of *Aristotle's Masterpiece* took a moralistic stance, saying there was too much lewd behaviour and ridicule of the married state. The writer wanted to show that marriage was the happiest state.[55] But near the end of the eighteenth century those concerned with sexual promiscuity became more outspoken, affecting many different forms of discourse, amounting to a new wave of moral reform.

Porter and Hall have shown that editions of medical treatises after 1790 were becoming more sexually repressive, increasingly concerned to confine sexual practice within the realms of marriage and procreation.[56] Attention was now directed not only at the aristocracy but also at the poor. Reformers became critical of labouring-class sexuality, blaming their miserable state on permissiveness, promiscuity, illegitimacy, obscenity and bawdiness.[57] In the words of one commentator,

> Bastardy is now scarcely deemed a disgrace … This species of profligacy, so detestable in itself, and so pernicious in its consequences, both to the individuals, and to the community at large, has increased of late years, especially in the metropolis, to an extent that is almost incredible. Adultery and concubinage in the lower classes of society are unhappily most prevalent.[58]

The census of 1801 and Malthus's essay on population contributed to the notion that uncontrolled sexuality was dangerous.[59] Malthus saw poverty, wars, famines and epidemics as the inevitable results of sexual promiscuity.[60] Men and women who saw themselves as middle-class or 'respectable' increasingly demanded that women be chaste and men exercise self-control.[61] The growth of Evangelicalism contributed to this campaign. Many Evangelicals felt sexual restraint was necessary for conversion.[62] Poverty could only be eradicated if the poor's moral character was improved first.[63] Even compassionate Evangelicals like Thomas Chalmers proposed that an objective for philanthropists' visits to labourers should be to rescue them from sensuality and lust.[64]

Hannah More typified this attitude on the part of social reformers toward labourers' sexuality. When she was preparing her tracts and her friend William Mason sent her some ballads he himself had written, she rejected most of them on the grounds that they contained either too much politics or too much love. Although not as bad as political ballads, bawdy songs were unacceptable. As she studied the literature sold by hawkers and peddlers, she was dismayed to discover that a huge portion of it was 'dirty and indecent stuff'.[65]

So on the one hand we have a Foucauldian proliferation of discourses in print about sexuality, and on the other hand we have the growing sexual repressiveness associated with the middle class but also shared by some genteel opinion. The question we have to ask is how do popular songs relate to these developments? The answer to this question will be necessarily speculative, as we cannot be certain that songs printed after 1790 did not have earlier precedents that have been lost or were not printed. What can be shown is what themes appeared in popular songs printed at the end of the century. As the century progressed, sexuality became more open and diverse, and the kinds of stories that were told increased in variety as did the sexual imagery. Also, more songs were printed in which women exhibited a greater degree of independence.[66] In this sense Peter Wagner's argument that the middle class's concern about bawdiness led to erotic poetry becoming solemn and bawdy verse being driven underground after 1800 is untenable.[67] Bawdy songs continued to be printed throughout the country, increasing during Victorian times in spite of the moralists.[68]

There is a relationship between this trend in popular art and some demographic patterns drawn by social historians. Higher birth rates, earlier marriages, and higher degrees of illegitimacy after 1750 are interpreted by both Porter and Gillis to reveal higher instances of extramarital sex among working people.[69] In villages and towns where young people had an independent source of income early on, parents would allow their children considerable independence. Young men would visit women at their parents' home and parents would withdraw, leaving the couple alone.[70] In those areas affected by industrialisation and the agricultural revolution, both work and leisure were less segregated for men and women leading to freer courtship and greater intimacy before marriage.[71] Night-visiting, bundling and cohabitation before marriage became more widespread.[72] Bundling was especially common among farm servants in Cheshire, where many a milkmaid must have worked.[73] Illegitimacy rates were growing and were particularly high in the countryside due to industrialisation – the irregular economy made it more necessary for husbands to move in search of work. By 1850 the rate of pre-marital pregnancy among agricultural women was over 30 per cent.[74] Also, men were now more likely to abandon their pregnant sweethearts.[75]

Porter and Hall's argument that sex was only allowed between courting couples where there was an expectation of marriage, and that loose women or men who brought bastards into the world would be condemned, is not verified by my evidence.[76] Of course, rural communities would have had limited tolerance for loose sexual behaviour. Jeffrey Weeks argues that peasants had a social morality: their concern was about the economic burden of bastards on the parish, not any notion of the immorality of sexual behaviour outside of marriage.[77] Perhaps this is why the ploughman who made many conquests, or the flirtatious milkmaid Smirky Nan, were often celebrated in song.[78] But even illegitimacy was often given a rather light-hearted and frivolous treatment, as if it were merely a part of everyday life. It was seldom described as the disaster we know it often was for working women.[79] 'The Praise of the Dairy-Maid', a very cheerful song celebrating the beauty of the milkmaid, ends with a little story of Rose getting pregnant outside of wedlock and advises other milkmaids to learn from her fall and never touch a man.[80] In typical fashion, illegitimacy is a problem for the woman, not the man, though Mr Edmond (the seducer) is censured for 'grafting a Thistle upon a Rose Bush', anti-Scottish feeling taking the upper hand, in spite of Mr Edmund's belonging to a higher social class than Rose.[81] These kinds of songs may have been more popular with a male audience. We will discuss this question in more detail below in relation to women's agency.

Ballads about couples of unequal social standing

Of all the texts discussed here, John Cleland's representation of peasant sexuality in *Memoirs of a Woman of Pleasure* was the closest to bawdy songs. Cleland defines the sexual prowess of milkmaids and ploughmen against that of the aristocracy, and judges it to be more powerful. For instance, Mrs Cole's voluptuous clients 'would at any time leave a sallow, washy, painted duchess on her own hands, for a ruddy, healthy, firm-fleshed country maid'.[82] Similarly, Fanny Hill assures the reader that country boys are the best endowed. Beauty is more important to her than titles, and she seduces Mr H's servant, whose member she lovingly refers to as a 'maypole'. After going to bed with this country lad she writes:

> May I not presume that so exalted a pleasure ought not to be ungratefully forgotten or suppressed by me, because I found it in a character in low life, where, by the by, it is oftener met with, purer and more unsophisticated, than amongst the false ridiculous refinements with which the great suffer themselves

to be so grossly cheated by their pride.[83]

Fanny's friend, Emily, was deflowered by a ploughboy when she ran away from home, and this remains one of her fondest memories. On the road she was overtaken by the youth who, she says, was 'ruddy, well featured enough, with uncombed flaxen hair, a little flapped hat, a kersy frock, yarn stockings; in short, a perfect ploughboy'.[84] His charm led her to follow all his entreaties and they got into bed together at a nearby inn. The seventeen-year-old Emily discovered the ploughboy's genitals, asking in her innocence what they were for. 'I will show you,' he replied, 'If you will let me.'

The reason why milkmaids and ploughmen were depicted in this way may have something to do with the text having a broad audience. Though it was not oral like ballads, it was more popular than treatises or paintings and so catered to a broader taste.

Songs took the representation of sexuality a step further, because they often allowed marriage between a peasant and a member of the gentry. Frequently, aristocratic sexuality was openly disparaged, and master and servant sexuality were set against each other. For instance, the ballad 'Drive on Coachman' pits the coachman Robin against the old Sir John. Sir John cannot satisfy his wife but he needs a male heir, so he looks the other way when Robin takes over, allowing him to 'drive in'.[85] In 'The Mouse's Tail', Jack and his master bet on who had the larger penis, but Jack beats his master by four inches. He then makes his master a cuckold.[86] Robert Burns proposed one explanation for this difference not found in the elite discourses described hitherto. As he put it in his song 'Why Should Na Poor Folk Mowe', great men have great exploits and conquests to bring them excitement, but poor people's only pleasure is sex:

And why shouldna poor folk, mowe, mowe, mowe,
And why shouldna poor folk mowe:
The great folk hae siller, and houses and lands,
Poor bodies hae naething but mowe.

But Burns also argued that sex was more pleasurable than silver and gold, not merely a substitute.[87]

Concern about the luxury of the leisured classes was also reflected in popular songs, where this was a prevailing trope. In bawdy satirical ballads against the aristocracy, rakes were seen as 'dissolute' and were not celebrated the way ploughmen and milkmaids were. The ballads that talked about rakes were scandalous, sensational stories: the aristocratic seducer was not an object of admiration. In popular culture the sexuality of the upper classes was seen as somehow immoral and perverse. While the stereotype of the aristocratic rake could be found in some songs, much anti-aristocratic erotica was often personal, referring to real people, which distinguished it from bawdy ballads involving rural stock characters. Peter Wagner makes a comparison between French and English anti-aristocratic erotica, arguing that the former was a vehicle of popular protest while the latter was merely social satire.[88] The fact that in English popular culture the peasants' sexual exploits were admired, while the aristocratic ones were censured, may not amount to social protest, but it certainly was at odds with the aristocratic notion that the master's masculinity is of a superior order to that of the servant.[89] There are occasions in ballads about the countryside when squires do not come off too badly as lovers, as they end up marrying a beautiful milkmaid, a farmer's daughter, or another attractive woman whose station is inferior to their own, but there is little tolerance for a nobleman's seduction and abandonment of a country girl.

Like medical treatises and writings about population, popular songs associated peasants with strong, healthy, beautiful bodies. Songs celebrated the beauty of the milkmaid over and over again, in roughly the same terms: black eyes and hair, fair skin with red cheeks and lips, dimples, curvaceous form. Here is one example that departs slightly from the formula describing golden tresses rather than black ones:

> Like Helen's is her face with Golden tresses,
> Which showes such splendant grace like young Narcissus
> Her eyes like lampes doe shine
> Her lookes are so Diuine
> She doth my loue confine
> Up to the elobowes.
>
> Her pretty Dimple Chin, Cheeks red as Cheries
> Her necke like Iuory thinne with Amber Berries
> Wast short and body tall
> And fingers long and small
> Forst me in loue to fall
> Up to the elbowes.[90]

'The Praise of the Dairy-Maid, with a Lick at the Cream-Pot, or a Fading Rose' even goes so far as to claim the dairymaid is the essence of womanhood. It argues the first dairymaid was Eve, followed by a line of royal milkmaids: in biblical times, it continues, even a queen 'of the highest degree' would milk the cows.[91]

The sexuality of the milkmaid was contrasted to that of the rich or urban lady. A 1700 ballad entitled 'The Bonny Milkmaid' describes how the

> Town Lass
> looks with her white Face,
> And lips of deadly pale,
> but it is not so
> with those that go
> through frost and Snow
> with Cheeks that glow
> to carry the milking pail.

The city girl has to resort to unnatural remedies like 'washes and paint' to give her complexion a fresh look and use cushions to make her figure look pleasantly curvaceous, while the milk maids are naturally 'plump and round' and 'sweet and sound'. It is no wonder they are the envy of the city girls, who grow old before their time while the milkmaids retain their freshness much longer.[92] Multiple reprints suggest that this song was very popular.[93] In another version of the song the sense that milkmaids are one with nature is even more prominent, as all the birds are said to sing in order to entertain the milkmaids.[94] The milkmaids' very movements are more graceful and beautiful than those of the city girls; they are full of energy and life.[95] Therefore, milkmaids are much better lovers – they are 'Girls of Venus Game' who make their lovers grow 'blind and lame'. The wise man will choose a milkmaid as his lover, concludes the song:

> If man were so wise,
> To value the prize
> Of the Wares most fit for Sale;
> What store of Beaus
> Would Daub their cloaths,
> To Save a Nose
> By following those
> That carry the Milking-pail.[96]

In similar fashion, ploughmen in songs were contrasted with urban men or with noblemen, in a manner reminiscent of Cleland's portrayal of ploughmen, described above. In J. Deacon's version of 'The Bonny Milkmaids' there is a second part called 'The Plowman's Answer'.[97] This points out that

> No Courtier May
> Compare with they,
> who cloath'd in gray,
> Do follow the painful plow.

The courtiers are degenerate, as is their love. They have no taste in beauty, and 'doat on every Sow' who is willing to oblige them. Having to pay for love often leads to their financial ruin. This detail puts the courtier's sexual prowess in doubt – no ploughman is ever reduced to having to pay for his pleasure. There is a moral censure implicit in this and it reveals the limits of what was sexually permissible in the eighteenth century: despite considerable sexual freedom, prostitution was not sanctioned, even in popular culture.[98] 'The Farmer's Courtship' contains a similar critique of the sexuality of the aristocracy and points to the ploughman's sexual prowess in even more explicit terms:

> Dear lady, believe me now,
> I solemnly swear and vow,
> No lords in their lives
> Take such pleasure in their wives,
> As a fellow that follows the plough.
>
> For what they do gain by their labour and pain,
> They do not to a harlot run,
> As courtiers do, I never knew
> A London beau, that could outdo
> A country farmer's son.[99]

It was this legend of the ploughman's beauty that Malthus was thinking of as he tried to describe the sad reality of the peasant condition in 1798:

> The sons and daughters of peasants will not be found such rosy cherubs in real life as they are described to be in romances. It cannot fail to be remarked by those who live much in the country that the sons of labourers are very apt to be stunted in their growth, and are a long while arriving at maturity. Boys that you would guess to be 14 or 15 are, upon inquiry, frequently found to be 18 or 19. And the lads who drive the plough, which must certainly be a healthy exercise, are very rarely seen with any appearance of calves to their legs: a circumstance which can only be attributed to a want either of proper or of sufficient nourishment.[100]

This brings us to the crucial question of courtship and social status as depicted in songs. How did songs deal with the case of two lovers of unequal social status? Song writers had different responses to this phenomenon. Some songs praised the girl who chose the ploughman or country boy over the squire, because the former was more attractive. But this could be read to mean that no one should marry above their station, a reaffirmation of the social hierarchy. Take for example the ballad 'The Shepherd's Daughter'.[101] The narrator meets the shepherd's daughter bathing in the Boyne. Captivated, he promises to marry her if she follows him, but she replies that his parents will find some wealthy grazier's daughter for him and he should leave her alone. The last verse reproaches 'Judas young men' who try to deceive girls, and praises the shepherd's daughter for her virtue:

> Now to conclude and finish,
> I mean to stop my pen;
> To all you Judas young men
> I this fair one recommend
> To all you Judas traitors,
> With me you will combine,
> She's the shepherd's virtuous daughter
> Who went bathing in the boyne.

She is commended because she preserves her honour, yet there is an implicit assumption that a well-to-do man can never marry a shepherd's daughter, only deflower her. Yet in other songs the unequal lovers get married and this too is a cause for celebration. We can use 'The Crafty Farmer' as an example.[102] A young farmer marries a rich lady of six thousand a year; her father, initially opposed to the match, ends up blessing the couple. A third kind of song, like 'The Two Unhappy Lovers', criticises women who are too proud to respond to the affections of men from their own class and set their heart on a person above their station.[103] The song 'No, my Love, No!' is another example of this. A haymaker refuses to marry a village lad because she thinks his degree is low and she can do better, though she does not refuse to make love to him:

> Her answer 'twas back again, no, my love, not I
> Suppose that I should marry you, should I not be to blame
> My friends and relations would laugh at my disdain,
> For you are such a low degree, and I'm so very high,
> Do you think that I would marry you, O, no, not I.

When she gets pregnant she tries to retract her refusal and insulting words, but it is now the lad's turn to reply 'No, my love, not I'. Thus she is punished for scorning her class.[104]

The song about lovers of unequal social status was not a new phenomenon in 1800. In fact, the majority of love songs from the eighteenth century dealt with this problem. Of the 230 or so songs that show up in the Bodleian Broadside Ballad catalogue under the subject title 'courtship', 210 are listed as dealing with unequal social status.[105] More such songs were printed after 1800, suggesting a growing market. It is tempting to argue that these were symptomatic of growing social tension in the countryside. However, it is important to note that in later songs wealthy suitors were not condemned and milkmaids were not depicted as victims.[106] They were either willing participants in the act of lovemaking or well able to defend their bodies and their pride. In 'Love in a Barn, or the Country Courtship', a London lord is smitten by the beauty of a young milkmaid.[107] Though he has seen many great ladies, he is dismayed to find he has fallen for a country girl. He decides to use his wealth to seduce her. He promises her marriage and the life of a lady in London. She replies humbly that she is more suited to her father's dairy, and that she cannot pass for a lady, being unable to dress elegantly and dance. The lord is not to be put off:

> You can dance in bed, my dear,
> And that's the prettiest sport;
> Aye, never fear, I'll warrant you Gafffer,
> As well as the best at court.

The lord thinks he has won but the narrator tells us

> Country girls are no such fools,
> For to be taken in,
> But now you shall hear the country bite,
> Which she put on him.

To make a long story short, she pretends to agree to sleep with him for £500. She comes to the appointed place, gets him drunk, and pays some gypsies to tie a gypsy child to his back while he is sleeping. When he wakes up he is frightened out of his wits, making a spectacle of himself in front of the whole town. Surprisingly, he is even more enchanted with the milkmaid after this prank and marries her. 'The Northern Ditty: or, the Scotsman Outwitted by the Country Damsel' is similar in nature.[108] A gentleman attempts to seduce a farmer's daughter on her way to market to sell her barley. He offers to buy all her barley for £20 and give her £20 on top if she would sleep with him. At first she refuses but later she seems to agree and he gives her the money. Then she jumps to the other side of the river with her mare and leaves the gentleman, too cowardly to do the same, without a penny:

> She leap'd her mare on the other side,
> And left me not one penny.
> Then my heart was sunk full low,
> With grief and care surrounded,
> After her I could not go,
> For fear of being drownded;
> She turn'd about and says behold,
> I'm not for your devotion,
> But Sir I thank you for your gold,
> 'Twill serve to enlarge my portion.

In songs, it was not only rich men who try to seduce milkmaids. The opposite was also true; rich ladies often married farm boys. In the song 'The Farmer's Son' a lady marries a farmer's son.[109] In 'The Surprised Lovers', the farmer's man

Will deflowers the miller's daughter. They are discovered making love inside the oven, but the miller and his wife decide to forgive them because Joan, the wife, herself had made love to the miller inside an oven before they were married.[110]

Farmers and ploughmen were frequently juxtaposed in later songs. Needless to say, it was usually the ploughman that won the day. In 'The Wealthy Farmer' a farmer is dissatisfied with the gendered division of labour in his family, complaining that his wife's work at home is easy while he has to work on the field with his ploughman, John.[111] They agree to trade jobs and the next day his wife goes ploughing with John. The outcome is predictable – the farmer goes to check on them only to find out that he is a cuckold. Having learned his lesson, he advises farmers never to busy themselves with women's work. Admittedly, this song reaffirms gender roles in agricultural labour, but it quite overlooks the act of adultery. Of course, Porter and Gillis' contention that such acts were unacceptable may still hold true when it comes to actual behaviour. But standards were more relaxed in popular songs. The ploughman is not condemned and neither is the wife. In fact, the whole thing is the farmer's fault and he gets what is coming to him.

Ploughboys were also set up as rivals in courtship to squires or 'men of fashion'. Again, the man of inferior social standing was represented as more masculine than his superiors. This may be because working men identified skill with manhood.[112] In 'Cupid the Pretty Ploughboy', the ploughboy is Cupid, or rather the ploughboy is so irresistible an object of desire that the woman sees him as Cupid, rejecting a wealthy young gentleman for his sake.[113] In 'Jemmy the Plough Boy' a girl announces to her mother that she 'can have none but Jemmy, my pretty Plough Boy'.[114] The mother advises her that Jemmy does not enjoy a great reputation and that she should try to marry a man of fashion. On top of his mean degree, Jemmy is a Tory and Tories are out of fashion. The mother prefers Tommy, the Irish Dissenter, as a son-in-law. The girl will have none of it:

> For I love an honest Churchman,
> like to my Jemmy dear,
> For he's a true born Englishman,
> he does no Colours bear.

Here the ploughman is associated with Church-and-King loyalty while the men of fashion and Tommy the Irish Dissenter are seen as morally corrupt. Another interesting song of this kind is 'Undaunted Mary, On the Banks of Sweet Dundee'.[115] Here a farmer's daughter with five hundred pounds as her portion rejects a squire (her uncle's chosen suitor) for William, the ploughboy.

The uncle has William impressed. The squire tries to rape Mary and she kills him in self-defence. The uncle tries to kill her but instead she kills him too. On his deathbed the uncle is remorseful and impressed with Mary's strength and determination, leaving all his money to her. Here the story of William is not resolved, but in a sequel, 'William's Answer', we learn that he returns to wed Mary. Roy Porter's point that the aristocracy feared plebeian sexuality may explain why this kind of competition had such wide appeal after 1800, when relations between landowners, farmers and labourers were increasingly strained.[116]

A growing audience for bawdy songs and new sexual imagery at the end of the century

As the perception of peasant sexuality began to change, the audience for bawdy songs began to increase. In 1750 the Bishop of London wrote that obscene and infamous ballads sung in the streets were corrupting the common people and *The Gentleman's Magazine* proposed that ballad singers be licensed so that young girls would not be exposed to bawdy songs. The outcries against bawdy songs, which continued over the next few decades, give the impression that they were popular among both men and women. Tim Hitchcock has distinguished between sexual representations found in trial reports, medical literature, extended metaphor and Grub Street sexual humour, on the one hand, and chapbooks and broadsheets, on the other: the former were associated with the middling sort, the latter with plebeians. Hitchcock's contention that the two 'contained different sets of assumptions' is supported particularly by their contrasting representations of the ploughman, which were discussed above.[117] Also, while medical treatises and Grub Street pamphlets had to be purchased, often at a significant cost, bawdy songs had a vigorous oral life. At the same time, there was some overlap and such distinctions can never be absolute when dealing with popular culture. According to Francis Place, bawdy songs could be heard among master artisans and tradesmen even when they aspired to the status of gentlemen as well as poorer people.[118] While the largest audience for bawdy songs consisted of working people, it is possible that the middling sort, unless they were pious Evangelicals, also did hear, read and enjoy love songs and bawdy songs during much of the eighteenth century. The songs may tell us something about what kinds of sexualities were associated in the popular mind with the different social groups one finds in the countryside. Their appeal, in particular their appeal among peasants or labourers, reveals one aspect of a rural labouring identity.

Class relations remained more or less the same in bawdy songs, but there were new sexual images added on. There may have been a precedent for this, and if so I've not found it yet, but in later songs milking the cow was often a metaphor for masturbation. In 'The Pretty Milkmaid' the milkmaid asks her suitor to let go of her hand because she 'must go milk the kine' and he replies that 'If that my Dame would not me blame, / I'd freely give thee mine'.[119] In 'The Milk Maid' we find the following verse: 'Young Collin so lov'd with his flail, / Shewn it to fill her milking pail.'[120]

It is also after 1800 that we find for the first time a song about milkmen. This may be indicative of Deborah Valenze's argument that dairying became increasingly dominated by men in the nineteenth century, but the centre of the song was still the female dairy workers. The milkman says he loves his job because he gets to make love to all the pretty milkmaids.[121]

Phallic imagery gained greater importance in songs after 1800, supporting Hitchcock's idea that sex came to be defined more exclusively as penetration.[122] The use of the image of ploughing for bawdy purposes became more elaborate and sophisticated. One song advises girls that plough boys cannot be trusted because 'They're used so much to ploughing their seed for to sow, / That under your apron it is sure for to grow'.[123] The song 'The Ploughman', from the 1820s, told from a female point of view, includes the oxen in the sexual metaphor:

As I was walking in a field,
I chanced to meet a plowman,
I told him I would learn to till,
If that he would prove true man. (refrain)

He said my dear, take you no fear,
But I will do my best, O,
I'll study for to pleasure thee,
As I have done the rest, O. (refrain)

He then assures the girl his oxen are stout and good, the foremost one is long and small, while the other ox is firm and round. He proceeds to plough, and when he comes between the stilts he feels like he is in heaven. The rest of the song describes the act of lovemaking between the ploughman and the village girl in similar terms, concluding with an invitation to drink the ploughman's health.[124]

Songs and women's agency

Anna Clark and Cindy Lynn Preston have suggested that ballads could serve misogynist ends. Clark has argued that a certain genre of bawdy song tried to control female sexuality because it was based on the assumption that 'no means yes' and that women would always yield to their seducers in the end.[125] Cindy Lynn Preston has suggested that most of these ballads may have appealed to a male audience because they used the female body as a site of class struggle. Women participated in the bawdy song tradition, but their doing so implied an acceptance of a predominantly male system of values. These arguments hold true for the ballads that Clark and Preston read, and for some of the ballads in this chapter, but they do not give a full picture of the role of women in popular ballads. Clark does allow that some northern ballads gave women more agency. In this section I would like to extend the exploration of this question of agency.

There were ballads that told the stories of women who were treated poorly by male lovers. These were tragic songs about seduction and abandonment like 'The Perjured Youth', where a farmer's son seduces a girl and abandons her after he makes her pregnant.[126] Some ballads about criminals depicted male violence toward women. This was particularly true of the Punch and Judy tradition, but was also to be found in songs with rural settings. Often songs about criminals included their sexual exploits, usually with whores. It is possible that these songs reflected the violence that was common in real-life relationships, which has been recorded in other sources. Historian V. A. C. Gatrell mentions commonplace books and diaries describing a brutal side to village life where men would beat their wives and even sweethearts on occasion.[127] Gatrell also suggests that rapes were more common in the countryside than legal records show. An example of violence in popular song is 'The Dorsetshire Tragedy', which tells the story of a shepherd's daughter seduced by the steward while 'she in Service dwelt'. When she becomes pregnant with his child he takes her to a wood and stabs her to death with a knife.[128] In many of the songs about lovers of unequal social status the parents or relatives of the wealthier lover murder the poorer one. However, ballads also depicted violence towards men. It was common for girls' families to have unwanted suitors impressed and even murdered. One example was 'The Merchant's Daughter and the Constant Farmer's Son', in which a London merchant's daughter loves a farmer's son, but her brothers oppose the match and murder the young man at a country fair.[129] Ballads did not sanction such behaviour with regard to either women or men.

The figures of the ploughman and the milkmaid never took part in such dark stories. In this sense the 'ploughman' and the 'milkmaid' were types rather than personalities taken from life.[130] In most bawdy songs, the man initiated courtship or lovemaking, but this did not necessarily mean women were forced into sex. For example, in 'The Milk Maid' a squire makes love to a milkmaid without having married her, but she is willing, not taken advantage of.[131] The most sinister seduction song, which also raises the question of illegitimacy, is a different 'The Milk Maid', which was revised later by collectors to become a popular nursery rhyme.[132] The seducer is of higher social standing than the milkmaid since she addresses him as 'Sir'. He asks what she would do if he got her pregnant. She replies he would have to become a father. He asks her what she would do for the baby's clothes and cradle, and she says her father is a linen draper and her brother is a cradle maker. Then he asks what she would do if he ran away and left her. She replies with a laugh that 'I never would run after you, kind sir'. This is a striking assertion of independence. In another version the girls' reply is 'The devil he would follow, kind sir'.[133] An extra verse was added at the end, where the gentleman asks what she would do if he came back again after his flight. She replies they would be married and her 'red rosy cheeks [would] grow paler'. In the R. Evans version the last line reads 'Your red rosy cheek would be paler then'.[134] The meaning of this is difficult to piece together, but it may be an indication the milkmaid does not want to be married to this man.[135] Once again, the ballad may deal with the theme of seduction and abandonment, but it cannot be said that it encouraged or supported the attitude of the seducer.

An important point that needs to be made is that ballads allowed women to express strong sexual desire. While in elite art the ideal of the milkmaid's beauty did not necessarily encourage sexual expression, in popular songs female beauty and sexuality were closely intertwined. The products of the milkmaid's labour – milk, curds and cream – were themselves symbolic of love and were often given by the milkmaid to her suitor, or vice versa, as a reward after lovemaking or as a form of seduction. In 'The Charming Month of May', the blushing milkmaid rewards her lover with curds and cream after they had made love.[136] In an untitled song of 1750 a lover seduces the country maid Molly by offering her milks, curds, cheese-cake and custards. Then he rewards her favours by settling her in a copyhold worth £40 a year and providing an income of £20 on top.[137] In 'Love in a Barn, or the Country Courtship', a young London lord often drinks warm milk offered him by the milkmaid he falls in love with. The milk acts as a kind of love potion:

> The draught of love he drank so sweet
> And gazing on her charms,
> This lovely beauty he would often
> Wish her in his arms.[138]

'The Praise of the Dairy Maid' argues milk and cream cure all ailments, such as the spleen, and 'makes an old Bawd like a Wench of fifteen'. The song also mentions syllabub, which fills the narrator with pleasant anticipation that is also sexually suggestive:

> with pleasure I rub,
> Yet impatient I scrub,
> When I think of the Blessing of a Syllabub.[139]

Thus the ballad was a flexible form that had room for more than one point of view. Bawdy ballads or ballads about sexuality allowed women a broad range of responses to sex. There were songs told in a female voice expressing sexual desire, songs in which women tricked lustful males by pretending to agree to sex and then stealing their money or humiliating them, songs in which women refused suitors, songs in which women not only refused but beat or assaulted suitors, and songs in which women got illegitimate fathers to claim their children.

An example of trickery is 'An Excellent New Song: Called the Cunnie's Garland' where a Lincolnshire country girl goes to market to sell her butter, eggs, cheese, chickens and two cunnies (rabbits), one of which she hides between her legs.[140] Playing on the double entendre of the word 'cunnie', she misleads a gentleman into making a bargain for the 'cunnie between her legs'. Thinking he is paying for sex, he offers her £50 but ends up with a rabbit. Angered, he takes the girl to court but the justice decides in her favour. Two songs discussed above in the context of class also involve female trickery against males. In 'The Northern Ditty' – of which there were many versions, testifying to its popularity – a country girl outwits a gentleman by stealing his £40 and running away without satisfying his passion. It is noteworthy that the reason he can not follow after her is that he is too afraid to jump over the ditch with his horse as the girl has done. Thus the girl is superior both in wit and bravery.[141] In 'Love in a Barn, or the Country Courtship', a milkmaid steals £500 from a nobleman without giving herself to him.

In many of the songs in this chapter we have seen women only accept suitors if they meet their demands, or refuse them outright. In 'Milking the Cows in the Farm', a farmer pleads with a milkmaid to walk with him and in return he will look after the ground and return the cows to the farm.[142] She replies that his neighbours have informed her that he would 'sleep sound' instead of looking after the land or the cows. She only yields to him after he promises to work hard. Some songs even had aggressive women physically attack unwanted suitors.[143] In 'Undaunted Mary', also discussed above, Mary's reaction to being forced to marry an unwelcome suitor is very strong: she gets into a fight with the squire and her uncle, killing both. The song does not condemn Mary; on the contrary, before he dies, the uncle begs Mary's forgiveness and leaves her all his money.[144] In 'The Taylor's Courtship', Dolly the milkmaid, angered by some of the sexual liberties the tailor takes, throws him down the well. He is saved, but she still refuses to marry him.[145] Anna Clark cites one such song in her study of sexual assault, allowing that it permits women some agency but concluding that it implicitly slandered women who could not resist male sexual aggression.[146] However, as we have seen, other songs go very easy on women who yield to men and even on women who get pregnant outside of marriage.

Making men responsible for illegitimate children was another form of agency given to women in popular songs. 'Bite upon Bite's Garland; or the Miser Out-witted by the West Country Maid' is about a girl tricking an old miser by getting him to keep her illegitimate child, though the child was from another union. This works because the child's name is Maidenhead and the miser thought he was paying £40 to have her maidenhead, but in fact had made a bargain for the child.[147] In 'The Politic Maid of Suffolk' a lawyer makes a country girl pregnant and refuses to marry her, but she makes him do so by dressing up as the devil and scaring him into marriage.[148]

Most of these elements did not change in 1800, except that there were more versions and reprints of songs about tricky or aggressive women.

The proliferation of sexual imagery in popular songs may be a kind of popular opposition to middle-class attempts to impose their ideas of sexuality on the rural poor.

The reprinting of ballads celebrating the sexuality of rural labourers and the production of new ballads dealing with unequal social status show common people's lasting identification with these themes. It is hard to come by evidence of how these songs were perceived by rural labourers, but Samuel Bamford's autobiography provides a rare glimpse into their readership. He tells us how he read Robert Burns's 'The Ploughman': 'There he was, a tall, stooping, lank haired, weather browned, dreamy eyed, God-crowned, noble minded ploughman.' Bamford was so moved that he started writing verse himself.[149] The fact that rural labourers enjoyed the celebration of their sexuality in song confirms historians' arguments that while rural labourers' lives got harder they developed a new pride in their identity. Anna Clark has argued that although the working class was more sexually permissive than the middle class, in response to new hardships and dislocation due to industrialisation, this sexual permissiveness only served to divide the working class into more segments – those who were for it and those who were against, men versus women, and so on – instead of creating class identity.[150] Here I have tried to show that the appeal of the characters of the ploughman and the milkmaid placed both rural men and women in the same category as against other segments of society.

Notes

1 'John and Nell' (Greenock: W. Scott, c.1815), Houghton Library Collection.

2 Michel Foucault, *The History of Sexuality: An Introduction*, Vol. 1 (New York: Random House, 1978; reprinted Vintage Books, 1990), 17.

3 Vic Gammon, 'Songs, Sex, and Society in England, 1600–1850', *Folk Music Journal* 4, No. 3 (1982): 210–11.

4 Lawrence Stone, *The Family, Sex and Marriage in England, 1500–1800* (New York: Harper Row, 1979), 395. See also Randolph Trumbach, *Sex and the Gender Revolution, vol. 1, Heterosexuality and the Third Gender in Enlightenment London* (Chicago and London: University of Chicago Press, 1998), 3–4, 9–10, 21. Trumbach argues that the new heterosexuality in the eighteenth century took the form of sexual freedom for men and a new emphasis on domesticity and romance for women. He has not paid sufficient attention to popular ballads.

5 Nicholas Venette, *Conjugal Love Revealed*, 7th edition (London, 1720), 2. Venette was a seventeenth-century French writer, but his treatises were translated into English and were among the most influential medical writings on sexuality in eighteenth-century England. On Venette's popularity See Roy Porter and Leslie Hall, *The Facts of Life: The Creation of Sexual Knowledge in Britain* (New Haven, CT: Yale University Press, 1995), 5.

6 Venette, *Conjugal Love Revealed*, 7.

7 Venette, *Conjugal Love Revealed*, 36.

8 Venette, *Conjugal Love Revealed*, 42, 45.

9 Venette, *Conjugal Love Revealed*, 55.

10 Porter and Hall, *The Facts of Life*, 112.

11 Porter and Hall, *The Facts of Life*, 33.

12 Quoted in Porter and Hall, *The Facts of Life*, 114.

13 Thomas Newenham, *A Statistical and Historical Enquiry into the Progress and Magnitude of the Population of Ireland* (London, 1805), 18.

14 James Graham, *A Lecture on the Generation, Increase, and Improvement of the Human Species* (London, 1780), 35.

15 Roger North, *A Discourse of the Poor. Shewing the Pernicious Tendency of the Laws Now in Force for the Maintenance and Settlement* (London, 1753), 54.

16 James Graham, *A Lecture*,19.

17 James Graham, *A Lecture*,27.

18 The Henry Harris Papers, quoted in Anthony Fletcher, *Gender, Sex and Subordination in England 1500–1800* (New Haven, CT, and London: Yale University Press, 1995), 343.

19 Thomas Malthus, *An Essay on the Principle of Population* (1798; edited Anthony Flew, Penguin Books, 1970), 130.

20 Donna T. Andrew, *Philanthropy and Police: London Charity in the Eighteenth Century* (Princeton, NJ: Princeton University Press, 1989), 54.

21 Andrew, *Philanthropy and Police*, 145–7. Andrew argues we do not see the concept of a useless population until the 1770s in the work of Sir James Steuart. Later this argument was continued by Joseph Townsend, *A Dissertation on the Poor Laws* (1797). As a result, London charities decreased aid to pregnant mothers, hoping to discourage them from having children, Andrew, 148, 180–1.

22 Graham, *A Lecture*, 4. See also Henry Fielding, *A Proposal for Making an Effectual Provision for the Poor, for Amending their Morals, and for Rendering them Useful Members of Society* (Dublin, 1753), 5.

23 North, *A Discourse of the Poor* (1753), 65, 67, 70.

24 North, *A Discourse of the Poor* (1753), 11.

25 North, *A Discourse of the Poor* (1753), 54.

26 North, *A Discourse of the Poor* (1753), 78.

27 Newenham, *A Statistical and Historical Enquiry* (1805), 281.

28 John Howlett, *An Examination of Dr Price's Essay on the Population of England and Wales and the Doctrine of Increased Population in This Kingdom Established by Facts* (1781; reprinted New York, 1968), x, 27.

29 Porter and Hall, *The Facts of Life*, 113.

30 Graham, *A Lecture*, 4.

31 Newenham, *A Statistical and Historical Enquiry* (1805), 280.

32 Howlett, *An Examination of Dr Price's Essay on the Population of England and Wales* (1781), 28.

33 Graham, *A Lecture*, 32.

34 For the latter see John Barrell, *The Dark Side of the Landscape: The Rural Poor in English Painting, 1730–1840* (Cambridge and New York: Cambridge University Press, 1972), 74.

35 Barrell, *The Dark Side of the Landscape*, 51.

36 Emily Brooks, 'The Milkmaid's Tale', *The National Trust Magazine* 93, no. 4 (2001), 42–3.

37 John S. Farmer, ed., *Merry Songs and Ballads, Prior to the Year AD 1800* (New York, 1964), 127.

38 Fletcher, *Gender, Sex and Subordination*, 339.

39 Fletcher, *Gender, Sex and Subordination*, 34.

40 Barrell, *The Dark Side of the Landscape*, 50.

41 Barrell, *The Dark Side of the Landscape*, 41.

42 David Foxon, *Libertine Literature in England, 1660–1745* (New York: University Books, 1965), 12.

43 Foxon, *Libertine Literature in England*, 13.

44 Venette, *Conjugal Love Revealed*, 37–8.

45 Howlett, *An Examination of Dr Price's Essay on the Population of England and Wales* (1781), 28.

46 Howlett, *An Examination of Dr Price's Essay on the Population of England and Wales* (1781), 27–9.

47 'Kick Him, Jenny', quoted in Peter Wagner, *Eros Revived: Erotica of the Enlightenment in England and America* (London: Secker & Warburg, 1988), 177.

48 John Barrell and John Bull, eds, *The Penguin Book of English Pastoral Verse* (London: Allen Lane, 1974), 377–81.

49 John Gay, 'The Shepherd's Week' (1714), in *The Poetical Works*, ed. G. C. Faber (London: Oxford University Press), 32.

50 Barrell, *The Dark Side of the Landscape*, 54.

51 Barrell, *The Dark Side of the Landscape*, 56.

52 *The Aviary or Magazine of British Melody Consisting of a Collection of 1417 Songs* (London, 1750), song no. 502.

53 See for example Stone, *The Family, Sex and Marriage*, where he speaks of how sexual permissiveness declined after 1770 due to the growth of Evangelicalism, 395.

54 For the Mohawk scare in the 1700s and the fear of rape see Jennine Hurl, *Voices of Litigation; Voices of Resistance: Constructions of Gender in the Records of Assault in London, 1680–1720*. Unpublished PhD dissertation (York University, Toronto, 2001), 189–205.

55 *Aristotle's Masterpiece* (London, 1749), 25.

56 Porter and Hall have made this argument for editions of *Aristotle's Masterpiece*. Its early eighteenth-century versions discussed sex openly, while its new Victorian version removed bawdy language and explicit references to the physical aspects of sex: *The Facts of Life*, 128.

57 John Gillis agrees with this view: *For Better for Worse: British Marriages, 1600 to the Present* (New York: Oxford University Press, 1988), 135.

58 Quoted in Anna Clark, *The Struggle for the Breeches: Gender and the Making of the British Working Class* (Berkeley, Los Angeles, and London: University of California Press, 1995), 44.

59 Clark, *The Struggle for the Breeches*, 125–7.

60 Boyd Hilton, *The Age of Atonement: The Influence of Evangelicalism on Social and Economic Thought, 1795–1865* (Oxford: Clarendon Press, 1988), 79.

61 Clark, *The Struggle for the Breeches*, 43.

62 Hilton, *The Age of Atonement*, 81.

63 Hilton, *The Age of Atonement*, 87.

64 Hilton, *The Age of Atonement*, 81.

65 M. G. Jones, *Hannah More* (Cambridge: Greenwood Press, 1952), 140.

66 Clark, who uses popular songs to supplement her evidence, says that the working class saw extra-marital sex as acceptable as long as the father provided for his illegitimate children, *The Struggle for the Breeches*, 47.

67 Wagner, *Eros Revived*,162–3.

68 See Jeffrey Weeks, *Sex, Politics and Society: The Regulation of Sexuality Since 1800* (London and New York: Longman, 1981), 19.

69 Weeks, *Sex, Politics and Society*, 14.

70 See the case of Elizabeth Cureton in V. A. C. Gatrell, *The Hanging Tree: Execution and the English People 1770–1868* (Oxford:Oxford University Press, 1994), 451 ff. Also, Gillis, *For Better for Worse*, 119.

71 Gillis, *For Better for Worse*, 109.

72 Gillis, *For Better for Worse*, 114, 209.

73 Gillis, *For Better for Worse*, 121.

74 Clark, *The Struggle for the Breeches*, 45. Jeffrey Weeks has argued that middle-class moralists were not interested in exporting their morality to the poor, but all the evidence points to the contrary. He says himself that middle-class reformers worried about working-class women spending time in the factories and thus hurting the family, see Weeks, *Sex, Politics and Society*, 32.

75 Cissie Fairchilds, 'Female Sexual Attitudes and Rise in Illegitimacy: A Case Study', *Journal of Interdisciplinary History* 8, no. 4 (1978): 627–67, as cited in Weeks, *Sex, Politics and Society*, 62.

76 Weeks, *Sex, Politics and Society*, 15.

77 Weeks, *Sex, Politics and Society*, 22. Stone also thinks that illegitimate children were accepted by society in general in the eighteenth century: *Family, Sex and Marriage*, 327.

78 Smirky Nan was the torment of many village lads. See the chapbook *Jubilee for Jubilee; or Fifty Year Shepherd for Fifty a King. To Which Are Added, The Cambridge Tender, With the Answer. The Death of General Wolfe. Smirky Nan the Milk-Maid. The Humble Beggar* (Glasgow: J. and M. Robertson, 1809).

79 This treatment of illegitimacy can also be found in earlier songs. One of Pepys's ballads, 'A Pleasant Country Maying Song', described peasants making love and tumbling on the grass. In passing it mentioned that 'This pretty maiden waxeth big: / See what 'tis to play the Rig', as if pre-marital pregnancy was quite natural. It also depicted girls showing off their legs, and boys lifting up the girls' petticoats. In the conclusion the narrator says he must end the song to avoid wronging his friends, suggesting an awareness of a more moralistic view of such free interaction between the sexes (1625–40): *The Pepys Ballads*, vol. 2.

80 Farmer, *Merry Songs and Ballads*, 131.

81 There are songs, especially older ballads, that treat the problem of illegitimacy more seriously. 'The Dorsetshire Tragedy' sees it as a serious problem. The heroine is 'defiled' by the pregnancy and she tells her lover she would rather die than be unmarried. With a cruel irony he murders her in response: *The Pepys Ballads*, vol. 7.

82 John Cleland, *Fanny Hill, or Memoirs of a Woman of Pleasure*, ed. Peter Wagner (London: Penguin Books, 1985; first published 1748–49), 134.

83 Cleland, *Fanny Hill*, 120.

84 Cleland, *Fanny Hill*, 135.

85 'Drive on Coachman. An Humorous Tale. Occasioned by an Affair Lately Discover'd in a Famly of Quality' (1739), described in Peter Wagner, *Eros Revived*, 106–7.

86 'The Mouse's Tail' (Yorkshire, 1753), quoted in Wagner, *Eros Revived*, 175.

87 Robert Burns, *The Complete Poetical Works*, ed. James A. Mackray (Darvel, Ayrshire, 1993), 476.

88 Wagner, *Eros Revived*, 100.

89 Clark, *The Struggle for the Breeches*, 2.

90 *The Pepys Ballads*, vol. 2. The song may be as old as 1614.

91 'The Praise of the Dairy-Maid, with a Lick at the Cream-Pot, or a Fading Rose', *Pills to Purge Melancholy* (1707; reprinted in Farmer, *Merry Songs and Ballads*), 127.

92 'The Bonny Milkmaid'. This is in the Deacon version. See footnote 94.

93 See version 'The Milking Pail', *The Milking Pail. To Which are Added The North Country Lass. Oxter My Laddie. Old King Goul. The Humble Beggar* (Glasgow, 1801), BL, Shelfmark HS 74 1250.

94 'The Bonny Milkmaid' (London: J. Deacon, 1671–1704), Bodleian Library, Don.b.13(63).

95 'The Milkmaid', *An Excellent Garland Containing Six Choice Songs* (Manchester: G. Swindells, d. 1796), L.C. 2955.

96 'The Bonny Milkmaid' (London: J. Deacon, 1671–1704), The song also praises milkmaids for their exceptional beauty.

97 See 'The Bonny Milkmaid', *A Collection of New Songs Call'd the Milk-maids Garland* (London, 1705). This song also argues that milkmaids are prettier than city girls.

98 On attitudes to prostitution in the eighteenth century see Porter and Hall, *The Facts of Life*, 14–15.

99 'The Farmer's Courtship' (London: John Pitts, 1819–44), Bodleian Library, Harding B11(1153).

100 Malthus, *An Essay on the Principle of Population* (1798), 93.

101 'The Shepherd's Daughter' (n.p., n.d.), Bodleian Library, 2806 b.11(194).

102 'The Crafty Farmer' (Sheffield: J. T. Saxton, 1790–1840), Bodleian Library, Harding B25(642).

103 'The two Unhappy Lovers' (1684), *The Pepys Ballads*, vol. 3.

104 'No, my Love, No!' (London: J. Evans, London, 1780–1812), Bodleian Library, Harding B25(1374).

105 Here is an older example of such a ballad. In the Pepys ballad 'Constancy Lamented' (1688), for example, a young man was in love with a poor serving maid, far below him in degree, to the displeasure of his mother. *The Pepys Ballads*, vol. 4.

106 There were sad songs about seduction and abandonment. An example was 'The Village-Born Beauty' (n.p., n.d.), Bodleian Library, Johnson Ballads, 2955. The girl was seduced by a London gentleman and kept as a mistress, then he tired of her and left her to her fate. She became a prostitute.

107 'Love in a Barn, or the Country Courtship' (n.p., n.d.), BL 11621.c.4.

108 'The Northern Ditty: or, the Scotsman Outwitted by the Country Damsel', by Thomas D'Urfey (1653–1723) (Newcastle, n.d.), Bodleian Library, Douce Ballads 3(70a).

109 'The Farmer's Son' (n.p., n.d.), Bodleian Library, Harding B25(632).
110 'The Surprised Lovers', quoted in Peter Wagner, *Eros Revived*, 174–5. Wagner gives no date, but it seems to be from the 1770s because he quotes it with other texts from that time.
111 'The Wealthy Farmer', *The Great Messenger of Morality* (Edinburgh: J. Morren, 1800–20), L.C. 2805.
112 Clark, *The Struggle for the Breeches*, 3.
113 'Cupid the Pretty Ploughboy' (London: J. Catnach, 1800–30), BL, Shelfmark 11621.k.4 vol. 2.
114 'Jemmy the Plough Boy', *Philander's Garland; Composed of Five Delightful New Songs* (n.p., n.d.), Houghton Library. This song may have been a Jacobite song originally, with Jemmy as James Stuart, but in this version the ploughboy is cast as the 'true born Englishman'.
115 'Undaunted Mary, On the Banks of Sweet Dundee' (n.p., n.d.), Bodleian Library, Firth c.12(260).
116 Porter and Hall, *The Facts of Life*, 28.
117 Tim Hitchcock, *English Sexualities 1700–1800* (New York: Macmillan, 1997), 8–23.
118 Place spoke of 'gentlemen', by which he seems to have meant master tradesmen, whom he deems 'respectable', see Gatrell, *The Hanging Tree*, 128.
119 'The Pretty Milkmaid', *The Pretty Milkmaid's Garland, Composed of Several Excellent New Songs* (n.p., n.d.), Houghton Library.
120 'The Milk Maid', Bodleian Library, Harding B 6(8). See also 'Rigs of the Fair', (n.p., n.d.), B.L., Shelfmark HS.74 11250: 'Johnny hires for the plough / And Molly for to milk the cow, / And little Jenny hires too, / To milk her master's doddle-do.'
121 'The Milk men' (London: J. Pitts, 1802–19), Bodleian Library, 2806 c. 18(205). See Deborah Valenze, 'The Art of Women and the Business of Men: Women's Work and the Dairy Industry c. 1740–1840', *Past & Present* 230 (1991): 142–69.
122 Tim Hitchcock, 'Redefining Sex in Eighteenth-Century England', *History Workshop Journal* 41 (1996): 85.
123 'A new song, called The Plough Boy', (n.p., n.d.), Bodleian Library, Harding B 25 (1507).
124 'The Ploughman', *Hark Away. The Boys of Kilkenny, the Land of Delight, The Plowman, Love in the Horrors. Glasgow* (n.p., n.d.), Bodleian Library, Houghton 25276.19* vol. 2. This is not confined to ploughmen: Clark has found a similar use of the attributes of an occupation as sexual metaphor in songs about weavers, *The Struggle for the Breeches*, 60.
125 Anna Clark, *Women's Silence, Men's Violence: Sexual Assault in England 1770–1845* (London and New York: Pandora, 1987), 37, 85.
126 'The Pergured Youth' (1690), *The Pepys Ballads*, vol. 3.
127 Gatrell, *The Hanging Tree*, 137.
128 'The Dorsetshire Tragedy' (n.d.), *The Pepys Ballads*, vol. 7.
129 'The Merchant's Daughter and the Constant Farmer's Son' (n.p., n.d.), Bodle-

ian Library Firth c. 12(438). See also 'The Bloody Gardener's Cruelty, Or the Shepherd's Daughter Betrayed' (London: J. Jennings, 1790–1840), Bodleian Library, Harding B1 (101), where a noble lord courted a beautiful shepherd's daughter. The lord's parents hired a gardener to kill the girl. When he learned of her death the young man committed suicide.

130 But this is not to say the content of the songs had no connection to the lives of agricultural labourers or that we need not try to historicise these songs, which certainly underwent variations and changes through time as would any other art form.

131 'The Milk Maid', *Six Favorite New Songs Called Life's Like a Sea. Davy Jones's Locker. Gorg is the Liquor of Life. The Sea-worn Tar. Green with Moorings. The Milk Maid* (n.p., n.d.), BL, Shelfmark 11606.aa.22.

132 'The Milk Maid' (Liverpool: G. Thompson, 1789–c.1828), Bodleian Library, 2806 c.17 (281).

133 'The Milkmaid' (Norwich: R. Walker, 1797–1834), Bodleian Library, 2806 c.18 (203).

134 'The Milk Maid' (Chester: R. Evans, 1780–1812), Bodleian Library, Harding B 25(397).

135 See also 'The Milkmaid' (London: J. Pitts, 1802–19), Bodleian Library, Harding B 25 (1250), where Polly was seduced by a gentleman. While he promised her marriage and a life of ease, she had already fallen in love with him before he made these promises. She got pregnant and the song ends without telling us if he kept his promises, but it seems unlikely. Also, 'The Pretty Milkmaid', *The Pretty Milkmaid's Garland, Composed of Several Excellent New Songs* (n.p., n.d.), Houghton Library. The seducer is of higher degree as she calls him 'Sir', but she willingly agrees to make love to him.

136 'The Charming Month of May', (early eighteenth century), BL, Shelfmark c.116. bb.11.

137 *The Aviary*, 266.

138 'Love in a Barn, or the Country Courtship' (n.p., n.d.), BL, Shelfmark 11621.c.4. See also 'A Summer Piece', *The Buxom Dame of Reading; or, the Cuckold's Cap* (Glasgow: J. & M. Robertson, 1802). In this song milkmaids made syllabub for their sweethearts. An early version of the association between dairying and love was Samuel Pepys's 'A Pleasant Country Maying Song', from the period 1625–40, where the country girls treated their lovers with syllabub and cream.

139 'The Praise of the Dairy Maid', *Pills to Purge Melancholy* (1707), Reprinted in Farmer, *Merry Songs and Ballads*.

140 'An Excellent New Song: Called the Cunnie's Garland' (n.p., n.d.), L.C. 2812.

141 'The Northern Ditty', by Thomas D'Urfey (1653–1723) (Newcastle, n.d.), Douce Ballads 3(70a).

142 'Milking the Cows in the Farm' (Haly, Cork, 18–), Bodleian Library, Harding B 26 (431).

143 'Love in a Barn, or the Country Courtship' (n.p., n.d.), BL, Shelfmark 111621.c.4.

144 'Undaunted Mary, On the Banks of Sweet Dundee' (n.p., n.d.), Bodleian Library, Firth c.12(260).

145 'The Taylor's Courtship' (London: J. Pitts, 1808–19), Bodleian Library, Firth c.18 (226).

146 The song is 'The Threshing Machine' (n.p., n.d.), BL, Shelfmark 11602.gg.28. Clark also suggests that such ballads were more prevalent in the north and that northern women generally expressed less shame about rape than women in the south. Clark, *The Struggle for the Breeches*, 26, 29.

147 'Bite upon Bite's Garland; or the Miser Out-witted by the West Country Maid' (Newcastle: Angus, 1774–1825), L.C. 2571.

148 'The Politic Maid of Suffolk; or the Young Lawyer Outwitted', *The Jovial Sailor's Garland, Furnished with Two Comical New Songs* (Newcastle: Angus, 1774–1825), L.C. 2751.

149 Samuel Bamford, *Early Days* (London, 1849), 288.

150 Clark, *The Struggle for the Breeches*, 62.

6

Hannah More takes on popular ballads: the effort to reform the morals of the poor

Hannah More's efforts to reform the poor have important implications for rural labourers' identity. Particularly noteworthy are three aspects of her work: her patronage of the milkwoman poet Ann Yearsley, her efforts to educate the poor of the Mendip villages, and her Cheap Repository Tract campaign. These three are intimately related. Ann Yearsley left a uniquely explicit record of how benevolent good intentions could have a bad effect; her relationship with More illustrates some of the more negative aspects of More's attitude to the poor. The work in the Mendip area provided material for the tracts and also served to create an audience for them: they were suggested reading at More's Sunday schools. Conversely, More's attitude to the Mendip poor (and to Ann Yearsley) helps put the purpose and message of the tracts in perspective.

Much has been written lately about Hannah More. Every aspect of her work has received historians' attention. I will deal with some of this historiography and with the issues of debate as I come to them in the course of this chapter. The evidence I have seen tends to support those historians who have empha-sised the authoritarian nature of her attitude toward the poor and her concern about social control. Although this is a somewhat old-fashioned way to view Hannah More, I hope to show that, when all three kinds of reform are looked at together, a clear pattern emerges.

My aim is not to add to our understanding of More herself. Rather, my purpose is to show how More's work relates to so many of the themes discussed in this book. If we agree with Susan Pedersen that More launched an attack on popular culture, we can see her opposition to popular ballads, to the language of complaint, to rural labourers' sexuality and to poaching as indicative of the importance of these themes in popular culture.[1] Popular resistance to her benevolence shows that the poor understood what she was doing and were not willing to be manipulated. Thus More's work is yet another argument in favour of the contention that popular ballads were an important expression of a rural labouring identity.

Educating the poor and suppressing ballads

Hannah More's campaign to reform the morals of the poor was not unique. It was part of the Evangelical revival and an overall concern with morality which became more widespread in the 1780s.[2] What made her different from other contemporaries who shared her politics was her insistence on literacy. Hannah More was adamant that the poor should be able to read. At the same time, she would have agreed with observers who argued the poor should be taught 'their duties to God and man' and how to lay the foundations of 'a religious and virtuous life',[3] and that reading should be taught together with religion and useful skills like spinning.[4] Therefore the existence of more conservative elements in eighteenth-century society and their opposition to literacy do not necessarily show that the Sunday schools were a haven for working-class culture or radicalism.[5] While literacy was a positive byproduct of the schools and could be used in a variety of ways by the poor, the More sisters intended the schools to teach obedience and gratitude. This is how Hannah More described the schools to her friend J. H. Addington:

> Allow me, my dear Sir, however to say that my notions of instructing the poor are extremely limited. I allow no writing, nor any reading but the Bible, Catechism and such little Tracts as may enable them to understand the Church Service; that they do not understand it is one reason why they do not like to go. Let me say that all the poor whom I have instructed are loyal to a man and that I am calumniated by the Methodists for attaching so many to Church and State.[6]

That the Mores' central concern was with preserving order and social harmony rather than with improving the lives of the poor (whether material or spiritual) is suggested by their intolerance of any competition for the time of the poor, even if it came from the Church of England, which they professed to love. At Rowberrow, when the new rector persuaded some of the older boys to join the church choir, which would keep them away from the Sunday school, Martha More saw it as a calculated action to increase his congregation and an affront to herself and her sister: 'It was a wicked action, and he will find he must account for it at the day of judgment.'[7] Any attempt to influence the poor that competed with their Sunday schools enraged the Mores.

Many of their contemporaries recognised the schools' potential for creating social harmony. If Martha More is to be believed, the reason why the sisters were invited to Blagdon to found a Sunday school was that a woman had been condemned to death for trying to start a riot and seizing some butter from a man who was selling it at too high a price.[8] In 1797, after the school had been in operation for two years, the authorities informed the Mores that two sessions and two assizes had passed without any incident and without any cases of wood stealing or pilfering.[9] Explicit exhortations to obedience and deference were part of the Sunday school curriculum. In one of their prayers they asked God to 'grant that every rebellious motion may be subdued that exalts itself against peace, and patience, and gentleness, and meekness of spirit …'[10]

It has been pointed out that the Sunday schools were a way to build an audience for the Cheap Repository Tracts. In fact the work in the Sunday schools and the Cheap Repository Tracts were mutually reinforcing. More said herself that her stories were connected to life and that she herself had observed the main circumstances but embellished them in order to serve a larger moral purpose.[11] We will see some examples of this below. Conversely, the Sunday school students came to serve as an audience for the tracts, which were the only reading allowed besides the Bible and the Book of Common Prayer.

Popular ballads were the major provocation for the Cheap Repository Tracts campaign. Although historians have pointed out that complaints about ballads were as old as ballads themselves, criticism seems to have grown louder in general at the end of the eighteenth century, as the threat to the social order became more real.[12] This widespread concern about popular songs shows that contemporaries recognised their significance and believed in the power of print to effect social change.[13] In 1792 an anonymous woman speaking on behalf of the loyalists suggested that ballads could be an effective tool to preach loyalty to the poor, because 'Every serving man and maid, every country Girl and her sweetheart … will buy a halfpenny ballad to a popular tune'.[14] Patriots other than Hannah More began using the ballad form as propaganda. William Jones was one writer whose love of his country took the form of song.[15] Other members of the elite were directly inspired by Hannah More's ballads and tales to adapt the genre to suit their political and social concerns. One such person was William Aldegrave (1753–1825), First Baron Radstock. Aldegrave published many halfpenny papers and More commended him with the following comment: 'Poor Lord Radstock is indefatigable in the cause, and pours out his well meant but not very powerful effusions in half penny papers without end.'[16] In contrast to the propaganda written by other loyalists, Hannah More's work had a definite rural flavour and most of her characters were rural.[17]

Although Hannah More's objection to popular literature extended to folk tales and her tracts included many prose stories, it was the 'wicked songs' that upset her most. This was part of a larger mistrust of all imaginative literature. Though she had written fiction herself, as she grew more religious More came to stress the Bible as the only source of truth, and she became more and more suspicious of works of the imagination.[18] When she was planning the Cheap Repository she once said its purpose was to replace ballad singing with sermons and hymns.[19] Though she felt compelled to adopt the genre of the street ballad for a number of her tracts, she was very unhappy with the form. Nevertheless, she thought it was her duty to do this work. More tried to make the tracts as similar to real popular literature as possible. With the ballads, Bishop Porteous suggested that she hire a music-master to set them to 'easy, popular, vulgar tunes, adopting, in preference to all others, the old favorite ones of "Chevy Chase", "The children in the Wood", etc.'[20] While More may not have hired a musician, she did make tune suggestions in her broadsides. For instance, 'The Riot' is set to the tune of 'A Cobbler There Was'.[21]

While it is more difficult to determine how the tracts were seen, there is little question about how they were intended. As Marlene Hess has pointed out, Hannah More espoused the pragmatic theory of art, which saw the purpose of art to be educational and instructional.[22] In both her ballads and prose tales More created characters who were punished for singing and selling ballads or who were corrupted by the baneful influence of songs. Thus in 'The Carpenter; or, the Danger of Evil Company' an originally virtuous family man is led astray by a singing cooper:

> This man could tell a merry tale
> And sing a merry song;
> And those who heard him sing or talk,
> Ne'er thought the ev'ning long.
>
> But vain and vicious was the song,
> And wicked was the tale;
> And every pause he always fill'd,
> With cider, gin, or ale.

The ballad singer and popular entertainer is immoral. Seduced by his charm, the carpenter begins to visit the alehouse on a regular basis, neglects his work and his family, drinks, and stops going to church. In a rare instance of charity More let the deluded carpenter off rather easily: he comes to recognise the cooper's wickedness and is reunited with his family.[23]

Much harsher is the fate of two female characters implicated in the ballad trade, Tawny Rachel and Sally Evans. Tawny Rachel is the wife of another wicked character, the poacher Black Giles, and she adds to her family's income by travelling around the countryside and selling dream books and 'wicked songs'.[24] Sally Evans, a dimwitted milkmaid, is interrupted at her work by Rachel's sweet singing:

> Sally was so struck with the pretty tune, which was unhappily used, as is too often the case, to set off some very loose words that she jumped up, dropped the skimming-dish into the cream, and ran out to buy the song.

Early modern dairywomen were notorious for their independence.[25] Here they get their comeuppance. Sally's foolishness is also evident in the way she searches Rachel's basket to find the songs with the most tragic pictures and the delight she takes in 'whatever is mournful'. Once Sally has been won over by the ballads, Rachel proceeds to tell her fortune. Following the wicked woman's advice, Sally rejects her upright suitor to marry Rachel's wicked accomplice, who is after her meagre savings. Like many of More's sinful characters she dies quite suddenly of a broken heart.[26] Rachel is also punished when the parson, Mr Wilson, catches her selling some 'very wicked ballads' to children. She is tried and sent to prison for deceiving the villagers. Sad is also the fate of Jack Brown in 'The Two Shoemakers', who is foolish enough to be blinded by a bunch of strollers and performers of 'that sing-song ribaldry by which our villagers are corrupted'. These scoundrels trick Jack of his rent money and he is promptly sent to jail, abandoned by his family and afflicted with jail fever.[27]

The depraved nature of ballads becomes an issue of contention between the agricultural labourer John and his daughter Hester in More's story 'The History of Hester Wilmot'. This story seems to have had a number of real precedents in the Mores' experience in the Sunday schools. At Cheddar, the location of one of the Mores' schools, a 14-year-old girl asked the teacher to lend her a prayer-book to take home so she could read it to her parents.[28] Another pious girl at the same school, Sally Thatcher, was punished by her wicked family for her affection for the school but she eventually converted them to the love of God.[29] In the tract, the opposition between piety and popular songs becomes an important theme. Hester is the most virtuous member of her family and since starting to attend Sunday school has taken to heart all they have been trying to teach her. One day her father, John, asks Hester to read to him and she readily pulls out the Bible. John laughs, calls Hester a fool and says she could read the Bible to him when he is on his deathbed but now he wants something more entertaining. He gives Hester a song-book which he has picked up at the local tavern. After looking over it Hester refuses to read it because it would offend

Hannah More, 'The Riot; or, Half a loaf is better than no bread. In a dialogue between Jack Anvil and Tom Hod' (1795)

God and hurt her soul. John calls her 'a canting hypocrite', threatens to throw the Bible into the fire and complains that she used to be the merriest girl in the village before she became religious.[30] There is no doubt whose side More was on. In the end John comes to recognise his daughter's righteousness and learns to stay away from songs, making the Bible his sole entertainment. In the same story farmer Hoskins, observing the piety of the Sunday school teacher, is edified and has a revelation that 'a psalm is better than a song'.[31]

While the best commentary on popular ballads was to be found in Hannah More's fictional works, she also criticised the genre in letters to friends and speeches made in her Sunday schools. In a letter to her friend Addison she related an anecdote about trying to set up a school in the village of Wedmore. Concerned the school might be Methodist, the villagers consulted a fortune-teller. The latter asked what kinds of tunes they used for their hymns at the school. After thinking about it, the villagers concluded none of the tunes were in 'Farmer Clapp's Book' and this must mean the school was Methodist. The villagers were looking for the popular tunes they were familiar with in order to be reassured. This kind of ignorance only strengthened More's determination to enlighten the folk of Wedmore.[32]

If not ballads, what should the poor read? In her schools More only permitted the reading of the Bible and her own tracts and by way of music 'God save the King' and the occasional religious psalm. She hoped the schools would teach the poor to sing hymns in praise of God instead of lewd songs.[33] The good characters in More's stories only like to read the Bible. The Shepherd of Salisbury Plain reads a verse every day, and instead of ballads on his cottage walls are pasted 'a hymn on the Crucifixion of our Saviour, a print of the Prodigal Son, the Shepherd's Hymn, and a New History of a True Book', the last of which is one of the Cheap Repository Tracts.[34] Aside from the Bible, Hester Wilmot buys the Cheap Repository's version of the Book of Common Prayer from a 'pious hawker' for three halfpence.[35] Sarah Trimmer, Hannah More's forerunner, had made the same point about suitable reading for the rural poor. Her virtuous hero, the farm boy Thomas, likes to repeat Dr Watt's hymns while at work, but his dream is to gain literacy so he can read the Bible. When offered a place at the Sunday school, Thomas sits in anticipation lovingly holding and eyeing the family Bible. Getting quite carried away he drops a tear of joy on it, but quickly wipes it off so as not to injure it.[36]

Improving social relations by suppressing the moral economy and the language of complaint

More was well aware of the deteriorating social relations in the countryside. References to greedy and tyrannical farmers and their contempt for agricultural labourers were everywhere in her letters and Martha More's journal. Martha described the parish of Congresbury in the Mendip area as divided into two classes: 'the very poor, and what is called gentleman farmers, wealthy, unfeeling, and hard.'[37] Martha and Hannah were both indignant at the attitude of many wealthy farmers toward the education of the poor. In Cheddar, where More started a Sunday school, the richest farmer objected to her project because he felt it would make the poor lazy and useless.[38] At Wedgemore, John Barrow, also the foremost farmer, argued the school would bring an end to property and cause revolution. He felt his ploughmen should not be wiser than he was and that he needed workmen rather than saints. His wife helpfully added that it was the will of providence that the lower class be ignorant, wicked and poor and that the More sisters had no business trying to change what was decreed.[39]

The Mores did have sympathy for the Mendip poor but they also saw many of them, even the children, as savages in need of civilisation.[40] When most of the schemes to teach the children skills like spinning failed, Martha blamed the 'idleness of the children', rather than poor management or failure to compete on the market.[41] A similar mentality is evident in the Mores' refusal to allow the poor even a moment of free time:

> As most of you are hard-working people, and have not much leisure, it might be well, perhaps, on a Sunday night, after you have been attending the Word of God both at church and here, to examine yourselves by that Word, and see whether you have been enabled, in any degree, to live up to it.[42]

This kind of authoritarian attitude led Hannah to suppress any indignation she felt at the attitude of rich farmers. In all her speeches to the schools as well as her tracts she instructed villagers to love and respect their social superiors and accept any treatment at their hands. In her tracts she emphasised the mutual dependence between rich and poor and the importance of the 'labour' of government performed by the elite. In her instructions to the poor she also repeated over and over again that social inequality was natural and divinely ordained, the very sentiments she and her sister had condemned from the lips of others:

That some must be poorer, this truth I will sing
Is the law of my Maker, & not of my King;
And the true rights of Man, & the life of his cause
Is not equal professions, but equal just laws.[43]

Her concern for social order made Hannah More turn her attention to food riots. Her attitude to the moral economy was ambivalent: she did believe that regraters and engrossers, greedy millers or farmers could make scarcity worse. The tracts concerning scarcity suggest that More may have sided with members of her class, such as Lord Kenyon, who believed that the market should be regulated during times of dearth.[44] Of course, she did not believe the poor had the right to organise a riot or even complain about scarcity. Nevertheless, her ballads about the moral economy were the most subtle, the least overtly didactic and the most similar to real popular ballads. 'The Honest Miller of Gloucestershire. A true ballad' is about the dearth of 1795 whose severity More had witnessed in the Mendip villages. The song begins with praise for the miller's profession, such as we saw in many of the songs in chapter 4: there are many important professions but none as important as the miller's. Then it tells about the good miller of Gloucestershire who refuses to make a profit from others' suffering. When England is hit by scarcity and frost (all the mills are frozen except that of our hero), the good miller is advised to raise prices and use the plea of his many children as justification. He firmly refuses to do this and grinds corn at the usual prices for both rich and poor:

'When God afflicts the land', said he,
Shall I afflict it more?
And watch for times of public woe
To wrong both rich and poor?

'Thankful to that Almighty pow'r
Who makes my river flow,
I'll use the means he gives to sooth
A hungry neighbour's woe.[45]

On the one hand this can be read as an instance of the moral economy – neighbourliness and a 'just price' are favoured over profit. On the other hand, it can be seen as an effort on the part of the Cheap Repository Tracts to strengthen the social fabric: the miller pities both rich and poor alike, and sells to both at the same price. The scarcity is God's will; no blame is to fall on middlemen. It is foolish to blame millers also, because there are good men among them, like the hero of the ballad. Thus it is best to bear the misfortune in peace.

'The Honest Miller of Gloucestershire' should be read side by side with its antithesis, More's 'The Roguish Miller'. Again, this ballad allows for different emphases or readings. It is the story of a wicked miller who appropriates too large a share of each customer's corn for himself. This confirms the anti-miller sentiments of the poor we have seen in other moral economy ballads. On the other hand, the bad miller is punished both in this world and the next. The miller goes a little too far when he steals a vast amount of corn from the Justice, who sends him to jail 'by the Law's just controul'. The last verse advises millers to be honest so they would be glad to meet their maker after death – this implies the punishment reserved for wicked millers in the next world. Therefore, wicked millers are taken care of by both divine and earthly justice, and there is no need to attack their mills or to complain about their unfairness.[46]

These two ballads are exceptional samples of More's work because they allow for different interpretations. The rest of her tracts were much more aggressive in their condemnation of disorder and murmuring. As with high prices and taxes, scarcity was always depicted as punishment from God for humans' wickedness:

He mark'd our angry spirits rise,
Domestic hate increase;
And for a time withheld supplies,
To teach us love and peace.[47]

The angry spirits appear to be due to pure spite here; no other cause is assigned. Instead of making people more angry, scarcity in this ballad has the unlikely effect of teaching a lesson of love and peace.

'The Riot' was specifically written to make an argument against food riots. Part of the rioters' plan is to pull down the mills. The ballad argues damaging mills is wrong because it would make food even harder to obtain:

What a whimsey to think thus our bellies to fill
For we stop all the grinding by breaking the mill!
What a whimsey to think we shall get more to eat
By abusing the butchers who get us the meat!
What a whimsey to think we shall mend our spare diet
By breeding disturbance, by murder and riot!

Because I am dry 'twould be foolish, I think
To pull out my tap and to spill all my drink;
Because I am hungry, and want to be fed,
That is sure no wise reason for wasting my bread;
And just such wise reasons for mending their diet
Are us'd by those blockheads who rush into riot.[48]

The second argument made by More is that the authorities are working hard to improve the situation by importing corn; furthermore, that the local gentry also want to help by giving up 'their puddings and pies'. The third argument is that you could save money by not drinking gin, ale and tea; fourth, if you wait patiently, the prices will fall; fifth, participating in a riot uses up valuable working hours when you could be making more money to buy bread; last, but not least, the penalty for riot is severe and so is it not better to be hungry than hanged?

Disorder must be contained, but so must its herald, complaint. In chapter 2 I talked about the fact that the end of the eighteenth century was characterised by a new language of anger and bitterness in popular songs. Deriving from a long-standing tradition of contrasting the lot of the rich with that of the poor, this language criticised the deteriorating social relations in the countryside. In addition to preventing riots, Hannah More wanted to suppress this language of complaint. A central part of the education of the poor was to teach them not to complain. This notion was taken up by other do-gooders like the publishers of *The Penny Magazine*, who said explicitly that the purpose of educating the poor should be to teach them to endure their lot: 'when poverty comes (as it sometimes will) upon the prudent, the industrious and the well-informed, a judicious education is all-powerful in enabling them to endure the evils it cannot always prevent.'[49] Hannah More's predecessor, Sarah Trimmer, used fiction to convey the same message. In one of her stories the school master gives little Thomas a sermon on gratitude:

> The design of charity schools is to give the children of poor people such a degree of knowledge, as may enable them to learn from the holy scriptures their duty to God and man. For this happy advantage they are indebted to the benevolence of persons in higher stations, and they ought to be very grateful for it; I therefore recommend it to you, Tom Simkins, as you are become my scholar, to be very thankful...[50]

Again, Hannah More's ideas were not exceptional. In the ballads and stories complainers and whiners are directly berated. The following verse from 'The Riot' points out that all must bear misfortune with patience:

> Besides I must share in the wants of the times,
> Because I have had my full share in it's crimes;
> And I'm apt to believe the distress which is sent,
> Is to punish and cure us of all discontent.
> But harvest is coming, potatoes are come!
> Our prospect clears up: Ye complainers be dumb![51]

Josiah Wedgewood argued in very similar terms that high prices were the result of a bad harvest imposed by God. He felt this knowledge should 'stop the most daring man, and induce him to bear with becoming patience his share of the public calamity, and submit quietly to the will of heaven, lest he be found fighting against his maker'.[52] Even apparently man-made afflictions like taxes and high prices were seen as the hand of providence:

> When taxes ran high, and provisions were dear,
> Still Joseph declar'd he had nothing to fear;
> It was but a trial he well understood,
> From him who made all work together for good.[53]

Tracing the origins of all social and economic problems to God equated complaining with blasphemy.[54]

The most extreme expression of dissatisfaction for a religious person like More was, of course, swearing. The unwise ploughboy whose difficult work leads him to swear at his oxen is immediately threatened with eternal damnation by Satan.[55] Thus expressions of dissatisfaction, whether they be complaining or swearing, became an offence against God himself. Charity itself was not for complainers but for 'the quiet, contented, hard-working man'.[56] Complaining must be replaced with gratitude: gratitude to the local gentry, gratitude to one's country and gratitude to God. Polite, deferential language to your betters reflected good character. The virtuous Shepherd of Salisbury Plain impresses Mr Johnson by his serious, solid manner of speaking – he is polite and respectful to the gentleman.[57] Later in the story the Shepherd and his poor wife thank Mr Jones and the village parson for their benevolence, crying on their knees.

Those who failed in gratitude could hope for no sympathy. More's quarrel with Ann Yearsley illustrates what More expected from the poor in return for aid. Yearsley's failure to be grateful to her benefactors provoked a huge outcry both from More and from her supporters. When Yearsley brought up for the first time her demand that she be allowed to control the profits from her own poetry, More and her sisters thought she was drunk.[58] Those who had previously praised her now berated her coarseness. In the words of Montagu, 'there are some ears which the lutes of Apollo would not charm more than the bagpipe of a pedlar'.[59] Referring to Yearsley's alleged charge that More was jealous of her talent, Montagu speculated that she must be mad and therefore not truly responsible for her wicked behaviour.[60] William Roberts, the editor of More's letters and an obvious admirer of More, had this to say about Yearsley:

The person alluded to in the preceding letter, was equally a stranger to gratitude and prudence; and inflated by the notice she had attracted, soon began,
to express in the coarsest terms, her rage and disappointment, at not having the
sum subscribed immediately put into her hands. Neither could she bear, as it
seems, to be represented to the public, in Miss More's preface to her works, as
an object of their charity. Not being able to gain her point, she soon broke out
into the bitterest invectives, and scrupled at no calumnies however absurd and
ferocious.[61]

Thus aid and compassion for the poor were predicated upon continuous
affirmations and expressions of gratitude. Yearsley's refusal to deliver these
placed her in the category of undeserving poor, and confirmed More's belief
that the poor could not handle wealth and that most of them would be
corrupted by even a minor worldly success: 'Prosperity is a great trial, and she
would not stand it.'[62]

The Mores also made sure Sunday school students expressed proper gratitude. One of the faults that was always mentioned in 'the charge' (a speech the
Mores made to their schools) was ingratitude.[63] Even aid in times of scarcity
should not be taken for granted but seen as a favour from the gentry requiring
profound gratitude. In a perverse kind of reasoning, the Mores argued the 1795
scarcity should make the poor especially grateful because it united all ranks
by showing the dependence of the poor on the rich and the dependence of
both on God. It enabled the poor 'to observe the benefits flowing from the
distinction of ranks and fortune, which has enabled the high so liberally to
assist the low'.[64]

Gratitude to the local gentry was closely related to gratitude to one's country;
one thing the poor should be grateful for was England's social institutions. We
see this expectation in the work of Sarah Trimmer, whose hero Thomas and his
mother express gratitude for the existence of parish relief. They are unwilling
to accept it not out of pride but because they are blessed with health and can
work for a living. Thus, despite the death of Thomas's father and their extreme
poverty, Thomas and his mother contrive to be grateful to both God and their
country.[65]

The notion that England was better off than the rest of Europe and that
therefore its people should be grateful to be English became widespread among
loyalists in the 1790s and continued to be emphasised in literature aimed at
the poor for decades. Early on it was voiced in William Jones's anti-French
pamphlet written in the voice of John Bull: the English were lucky because
their cattle were safe in their stalls, their corn was growing well, and their
landlords were kind, unlike the French who were miserable in every way.[66] In

the 1830s *The Penny Magazine* wrote that England's poor were better lodged than in any other European country and every parish was filled with 'an amazing number of snug little houses in which provision is generally made for the comfort of those who inhabit them'. More also depicted poor relief and almshouses as blessings unique to England. In 'The History of Mary Wood' the lucky Mary and her mother are sent to an almshouse built and endowed by Lady Worthy where they receive good care.[67] Even when times seem hard we should remember that England has a special place in God's heart:

> I would not take comfort from others distresses,
> But still I would mark how God our land blesses;
> For tho' in Old England the times are but sad,
> Abroad I am told they are ten times as bad:
> In the land of the Pope there is scarce any grain,
> An 'tis still worse, they say, both in Holland and Spain.[68]

More's ballad 'Will Chip' encourages gratitude to English legal institutions as well as rights such as habeas corpus and the right of property. These are again contrasted with French tyranny, where one could be sent off to the Bastille any time without an explanation. More also praises the right to vote bestowed on any Englishman who could 'scrape up but forty good shillings a year'.[69]

Instead of complaining, the good peasants in More's ballads and tales are always singing God's praise. Before he meets a wicked cooper, the carpenter of More's ballad by that name is grateful to God for his many blessings such as good health, strength and youth:

> Where is the lord, or where the squire,
> Had greater cause to praise
> The goodness of that bounteous hand,
> Which blest his prosp'rous days?[70]

One could always find a blessing to thank God for, no matter how dire things seemed. In the ballad 'The Riot' the poor are advised to be grateful for their health – their only possession:

> And though I've no money, and though I've no lands
> I've a head on my shoulders, and a pair of good hands;
> So I'll work the whole day, and on Sundays I'll seek
> At church how to bear all the wants of the week.[71]

The same expectation of gratitude during adversity is found in Martha More's journal. A pious farmer at Yatton praised God even during the funeral of his beloved wife. Martha was extremely pleased by his attitude.[72]

A good way to suppress complaint and criticism would be to teach the poor that they do not have the intelligence to understand politics and should refrain from making any comment on it. One historian has argued that we can read into More's work respect for the opinion of the poor and an implicit argument that they should be included in the political debates of concern to the nation. Supposedly, by giving a voice to Tom and Jack in 'Village Politics', More shows that they are capable of sound political conclusions and deserve to be heard.[73] Perhaps this can be read into some of the tracts, but for the most part – and this is true even of 'Village Politics' – More tried to educate the poor to understand that they were simply too ignorant to know how the state should be run and that they should leave important decisions to those who were qualified to make them – that is, their betters. Time after time one character is told by another that he must know his place and not meddle in affairs he does not understand, or a character comes to the realisation that he is not the brightest and therefore should defer to the opinion of others. This is the conclusion Jack makes in 'The Riot':

> If the thing can be help'd I'm a foe to all strife,
> And pray for a peace every night of my life;
> But in matters of state not an inch will I budge,
> Because I conceive I'm no very good judge.

In 'Turn the Carpet; or, the Two Weavers' Dick is upset about the price of meat and the gap between rich and poor, but John persuades him that they are too ignorant to understand why God has made the world the way it is and that if they wait patiently they will find out when they die and go to Heaven.[74]

Controlling sexuality

Apparently More's disgust with popular songs finds sympathisers to this day – one historian has argued that many of the ballads to which More objected would still be found improper today because they included young women giving 'graphic accounts of their fall from virtue or their frustration at not being seduced'.[75] As a foil for such songs More wrote the ballad 'Sinful Sally', whose heroine's life of pleasure ends in an early death and condemnation to Hell.[76] Initially an innocent country girl, Sally is seduced by the local rake Sir William. In contrast to the popular ballads discussed in the sexuality chapter, Sally does not outwit Sir William, nor is he moved to marry her because of her charm. They move to London, where Sally's moral degradation is signalled by her abandonment of the Bible for the sake of 'filthy novels'. It is interesting that More associated rural popular culture with 'wicked songs' and urban popular culture with 'wicked novels'. Sally is conscious that the life of pleasure is a life of sin, but lacks the discipline to do anything about it. Abandoned by her lover who has grown tired of her, she dies of disease with the threat of hell hanging over her.[77]

The More sisters' dislike of labourers' sexuality was evident in their treatment of Sunday school teachers, most of whom were literate agricultural labourers or miners. Whenever these unfortunates were seen to get too close to a member of the opposite sex they were let go. This also happened to teachers who married without the Mores' approval. This negative attitude is readily apparent in the Mores' reaction to the glass-house at Nailsea. Apparently the workers' bodies were not sufficiently covered because of the great heat: 'the body [is] scarcely covered, but fed with dainties of shameful description.' The Nailsea labourers also failed to keep a proper distance between men and women in their homes: 'Both sexes and all ages herding together; voluptuous beyond belief.'[78]

To the playful milkmaid or ploughman of the popular songs, the Mores opposed the serious and pious milkmaid or ploughman. Real prototypes of these were to be found in the Mendip area and Martha held them up as examples of the deserving poor in the *Mendip Annals*. The reputation of Patience Seward, the pious milkmaid, preceded her. The daughter of a poor farmer, Patience had set up her own Sunday school. She had collected thirty poor children and bought books for them from her own money. She also offered rewards of gingerbread to her good scholars. The Mores sought out Patience and found her milking her cow: 'She possessed a good understanding, had received a better education than commonly falls to the lot of people in her station, could read and write very prettily, was deeply serious, and seemed pretty well acquainted with the Scriptures.' The Mores were even more excited to hear that Patience had a half-sister, Flower Waite, who was equally intelligent and devout. Hannah and Martha instantly secured the services of the two milkmaids for their Sunday school and instructed them in their 'method and manner of teaching'.[79]

The pious ploughman was a labourer at Cheddar by the name of Robert Reeves, whose devotion succeeded in bringing his master to the evening reading at the school. He also converted the next farmer he worked for. Martha praised him very highly: 'Wherever Robert is good instantly arises, converts are made, and the very spirit of prayer seems to go forth.' Robert further proved his mettle, together with other loyal souls at the village of Shipham, by burning Tom Paine in effigy.[80]

Protecting the commons from the undeserving

When More tried to persuade rich farmers to accept her Sunday schools she often used the argument that the schools would teach the poor not to steal from farmers' orchards, not to shoot their rabbits, and not to steal their game.[81]

More's attitude towards enclosure was ambivalent, like her attitude towards the moral economy. She saw that common right could be good for the deserving poor who used it well. The daughter of the Shepherd of Salisbury Plain, too young to work, gleaned wool from the bushes and was grateful for this blessing – this was acceptable. In addition to working as bird-scarers, his boys also gleaned and picked stones. The use of the common did not make them idle.[82] However, in the hands of the undeserving it became another corrupting influence. Thus the poacher Black Giles promotes his children from the trade of begging to the trade of 'thieving on the Moor':

> Here he kept two or three asses, miserable beings, which, if they had the good fortune to escape an untimely death by starving, did not fail to meet with it by beating. Some of the biggest boys were sent out with these lean and galled animals to carry sand or coals about the neighbouring towns. Both sand and coals were often stolen before they got them to sell, or if not, they always took care to cheat in selling them.[83]

More also condemned boys who gathered nuts on Sundays, not because they were stealing property but because the activity interfered with their devotions.[84]

While allowing the use of some materials from the common, More agreed with most of her class that any form of poaching for any reason was wrong because it was against the law. Black Giles's death was a lesson to all poachers that seemingly minor transgressions could be a great sin. Poaching could tempt even a good man like Giles's neighbour, Jack Weston, who catches a hare to give as a gift to the kind local justice. Jack is caught in the act and, despite his good intentions, the strict and utterly fair Justice sentences him to a stiff fine. Justice Wilson gives a long speech against poaching, arguing that it was connected to a 'habit of nightly depredation' which gives one a distaste for day labour, that catching hares could set one on the path of vice, and that plundering the warrens is no better than stealing sheep:

> He who begins with robbing orchards, rabbit warrens, and fish-ponds, will probably end with horse-stealing or highway robbery. Poaching is a regular apprenticeship to bolder crimes. He whom I may commit as a boy to sit in the stocks for killing a partridge, may be likely to end at the gallows for killing a man.[85]

Justice Wilson also does not omit to warn Jack that men like him have no business pondering whether the law is fair; their sole duty is to obey it.

Impact of the tracts and resistance to More's reforms

Hannah More and her supporters rejoiced in the success of the Cheap Repository Tracts and their staggering sales numbers. Some historians, impressed by the figures, have argued that the tracts made a huge impact on rich and poor alike.[86] I would like to argue that, first, the millions sold were seldom purchased by the poor themselves; second, that the proverbial entertainment value of the tracts is dubious, with the exception of some of the more subtle ballads; and, third, that the poor were fully capable of recognising the overtly didactic tracts as propaganda.

Hannah More certainly believed her tracts made a significant impact. At first she thought they would not be able to change the dangerous political situation in England for the better but, once persuaded by Bishop Porteous, she became convinced of their effectiveness.[87] This is why she wanted to reprint them in the troubled period 1816–19. In a letter to Mrs Addington she explained that the ballad 'The True Rights of Man' could be very effective in calming the countryside, though curiously she thought urban radical culture was too sophisticated to fall for it.[88] She also planned to rework 'Village Politics', which she still considered perfect for the times, even though it was originally written during the 1790s.[89] In 1816 Hannah More paid for some of the reprinting herself, but she was pleased with the subsequent sales. However, the practice of bulk pricing used by many printers resulted in most songs being sold to the middle ranks for distribution among labourers.[90] For example, the new version of 'Village Politics' published as 'The Village Disputants' in 1817 was sent to six gentlemen in Manchester (100 each) to distribute.[91]

More's admirers liked to tell stories of how her tracts prevented riots, and were eager to introduce them into areas of unrest.[92] The introduction to the 1817 edition of the tracts spoke of sedition and unrest and of how the tracts would help calm the country down.[93] It was even argued that the singing of More's song 'The Riot' prevented a serious food riot in Bath in 1796. In support of this, the historians Jeremy and Margaret Collingwood have pointed out that the Mendip peasantry, educated by Hannah More's schools, was loyal throughout the years of unrest in the early nineteenth century, and in 1819 signed a loyal address disapproving of disorder.[94]

Ballad historian Ian Dyck concedes that conservative propaganda was overwhelming in the 1790s and afterwards, but he has found little evidence that the Cheap Repository Tracts were bought by labourers.[95] Robert Hole agrees that the tracts found an enthusiastic readership mainly among 'the middle and upper orders, whose views they confirmed'. He argues this was true of both the 1790s tracts and the 1816–19 reprints.[96] Anne Stott also found that many of the buyers were More's friends and that the middle class were the most avid readers. Among the subscribers to the tracts were William Pitt, those associated with the reformation of manners movement, and Evangelicals.[97] These conjectures find support in the estimates of the tracts' publishers. According to the Advertisement to the 1798 edition of the shorter tracts, two million of them were sold in the first year of the enterprise 'besides great numbers in Ireland'. Nevertheless, the main clients were benevolent individuals and 'good and respectable Societies in various towns':

> Many persons have exerted their influence, not only by circulating the Tracts in their own families, in schools, and among their dependants, but also by encouraging booksellers to supply themselves with them; by inspecting retailers and hawkers, giving them a few in the first instance, and directing them in the purchase; also by recommending the Tracts to the occupiers of a stall at a fair, and by sending them to hospitals, workhouses, and prisons. The Tracts have also been liberally distributed among Soldiers and Sailors, through the influence of their commanders.[98]

The decision of Marshall (More's publisher) to print his own Cheap Repository Tracts after More put an end to the relationship, as well as other printers' interest in reprinting them, reflects their popularity but does not necessarily indicate that the poor themselves bought and read them.[99]

When the Cheap Repository Shorter Tracts were bound into a volume in 1798, More described their purpose in the Advertisement as supplanting 'the multitude of vitious Tracts circulated by hawkers' with 'some useful reading, which will be likely to prove entertaining also'.[100] Scholars of More have likewise dwelt on the artistic or 'entertainment value' of More's tracts. Praising the amusing nature of the stories, they have commented on the realistic dialogue filled with 'interjections, humorous word plays and lively language'.[101] It is worth examining this claim about the enjoyment to be derived from the tracts more closely. Let's take 'The History of Mary Wood' as an example. Using the 17-year-old Mary as a microcosm of sinful behaviour, time after time More tells the reader that it is the greatest sin for a farm servant to lie to her master, that she must return immediately after being sent on an errand, that any attempt to reduce her working hours is a sin, that going to a fair is a sin, and that she must always report to her master any transgressions her friends may have made against him if she cares about her reputation. Because Mary fails to observe these stern rules she is punished by death at the tender age of 18: 'Thus death, brought on by grief and shame at eighteen years of age, was the consequence of bad company, false promises and FALSE EXCUSES.'[102] Perhaps it was possible to derive enjoyment from this and get caught up in the narrative, but it can hardly compare to the popular ballads discussed in previous chapters. Some have tried to relate the moralistic aspect of the tracts and the cruelty of the punishment to folk tales and to criminal stories. While the Brothers Grimm tales were certainly quite violent, this element was missing from most English folk tales, which were frequently about a simple, humble, often lazy character who found a great fortune or was married to a rich partner purely through luck or wit. As for crime stories, it is true that they were violent and the criminal was harshly punished, but the offence was a serious transgression against the law, not a character flaw like superstition or a tendency to tell falsehoods. Also, we know that in many cases criminals, especially thieves, were seen as popular heroes rather than sinners going to hell. Thus Hannah More's tracts were in a category of their own; they were more overtly didactic and harsh than much of the rival popular fiction at the time.

Hannah More's charitable work often had an equally harsh and didactic tone as well as an element of coercion. In the *Mendip Annals* it is obvious that the teachings of the Mores resonated with some Sunday school students. The religious message did appeal to them and they did accept the Mores' definition of a good Christian. Apart from doctrine, much of the Mores' charity was undoubtedly beneficial to the poor. Nevertheless, they did not all passively accept Hannah More's influence as patron, educator or writer of popular fiction. Ann Yearsley, the milkwoman poet, is a good example of the kind of resistance More sometimes had to face. Recent studies of the More–Yearsley relationship have tended to emphasise the collaboration between the two women or to apportion equal blame to both More and Yearsley for their falling out.[103] However, no one can doubt that Ann Yearsley wished to be free of her patron's influence.

Rescued from complete destitution by a benevolent gentleman, Yearsley attracted More's interest because of her talent for poetry. Her connection to the countryside through her trade (she was a milkwoman) and her love of Virgil's *Georgics* must have served as further attraction for More, who tended to associate the city with vice. While More tried hard to obtain money and attention for her charge, she was 'utterly against taking her out of her station' for fear she would become idle and corrupt. Despite what historians have said about Yearsley's difficult character, it seems More played the role of patron with considerable insensitivity. At first More and her friends marvelled at the talent displayed by a woman of such a low station. Elizabeth Montagu praised Yearsley's poems and called her a 'miracle of nature' and 'noble creature'.[104] But problems soon began to arise. More attempted to separate Yearsley from her husband – perhaps he was not interesting enough since he did not write verse – edited her poems in ways Yearsley was not happy with, and took control of the earnings from the poetry, allowing Yearsley only a small sum at a time.[105] More and her friends, particularly Elizabeth Montagu and Horace Walpole, believed that the poor could not handle too much wealth and that to give Yearsley all the money at once would destroy her moral integrity.[106] More was also concerned that Yearsley would not spend the money prudently.[107] The mother of six children who had experienced extreme want, Yearsley was anxious to have control over the profits and demanded the whole sum.

According to Mary Waldron, Yearsley was angry that More had advertised her poems by emphasising her humble station, as if the poems had no merit on their own.[108] She also objected to More's revisions of her work. While many of her poems were dedicated to her patron, scholars like Moira Ferguson have read them as questioning middle-class benevolence.[109] The ability of this poor woman, whose rise to fortune was utterly dependent on More's help, to resist certain aspects of More's benevolence is impressive. Not only did she have her own opinion of what her rights were as a writer, but she had an independent opinion of what constituted good poetry.

Resistance to More's benevolence was also a definite if often understated presence in Hannah and Martha More's accounts of their charitable activities in the Mendip area. Women objected to the creation of female clubs or friendly societies, and when they agreed to them they insisted that their own ideas of what constituted their welfare be respected. The women at Rowberrow and Shipham preferred to not spend money on lying in but rather to be given an allowance for a good funeral. Though the Mores found this absurd, they were forced to 'submit to their folly and stupidity'.[110] They also had to agree to the funeral money in Cheddar.[111]

The poor also opposed some of the teaching imposed on them by the Mores in Sunday schools.[112] Unfortunately, the word 'opposition' appears much more often in Martha's journal than a discussion of what it was villagers opposed, which of them opposed it and on what grounds. Particulars are only given when the opposition came from rich farmers, perhaps because the journal was so concerned to present the More sisters as the friends of the poor. Disagreement about how the schools should be run was so powerful at Yatton and Congresbury that the Mores had to abandon them.[113] The rowdy villagers made frequent exhortations to obedience necessary. In the Mores' annual 'charge' to the schools, obedience was a central theme. In a charge made to the school at Shipham in 1795 the Mores stipulated that 'we are much better judges of who should preside over the school than you'. They also chided the villagers for petitioning 'against the hand that brought them assistance'.[114] Unfortunately they do not say what the issue was in the petition. In the same year at Nailsea the Mores had to remove the Sunday school teachers due to popular demand. Instead of appointing new teachers the Mores punished the villagers by closing one branch of the school. They deemed the villagers to be unworthy of it.[115]

It is hard to know whether the Mendip labourers' reaction to the Mores was unusual or whether they would have met with equal opposition elsewhere. The Mendip Hills were undergoing intensive enclosure between 1795 and 1819, around the time the Mores were active there.[116] Although the Mendips did not suffer as much as the Levels, a more fertile part of Somerset, 17.7 per cent of all land enclosed in the county mostly between 1770 and 1815 was in the Mendips.[117] The standard of living of agricultural labourers in the area is described as very low by contemporaries (including the Mores), and some historians have linked the distress to enclosure.[118] Lead mining, which had been an important industry, was on the decline, but the coal mines at Nailsea and the zinc mines in Shipham were still doing well in the 1790s and provided employment for many of the inhabitants.[119] Despite the economic difficulties in the Mendip area, many parts of England had a more difficult time during these years. It is possible the independent spirit of the inhabitants had something to do with the miners' culture, which has a rich tradition of resistance to authority. But it is also very likely that the character of the Mores' benevolence made passive acquiescence difficult.

Gratitude to the Mores did not come naturally to the beneficiaries of their charity, and this is evident in the efforts they had to make to extract explicit expressions of appreciation from the poor:

> They have so little common sense, and so little sensibility, that we are obliged to
> beat into their heads continually the good we are doing them; and endeavouring
> to press upon them, with all our might, the advantages they derive from us.[120]

Not only did they fail to be properly deferential, the poor even argued with the Mores, which provoked reflections from Martha on the 'depravity of the human heart'.[121]

Similar resistance must have been encountered by More's tracts. Despite the apparent universal middle-class and elite admiration for the tracts, they had their critics even here. Horace Walpole thought More was being cruel when she made the poor characters in her tracts spend all their leisure time reading religious material and deprived them of their Sunday pleasures.[122] Other commentators were concerned that depriving the poor of all sport and play would cause further dissatisfaction with the status quo, leading to unrest.[123]

How did the poor react to More's tracts? According to Marlene Hess, the didactic function of poetry was a commonplace since the Renaissance and it was not only an intention on the part of the author but part of the audience's expectation.[124] However, the street ballad was not didactic.[125] The poor would not necessarily have expected moral instruction from a chapbook ballad or tale, so it is possible they were duped by Hannah More's arguments. Evidence of this kind is hard to come by but we do have one example of an agricultural labourer who read and did not like one of More's tracts. Although a devout Baptist who often worried about the state of his soul and his chances of attaining salvation, Joseph Mayett knew when he was being put upon. When his minister put some educational tracts into his hands he wrote the following in his diary:

> at this time there was a great many tracks Came out and their Contents were Chiefly to perswade poor people to be satisfied in their situation and not to murmur at the dispensations of providence for we had not so much punishment as our sins deserved and in fact there was but little else to be heard from the pulpit or the press and those kind of books were often put into my hands in a dictatorial way in order to Convince me of my errors for instance there was the Sheperd of Salsbury plain…the Farmers fireside and the discontented Pendulum and many others which drove me almost into despair for I could see their design[126]

The Baptists have been described as being among the Dissenting churches that enjoyed 'the most democratic government of any permanent institutions in England and Wales' and as much more accommodating of radicalism than other nonconformist churches, who tended to expel radical members. A number of Baptist ministers were involved in Chartism.[127] Nevertheless, Joseph Mayett's church appears to have had very little tolerance for any opposition and insubordination. His environment cannot be described as 'radical'.

Mayett may have been exceptional in that he had a keen intelligence and an independent nature. But he was no rebel, and was eager to support his local church. He worried about his wickedness and was racked by guilt for sins like swearing, going to the alehouse or robbing a pear tree.[128] Even so, he did not

take the Cheap Repository Tracts in a simplistic and literal way. He understood very well the purpose of the kind of 'education' proposed by Evangelical
reformers. Frequently, it consisted in trying to persuade him that it was his
duty to contribute money to the church and that damnation awaited him if
he failed to do so.[129] Mayett's reaction to 'The Shepherd of Salisbury Plain' was
very different from that of More's own class. When the Dissenting minister
William Jay read the tract out loud to a gathering of More and her friends he
burst into tears at the touching story.

Hannah More believed in literacy for the poor, but the role of literacy was
to strengthen the social fabric. Education would impress upon labourers their
obligations to society and to their betters in particular. It would emphasise
religion, reading, and useful skills like spinning. The potential of the Mendip
schools for preventing disorder was recognised by both the Mores and their
contemporaries.

More's ideas about education are also evident in her attitude towards the
popular ballad. She saw the role of imaginitive art as strictly didactic, teaching
the same values she taught in the Mendip schools. Popular ballads did not
conform to this ideal and were therefore dangerous. Reading for the poor
should consist of the Bible or Cheap Repository Tracts; music should be either
'God Save the King' or the occasional religious psalm. More attacked ballads
in tracts, in her speeches to her schools and in letters to friends.

This attack targeted the themes found in popular ballads, which were either
directly addressed in Hannah More's tracts or played a role in her charitable
work and her patronage of Ann Yearsley. She wanted to replace the language of
complaint with a language of gratitude to the gentry, to one's country and to
God, which implied an acceptance of the social hierarchy. More's strict standards of chastity and self-control for her teachers suggest a belief that labourers'
sexuality needed to be replaced with prudence and piety. Compassion for
beggars and vagrants was to give way to compassion for the self-sacrificing
philanthropist – an almost Christ-like figure who took the suffering of others
upon herself. The use of commons was to be reserved for the deserving poor,
and poaching was to be strictly punished. Her concern about these issues
reflected a belief that these aspects of rural life had the potential to cause
disorder.

Although I have tried to show that More's tracts may not have made as
significant an impact on the lives of the poor as some historians have suggested,
the sheer volume of broadsides and chapbooks printed means that some of
them must have been read by the poor. The participants in More's Sunday

schools certainly read them, as did Joseph Mayett. However, the poor's resistance to all of More's work as well as to the tracts shows that they were not ready to accept her version of the good rural society. As More complained to Mr Addington, too many of the rural poor preferred the songs from 'Farmer Clapp's Book' to 'The Shepherd of Salisbury Plain'. In other words, Hannah More's tracts illustrate that the poor could distinguish between culture that was created by them or reflected their values and culture that was imposed on them from above. It is important to note that the men and women who fit under the category of 'the poor' in this chapter are quite diverse: Mendip miners and agricultural labourers, a Bristol milkwoman, a devout Baptist. Yet they all refused to passively accept More's benevolence. This finding can add to our understanding of the impact of philanthropy and propaganda literature on ordinary people in the 1790s and early 1800s.

Notes

1 For the relationship between Hannah More's tracts and popular culture see Susan Pedersen, 'Hannah More Meets Simple Simon: Tracts, Chapbooks, and Popular Culture in Late Eighteenth-Century England', *Journal of British Studies* 25, no. 1 (1986): 84–113.

2 Charles Howard Ford, *Hannah More: A Critical Biography*. Unpublished dissertation, Vanderbilt University, Nashville, TN, May 1992, 219. Ford sees the 1780s as bringing about an overall assault on popular culture.

3 David Davies, *The Case of the Labourers in Husbandry* (1795; reprinted Fairfield: Augustus M. Kelly, 1977), 29.

4 Davies, *The Case of the Labourers in Husbandry*, 93–4.

5 For the positive role some Sunday schools played in working-class life see Thomas Laqueur, *Religion and Respectability: Sunday Schools and Working-Class Culture, 1780–1850* (New Haven, CT: Yale University Press, 1976), 186–9. For the opposite viewpoint, see E. P. Thompson, *The Making of the English Working Class* (1963; reprinted with a new preface by Pelican Books, 1980), 412–15. See also Michael R. Watts, *The Dissenters*, vol. 2 (Oxford: Clarendon Press, 1995), 302.

6 Hannah More to Mr Addington, 23 September 1799, Letter no. 3 in Bonnie Lorraine Herron, ed., *'An Old Ballad Monger': Hannah More's Unpublished Letters, 1798–1827*. Unpublished dissertation, University of Alberta, 1999, 77. Hiley Addington was brother to the prime minister and More's neighbour and friend: M. G. Jones, *Hannah More* (New York: Greenwood Press, 1968), 206.

7 Martha More, *Mendip Annals: Or, A Narrative of the Charitable Labours of Hannah and Martha More in their Neighbourhood*, ed. Arthur Roberts (London: James Nisbet and Co., 1859), 217.

8 More, *Mendip Annals*, 167.

9 More, *Mendip Annals*, 198.

10 More, *Mendip Annals*, 238.

11 Marlene Alice Hess, *The Didactic Art of Hannah More*. Unpublished dissertation, Michigan State University, 1984, 109. One of the changes she made was to 'found all goodness on religious principles'.

12 Ann Stott, *Hannah More: The First Victorian* (Oxford: Oxford University Press, 2003), 172.

13 Clare Macdonald Shaw, Introduction to Hannah More's *Tales for the Common People and Other Cheap Repository Tracts* (Nottingham: Trent Editions, 2002), xix. Shaw gives credit to More for appreciating the significance of popular literature. For the relationship between print and social change see Mona Scheurmann, *In Praise of Poverty: Hannah More Counters Thomas Paine and the Radical Threat* (Lexington, KN: the University Press of Kentucky, 2002), 207.

14 BL, Add. MS 16920, Reeves MS, fo. 99. Quoted in Stott, *Hannah More*, 137–8.

15 See William Jones's anti-French song in his *Liberty and Property Preserved against Republicans and Levellers* (London, 1792), 15.

16 Letter no. 74 in Herron, 'An Old Ballad Monger', 194.

17 Francis Place thought her tracts sold mainly in rural areas: Stott, *Hannah More*, 207.

18 See Jane Nardin, 'Hannah More and the Rhetoric of Educational Reform', *Women's History Review* 10, no. 2 (2001): 217.

19 Stott, *Hannah More*, 170. See also Shaw's Introduction to *Tales for the Common People*, xvii. Shaw argues More saw the destruction of ballads as a prerequisite for widespread religious conversion.

20 Hess, *The Didactic Art of Hannah More*, 123.

21 Hess, *The Didactic Art of Hannah More*, 124.

22 Hess, *The Didactic Art of Hannah More*, 2–4.

23 'The Carpenter; or, the Danger of Evil Company', *Cheap Repository Shorter Tracts* (London, 1798), 373.

24 Hannah More, 'Black Giles the Poacher', in *Tales for the Common People*, 71.

25 See above, Chapter 5.

26 Hannah More, 'Tawny Rachel', in *Tales for the Common People*, 90, 94.

27 Ford, *Hannah More*, 233–4.

28 More, *Mendip Annals*, 47.

29 More, *Mendip Annals*, 104–5.

30 Hannah More, 'The History of Hester Wilmot, Part II', in *Tales for the Common People* , 108.

31 Hannah More, 'The History of Hester Wilmot, Part II', in *Tales for the Common People* , 112.

32 Hannah More to Mr Addington, 23 September 1799, Letter no. 3 in Herron, 'An Old Ballad Monger', 77. See Herron's note 31. Herron believes 'Farmer Clapp's Book' was a chapbook of songs containing 'impropriety or irreligion'.

33 More, *Mendip Annals*, 88, 153.

34 Hannah More, 'The Shepherd of Salisbury Plain, Part II', in *Tales for the Common People*, 35, 37.

35 Hannah More, 'The History of Hester Wilmot, Part II', in *Tales for the Common People*, 114.

36 Sarah Trimmer, *The Servant's Friend, An Exemplary Tale; Designed to Enforce the Religious Instruction Given at Sunday and Other Charity Schools, By Pointing out the Practical Application of them in a State of Service* (London, 1787), 8, 10.

37 More, *Mendip Annals*, 34.

38 Stott, *Hannah More*, 108.

39 Martha disapproved of a rich farmer's wife at Axbridge who said the poor were where they were because of Providence, that God intended them to be ignorant servants and slaves and there was no point trying to alter divine decrees: More, *Mendip Annals*, 34. See also Jeremy and Margaret Collingwood, *Hannah More* (Oxford: Lion Publishing, 1990), 91.

40 More, *Mendip Annals*, 28. This referred to the villagers at Shipham and Rowberrow. See also More's letter to Mrs Kennicott in *Mendip Annals*, 39, 23.

41 More, *Mendip Annals*, 24.

42 More, *Mendip Annals*, 234.

43 Hannah More, 'Will Chip's True Rights of Man in Opposition to the New Rights of Man by a Journey Man Carpenter'. This is a reworking of an earlier ballad, found in letter no. 74, Herron, *'An Old Ballad Monger'*, 195. Hannah More meant here that 'equal just laws' existed already in England, making any further political reform unnecessary. On the ideology that argued the English law guaranteed equal rights for everyone see Douglas Hay, 'Property, Authority and the Criminal Law', in *Albion's Fatal Tree* (New York: Pantheon Books, 1975), 36–7.

44 Douglas Hay, 'The State and the Market in 1800: Lord Kenyon and Mr Waddington', *Past and Present* 162 (1999): 102–3. On how town authorities in Bristol regulated the market through such measures as prohibiting exports in order to avoid disturbances in times of crisis see Steve Poole, 'Scarcity and the Civic Tradition: Market Management in Bristol, 1709–1815', in *Markets, Market Culture and Popular Protest in Eighteenth-Century Britain and Ireland* (Liverpool: Liverpool University Press, 1996), 91–115. Also in the same collection of essays Adrian Randall, Andrew Charlesworth, Richard Sheldon and David Walsh, 'Markets, Market Culture and Popular Protest in Eighteenth-Century Britain and Ireland', 17. The authors argue that well into the nineteenth century not only plebeians but also the elite resented those who acted against the community's customary expectations.

45 Hannah More, 'The Honest Miller of Gloucestershire. A true ballad', *Cheap Repository Shorter Tracts*, 408.

46 Hannah More, 'The Roguish Miller; or, Nothing Got by Cheating: A True Ballad' (Bath, 1800?).

47 Hannah More, 'A Hymn of Praise for the Abundant Harvest of 1796. After a year of Scarcity' (London, 1798).

48 Hannah More, 'The Riot; or, Half a Loaf is Better than No Bread. In a Dialogue between Jack Anvil and Tom Hod. To the Tune of "A Cobbler there was". Written during the Scarcity of 1795', *Cheap Repository Shorter Tracts*, 431.

49 'How to Endure Poverty', *The Penny Magazine*, 28 April 1832.

50 Trimmer, *The Servant's Friend*, 11.

51 Hannah More, 'The Riot'.

52 Josiah Wedgwood, *An Address to the Young Inhabitants to the Pottery* (Newcastle, 1783), 1.

53 Hannah More, 'Patient Joe; or the Newcastle Collier', *Cheap Repository Shorter Tracts*, 387.

54 John Barrell has connected Hannah More's explanation for poverty to a broader discourse which interpreted poverty as 'natural' and ordained by God. Artistic expressions to this view were given by Crabbe and Gainsborough, among others. When they explained social distress as punishment from God for 'sins' and 'crimes', these authors overlooked the personal responsibility of the rich in such sins: John Barrell, *The Dark Side of the Landscape: The Rural Poor in English Painting 1730–1840* (Cambridge: Cambridge University Press, 1980), 82–5.

55 Anon., 'The Plow-Boy's Dream', *Cheap Repository Shorter Tracts*, 416.

56 Ford, *Hannah More*, 266.

57 Hannah More, 'The Shepherd of Salisbury Plain', in *Tales for the Common People*, 34.

58 Mary Waldron, *Lactilla, Milkwoman of Clifton: The Life and Writings of Ann Yearsley, 1753–1806* (Athens, GA, and London: the University of Georgia Press, 1996), 70.

59 Note the derogatory slur aimed at popular music.

60 Elizabeth Montagu to Hannah More, Sandleford, 1784 in William Roberts, ed., *Memoirs of the Life and Correspondence of Mrs Hannah More*, vol. 2 (London: R. B. Seeley and W. Burnside, 1834), 373–4.

61 Roberts, *Memoirs of the Life and Correspondence of Mrs Hannah More*, 369–70.

62 More to Mrs E. Carter, Bristol, 1785: Roberts, *Memoirs of the Life and Correspondence of Mrs Hannah More*, 391.

63 See for example More, *Mendip Annals*, 146. See p. 243 on being grateful to the Mores for establishing the female clubs.

64 More, *Mendip Annals*, 243. 'The charge' is the name Hannah and Martha More gave to their annual speeches to the Sunday schools.

65 Trimmer, *The Servant's Friend*, 7.

66 Jones, *Liberty and Property Preserved* (1792), 2.

67 Hannah More, 'The History of Mary Wood, the House-Maid; or, The Danger of False Excuses' (Dublin: Sold by William Watson and Son, 1797?).

68 More, 'The Riot'. The song also argued one should be grateful to one's country because the poor rates allowed the sick to be 'maintained like lords' at the expense of the parish. For similar arguments see Hannah More, 'Village Politics', in *The Works* (London, 1853), 231.

69 Hannah More, 'Will Chip's True Rights of Man', included in her letter to Mr Addington, Letter no. 74 in Herron, *'An Old Ballad Monger'*.

70 Hannah More, 'The Carpenter; or, the Danger of Evil Company', *Cheap Repository Shorter Tracts*, 374.

71 More, 'The Riot'.

72   More, *Mendip Annals*, 44.

73   Stott, *Hannah More*, 143–4.

74   Hannah More, 'Turn the Carpet; or, the Two Weavers', *Cheap Repository Shorter Tracts*, 450.

75   Shaw, Introduction to *Tales for the Common People*, xvii.

76   This is Shaw's interpretation of the song, Introduction to *Tales for the Common People*, xvii.

77   Hannah More, 'The story of Sinful Sally, Told by Herself', *Cheap Repository Shorter Tracts*, 462.

78   More, *Mendip Annals*, 61.

79   More, *Mendip Annals*, 28.

80   More, *Mendip Annals*, 92–4.

81   Stott, *Hannah More*, 108. Hannah More also argued the schools would teach the poor to stay off poor relief.

82   'The Shepherd of Salisbury Plain', in *Tales for the Common People*, 37.

83   More, 'Black Giles, the Poacher', in *Tales for the Common People*, 68–9.

84   More, 'Black Giles the Poacher', in *Tales for the Common People* , 79.

85   More, 'Black Giles the Poacher', in *Tales for the Common People* , 73–4.

86   See Jeremy and Margaret Collingwood, *Hannah More* (Oxford: Lion Publishing, 1990), 112–13. The Collingwoods believe the tracts were popular with the poor and came to form a central part of their libraries.

87   Hess, *The Didactic Art of Hannah More*, 93–4.

88   Hannah More to Mrs Addington, 18 November 1816. Letter no. 61, Herron, 'An Old Ballad Monger', 183.

89   Hannah More to Mr Addington 11 December 1816, Letter no. 65, Herron, 'An Old Ballad Monger', 194.

90   Hannah More to Mr Addington. Letter no. 74, Herron, 'An Old Ballad Monger', 194; see also Herron's note 352.

91   Letter no. 74, Herron, 'An Old Ballad Monger', 195.

92   The same claims were made for the Sunday schools. See Stott, *Hannah More*, 143–; Hess, *The Didactic Art of Hannah More*, 124.

93   Scheurmann, *In Praise of Poverty*, 31–2.

94   Collingwood and Collingwood, *Hannah More*, 117.

95   Ian Dyck, *William Cobbett and Rural Popular Culture* (Cambridge: Cambridge University Press, 1992), 94.

96   Robert Hole, 'Hannah More on Literature and Propaganda, 1788–1799', *History* 85, no. 280 (2000): 622.

97   Stott, *Hannah More*, 172, 177.

98   Advertisement, *Cheap Repository Shorter Tracts* (London, 1798).

99   Stott, *Hannah More*, 206–7.

100 Advertisement, *Cheap Repository Shorter Tracts* (London, 1798).

101 Ford, *Hannah More*, 209 and Hess, *The Didactic Art of Hannah More*, 95. Hess even goes so far as to say that 'The Shepherd of Salisbury Plain' is a masterpiece of its kind: 115.

102 Hannah More, 'The History of Mary Wood, the House-Maid; Or, The Danger of False Excuses' (Dublin: Sold by William Watson, and Son, 1797).

103 See Madeline Kahn, 'Hannah More and Ann Yearsley: A Collaboration Across the Class Divide', *Studies in Eighteenth-Century Culture* 25 (1996): 203–23 and Patricia Demers, '"For Mine's a Stubborn and a Savage Will". "Lactilla" (Ann Yearsley) and "Stella" (Hannah More) Reconsidered', *Huntington Library Quarterly* 56, no. 2 (1993): 136.

104 Mrs Montagu to Miss H. More, Sandleford, 1784, Roberts, *Memoirs of the Life and Correspondence of Mrs Hannah More*, vol. 2, 363.

105 Stott, *Hannah More*, 73.

106 Montagu warned against this early on due to her own patronage experience. See her letter to More, Sandleford, 1784, Roberts, *Memoirs of the Life and Correspondence of Mrs Hannah More*, 364. For Montagu's own failed patronage experiment with Bryant, the pipe-maker poet of Bristol, see Waldron, *Lactilla, Milkwoman of Clifton*, 77.

107 Waldron, *Lactilla, Milkwoman of Clifton*, 65.

108 Waldron, *Lactilla, Milkwoman of Clifton*, 66.

109 See Moira Ferguson, *Eighteenth-Century Women Poets: Nation, Class, and Gender* (New York: State University of New York Press, 1995), 48. Ferguson argues that the quarrel with More had a serious impact on the rest of Yearsley's life, 92.

110 More, *Mendip Annals*, 66.

111 More, *Mendip Annals*, 67. Criticism of More's creation of friendly societies for poor women was also voiced by members of her own class. Hiley Addington, for instance, argued they should only be established if 'they [were] positively wanted' and if the poor could afford to contribute to them.

112 Martha commented on the villagers of Shipham and Rowberrow's refusal to accept the doctrines of their curate 'though these were truly evangelical', More, *Mendip Annals*, 28. Anne Stott has argued persuasively that what went on in the Mendip schools was the result of negotiation between More and villagers. Stott, *Hannah More*, 106.

113 More, *Mendip Annals*, 145.

114 More, *Mendip Annals*, 151.

115 More, *Mendip Annals*, 169–70.

116 By Acts of Parliament: Cheddar, 4,400 acres awarded in 1801; Chilton, 620 acres awarded in 1800. By private acts: Nailsea, 2,000 acres in 1819; Shipham, 1,080 acres in 1799. Blagdon had been enclosed in 1787: W. E. Tate, *A Domesday of English Enclosure Acts and Awards*, ed. M. E. Turner (Reading: The Library, University of Reading, 1978), 228–32.

117 Michael Williams, 'The Enclosure of Waste Land in Somerset, 1700–1900', *Transactions of the Institute of British Geographers* 57 (1972): 105. Williams argues that the most heavy enclosure in the Mendips took place between 1790 and 1799.

118 William Page, ed., *The Victoria History of Somerset*, vol. 2 (London: Published for the University of London Institute of Historical Rsearch, 1969), 321–2.

119 Page, *The Victoria History of Somerset*, 380–5.

120 More, *Mendip Annals*, 67. This refers to the villagers of Rowberrow and Shipham.

121 See for example More, *Mendip Annals*, 82.

122 More to her sister, 1795, Roberts, *Memoirs of the Life and Correspondence of Mrs Hannah More*, vol. 2, 432, quoted in Ford, *Hannah More*, 237.

123 Ford, *Hannah More*, 237–8.

124 Hess, *The Didactic Art of Hannah More*, 4.

125 Hess also thinks the moral tales were more eagerly read than the ballads but produces little evidence to this effect: Hess, *The Didactic Art of Hannah More*, 108.

126 Joseph Mayett, *The Autobiography of Joseph Mayett of Quainton 1783–1839*, ed. Anne Kussmaul (Buckinghamshire Record Society, 1986), 70.

127 Watts, *The Dissenters*, vol. 2, 192, 515, 521.

128 Mayett, *The Autobiography of Joseph Mayett of Quainton*, 14.

129 Mayett, The Autobiography of Joseph Mayett of Quainton, 70.

Conclusion

This book has argued that popular songs contain a popular voice. It has contributed to the work done on ballads by bridging the gap between Pepys and 1800 and showing how ballads drew on a tradition but took it a step further to articulate discontent or pride in an occupational rural identity. It has also placed songs in a larger cultural context, showing where they overlapped with other forms of discourse and where they diverged.

Broadside and chapbook ballads were printed in different places but they formed a coherent whole, a 'ballad culture'. They connected an oral and illiterate world to a literate world of print. Thus, low literacy does not indicate that this discourse was not widely shared. Ballads also connected the rural with the urban, as their construction of a rural identity was recognised by urban and rural dwellers. Printing ballads was a commercial endeavour and testifies to the ballads' popularity. The growth of the printing trade at the end of the eighteenth century indicates a growth in the audience for ballads. Nevertheless, the ballad seller and the ballad singer remained subversive figures throughout the period, associated by the elite with criminals and vagabonds. Despite an overlap between high culture and balladry, the distaste of much of the elite for the purveyors of the ballad trade suggests its difference from and opposition to elite art.

Like other texts, songs represented rural relations as in a state of decay. To develop a language of complaint they drew on a tradition of the moral economy which blamed middlemen and farmers for high grain prices. They borrowed a discourse about the negative effects of luxury and turned against 'new-fashioned farmers' who were no longer willing to socialise with their labourers. After 1770, the new moral economy songs placed more emphasis on the farmers' responsibility for high grain prices. Songs distinguished between small and large farmers, sympathising with the former. These sentiments can be found in other sources, but songs deviated from other texts in their strong anti-gentry sentiments as they connected high grain prices to high rents. A sub-genre of ballads described tension between tenant farmers and landlords, but the majority of songs assumed the voice of a tradesman or agricultural labourer and tended to place farmers and the gentry in the same category as trying to ruin the poor. It seems that the role of paternalism declined in songs after 1800. Songs about social relations can be understood within a context of hostility expressed by farmers towards labour and gentry, by gentry towards farmers and the poor, and by the poor towards farmers and gentry.

Although there was some room for the point of view of small farmers, the majority of songs represented the labourers' point of view. Significantly, the narrative in ballads is never told from the point of view of the gentry.

A second element in songs that critiqued the social order were arguments against enclosure and the loss of access to the land. Song writers joined poets in denouncing enclosers; they argued that enclosure impoverished the peasantry. The motivation behind enclosure was judged to be greed rather than a concern about the national interest. Ballads and poems also spoke of the social cost of enclosure: the growing animosity between labourers and enclosing farmers or gentlemen and the loss of a public space where villagers could socialise and play sports. There was also an aesthetic loss as a more natural and expansive landscape was subdivided into small fields. Finally, enclosure was connected to a loss of freedom, as commoners became more dependent on employers. The enclosers were described as oppressors. Some songs and poems expressed their opposition to enclosure by supporting infringements on private property such as poaching or stealing fuel.

In contrast to songs of complaint, songs about sexuality and agricultural labour had a positive tone. This book has suggested that such songs should not be dismissed as 'unrealistic' but should be seen in light of the fact that they enjoyed a broad audience which included labourers and artisans. Trying to understand the possible appeal of such songs can yield a reading that emphasises their construction of a positive rural identity. Bawdy songs contrasted rural labourers' sexuality with aristocratic sexuality. The elite was divided on the issue of labourers' sexuality. Eighteenth-century medical writings connected sexual prowess to physical activity and health and thus to agricultural labourers. Fear of depopulation and a concern about the degenerative effects of luxury on the aristocracy made labourers' sexuality seem useful. At the same time, in much elite literature peasants were mocked for being bumpkins and incapable of refined courtship. But such satire had a lightness to it that was lacking from

much elite discourse at the end of the eighteenth century. A stronger opposition to peasant sexuality was voiced when Evangelical reformers set out to
improve the morals of the poor. The triumph of the Malthusian account of
population made sexual restraint seem a necessity. New editions of medical
treatises reflected these concerns as they edited out sexually explicit content.
At the same time, the audience for bawdy ballads grew and they continued
to be printed in large numbers. In the more hostile climate the celebration of
plebeian sexuality in song was a kind of defiance. Bawdy songs celebrated both
male and female sexuality, allowing women considerable agency. The sexuality
of both ploughmen and milkmaids was described as superior to the sexuality
of aristocratic men and women.

By comparison, songs that celebrated agricultural labour during the French
Wars cannot be said to be subversive because they had a number of similari-
ties with the rustic tradition in painting and with the georgic tradition in
poetry. But, unlike those other genres, working songs were willing to depict
the hardship of labour and the difficult economic conditions that might be
faced by agricultural workers. Songs acknowledged the painful side of work.
They described the hardship of enduring hot and cold weather and the extreme
physical exertion and exhaustion suffered by agricultural labourers. In addition,
they spoke of the difficult conditions surrounding work: high prices of provisions, low wages, underemployment, bad masters. Nevertheless, songs pointed
out that agricultural labourers had certain compensations: at least they were
better off than industrial labourers, whose work was much more monotonous.
Songs perpetrated the stereotype of the healthy agricultural labourer arguing
that country surroundings were more beneficial than an urban environment.
Agricultural labourers could also cultivate an aesthetic appreciation of nature.
Finally, they were amply rewarded for their efforts by domesticity: a loving
wife and children made the work worthwhile. In addition to compensations,
songs conveyed a sense of pride in the agricultural labourers' occupation. They
praised his or her skill and strength and the importance of agricultural work to
the British economy. They also described the labourer as an honest patriot who
appreciated the advantages of being English. These songs bear a resemblance to
church and king songs but they are not as militant and didactic. They may have
resonated with a broad audience with a taste for pastoral or responded to a
concern about agriculture's role in the war effort. Nevertheless, their argument
in favour of agricultural labourers' importance to England could have had
resonance with agricultural labourers themselves.

Hannah More's negative reaction to ballads confirms many of the points made in this book. It is part of her overall attitude to the poor and relates to her work in the Mendip area and her work as patron. These three spheres of activity show More's attitude towards the issues discussed here. More wanted to suppress popular ballads, which she saw as dangerous, and replace them with the Bible, hymns and Cheap Repository Tracts. She hoped to replace the language of complaint with gratitude to philanthropists, to one's country and to God. In her Mendip schools she suppressed labourers' sexuality and encouraged chastity and religious devotion. More also wanted to protect commons and wastes from the encroachment of undeserving vagabonds who used them to support a life of crime and idleness. The poor's resistance to Hannah More illustrated by the Mendip villagers, by Anne Yearsley and by Joseph Mayett shows that they understood the difference between her version of popular culture as expressed in the Tracts and their own popular culture.

This book has extended our knowledge of the place songs occupied in popular culture. In some ways it has raised more questions than it has answered. More work is necessary on women's role in both the production and consumption of popular ballads. Historians often make references to women selling ballads in the street, singing them, or buying them and, indeed, such references can be found in contemporary accounts, but we do not know which songs women are likely to have sung or whether they wrote any of them.[1] The existence of female self-taught poets suggests there may have been women who wrote ballads as well. Vicinus has observed the development of a feminine point of view in many ballads: 'By the eighteenth century women had become the main repositories of traditional songs, and the major purchasers of romantic broadsides.'[2] It stands to reason that there may have been women authors as well. Women's participation in the printing industry would be another way to try to find out what their relationship to broadside and chapbook ballads may have been. Another important area of investigation would be the nature of the elite's interest in the popular ballad. Why did some members of the gentry collect popular ballads when so many of them expressed anti-gentry sentiments? Did they include anti-gentry songs in their collections? It appears that their preference was for traditional ballads rather than for the newer, critical songs, but this hypothesis needs to be tested. Did elite women collect ballads? Third, it would be interesting to know more about loyalist songs, where they were performed and by whom, and to what extent the labouring population shared in their sentiments, for the entire eighteenth century, but especially during the French Wars. In connection with this it might be useful to investigate the relationship between broadside and chapbook songs and the songs of Charles

Dibdin. Dibdin was seen by the elite as a man who truly loved his country, but some of his songs bear a resemblance to some of the songs discussed in this book. A more precise knowledge of the theatrical contexts in which his songs were performed and of audiences' reactions might give us a different reading of the genre of popular song from the one argued here. It would also be good to learn the precise nature of the slow-down in the ballad trade during the first 50 years of the eighteenth century: what were its causes, and why did the trade revive? It appears that chapbooks were more widespread during this period than broadsides, but both seem to have been printed in much lower numbers than before or after.

It would also be interesting to learn more about censorship, whether it extended to songs, and what kinds of songs were targeted. We know that censorship was more strict during the French Revolution and the war with France, but we do not know enough about how this may have affected the trade in street literature.[3]

This book has shown that popular songs' appeal to a labouring audience was due to their criticism of social conditions and celebration of rural labourers' identity. In so doing it has contributed to our understanding of popular culture in eighteenth- and early nineteenth-century Britain.

Notes

1 On women selling and singing ballads in the streeet see Roy Palmer, *The Sound of History: Songs and Social Comment* (Oxford and New York: Oxford University Press, 1998), 3. See also Tim Harris, 'Problematising Popular Culture', in Tim Harris, ed., *Popular Culture in England, c. 1500–1850* (New York: St Martin's Press, 1995), 69–95, and Jonathan Barry, 'Literacy and Literature in Popular Culture: Reading and Writing in Historical Perspective', in Tim Harris, ed., *Popular Culture in England, c. 1500–1850* (New York: St Martin's Press, 1995). Barry describes the growth of female readership in the eighteenth century.

2 Vicinus, Martha, *The Industrial Muse. A Study of Nineteenth-Century British Working-Class Literature* (London: Croom Helm, 1974), 9.

3 Barry, 'Literature and Literacy', 88. According to Barry, censorship turned its attention to popular literature after the Civil War and again in the period 1790–1815, but because Barry's focus is literacy he says little about the precise nature of the material that was targeted.

Bibliography

Songs

A Note on the dating

In general, white-letter ballads, which have been used in this book, are associated with the eighteenth and nineteenth centuries. When there is no precise date given for a ballad the dates listed are those during which the printer was in business. Dating printers is itself problematic. Unless specified otherwise, the dates for printers are supplied by the library catalogues where the ballads are found – in other words, the Lauriston Castle Catalogue, the British Library Catalogue and the Bodleian Library Catalogue. Victor E. Neuberg's *Chapbooks: A Bibliography of References to English and American Chapbook Literature of the Eighteenth and Nineteenth Centuries* (London: The Vine Press, 1964) has been used to date some printers.

Lauriston Castle Collection (National Library of Scotland)
seventeenth–nineteenth centuries

'Beggars and Ballad-Singers', *Sweet Echo, Or The Vocalist's Companion* (London: John Pitt, n.d.), L.C. 2087. Pitt's years: 1819–44, according to the Bodleian Library.

'A Brave Old Country Gentleman', *The Merryman Songster* (Glasgow, n.d.), L.C. 2847.

'Clean Pease Strae' (Glasgow, n.d.), L.C. 2845.

'The Cottager's Saturday Night: A Poem' (London: J. Evans & Son), L.C. 2729. Bodleian Library Catalogue dates J. Evans & Son 1813–20.

'The Corn Laws, A New Song' (Glasgow: R. Hutchinson, n.d.), L.C. 2842. The song is about the Corn Laws of 1814 so it must have been written during or shortly after that year. Robert Hutchinson's years are roughly 1815–30.

'The Covetous Miller', *The Covetous Miller with other Tales* (London: Dean and Munday, n.d.), L.C. Folio.79.rb.s.435. The printers Dean and Munday were in business between the years 1811 and 1841.

'An Excellent New Song; Entitled the Farmer's Glory', L.C. 2846 (another version of 'Painful Plough', of which there is a Catnach version, 1813–38).

'Father and I' (London: J. Pitts, 1819–44), L.C. Folio.79.rb.m.168.

'The Gleaners', *Beauties of Glasgow* (Glasgow, 1802), L.C. 2836.

'The Goodman of Auchermouchtie; or, the Goodwife Turn'd Goodman' (Glasgow: J. and M. Robertson, 1802), L.C. 2837.

'The Grateful Cottager', *The Convivial Songster* (London: John Pitts, n.d.), L.C. 3087. Pitts: 1819–44.

'The Happy Beggars and The Turkish Lady' (Glasgow: J. and M. Robertson, 1802), L.C. 2837.

'The Joys of the Harvest' (n.p., n.d.), L.C. 2846.

'The King and the Miller' (n.p., n.d.), L.C. 2837.

'Luckidad's Garland', *Luckidad's Garland; or, When my Old Hat Was New* (n.p., n.d.) L.C. 2846.

'The Milkmaid', *An Excellent Garland Containing Six Choice Songs* (Manchester: G. Swindells, d. 1796), L.C. 2955.

'A New Song Called the Farmer's Rant or Jockey's Dream Shewing the Pride and Ambition of the Farmers and Factors, and the Distressed and Deplorable Condition of the Poor at this Day' (Newcastle, 1800?), L.C.

'A new song on the Farmer's Glory', *Bonny Jockey's Garland, Beautified with Several Merry New Songs* (Newcastle: Angus, n.d.), L.C. 2751. This must be one of the Angus family who were in business c.1774–c.1825. Dates provided by the Bodleian Library.

'The Ploughman', *Six Favourite Songs* (Falkirk: T. Johnston, n.d.), L.C. 2829. T. Johnston's years: c.1798–1827.

'The Ploughman Turn'd Sailor' (n.p., n.d.), L.C. 2808.

'The Poor Man's Labour's Never Done', *The Poor Man's Labour Never Done or, the Mother's Advice* (Glasgow, 1802), L.C. 2837.

'The Scotch Shepherd', *When Late I Wandered* (Stirling: M. Randall, c.1814–20), L.C. 2870.

'Sheep Shearing', *Batchelar's Rural Songster. An Excellent Collection of Popular Songs* (London: T. Batchelar, 1813–15), L.C. 3087.

'A Sweet Country Life', *The True Hearted Maiden* (Glasgow, 1802), L.C. 2837.

'The Travelling Chapman', *Five Popular Songs* (Edinburgh, 1824), L.C. 2837.

'The True Hearted Maiden' (Glasgow, 1802), L.C. 2837.

'The True Joke, Or the Poor Man's Complaint', *The True Lovers' Garland; Consisting of Three Good Songs* (Warrington: W. Eyres, n.d.), L.C. 2837.

'Thrasher', *Batchelar's Rural Songster. An Excellent Collection of Popular Songs.* (London: T. Batchelar, 1813–15), L.C. 3087.

'The Wealthy Farmer', *The Great Messenger of Morality* (Edinburgh: J. Morren, 1800–20), L.C. 2805.

British Library

'Answer to Nae Luck about the House. A favourite Scottish Song' (Salisbury, 1785), B.L., Shelfmark HS 74 1250.

'The Apron Farmer', by John Crane (Birmingham: Grafton and Reddell, 1802), B.L., Shelfmark 992.g.11.

'Bacchus's Calendar', *The Cabin Boy; or, the First Step to Fame, a New Song Book. Wherein are all the New Songs Sung in Harlequin and Mother Goose, Arbitration, Tekeli, &c.* (London, 1807), B.L., Shelfmark 11602.e.28.

'The Badger Completely Done Over, an Extemporary Dash of the Pen, in the Year 1801', *Collins, Scripscrapologiea; or, Collins's Doggerel Dish of all Sorts. Consisting of Songs Adapted to Familiar Tunes* (Birmingham: Published by the Author, Printed by M. Swinney, 1804), B.L., Shelfmark 11633.aaa.10.

'The Ballad Singer', *The New Vocal Harmony, or the Merry Fellow's Companion. Being a Choice Collection of Songs, Sung at All the Places of Public Entertainment* (London: J. Davenport, n.d.), B.L., Shelfmark 11643.bb.33. Bodleian Library catalogue lists Davenport as 1799–1807.

'The Beggar Girl', *A Garland Containing Four Excellent Songs* (Alston: J. Herrop, 1820?) B.L., Shelfmark BL 11621.b.9.(9.)

'The Beggar's Petition', *The History of Whittington, Who Was Afterwards Lord Mayor of London, And His Cat, to Which Are Added Two Poems* (Newcastle, n.d.) B.L., Shelfmark 11621.c.10.

'The Charming Month of May' (n.p., early eighteenth century), B.L., Shelfmark c.116. bb.11.

'The Churlish Farmer' (n.p., n.d.), B.L., Shelfmark 1161.a.5.

Collins, *Scripscrapologiea; or, Collins's Doggerel Dish of all Sorts. Consisting of Songs adapted to familiar Tunes.* (Birmingham: Published by the author, printed by M. Swinney, 1804).

'The Contented Ruricolist' (Glasgow, 1802), B.L., Shelfmark 11605.aa.23.

'The Cot on the Hill', *The Smithfield Bargain. Added: The Cot on the Hill. The Deserter.* (Dublin: Hawke, 1820?), B.L., Shelfmark 11622.b.43.(23).

'The Cottager's Daughter' (London: J. Catnach, 1814–42), B.L., Shelfmark rb.m.93.

'The Cries of the Poor Against the Oppresion of the Rich', *Two Excellent Old Songs. Entitled, I. The humours of the Age, II. The cries of the Poor Against the Oppression of the Rich.* (London? 1815?), B.L., Shelfmark 11621.b.7.(18).

'Cupid the Pretty Ploughboy' (London: J. Catnach, n.d.), B.L., Shelfmark 11621.k.4 vol.2. 1803–38.

'The Distressed Pedlar', *The Clown. To which is Added Poor Allan, the Pedler. Cape of Good Hope* (Falkirk: T. Johnston, 1801), B.L., Shelfmark 11606.aa.22.

'Do you see the old beggar who sits at yon gate?' *Universal Songster; or, Museum of Mirth* (London: Jones and Co., c.1835), B.L., Shelfmark 11661.eee.22.

'An excellent new ballad, giving a full and true relation how a noble lord was robb'd of his birth-day cloaths' (1713). B.L., Johnson Ballads, fol. 342.

'Farewell to Spring' (Glasgow, 1802), B.L., Shelfmark 11606.aa.23.

'The Farmer', *A Garland of New Songs, Containing How Stands the Glass. The Cobbler, No Rest in the Grave. The Farmer* (n.d., n.p.) B.L., Shelfmark 11606.aa.22.

'The Farmer's Boy' (Birmingham: Watts, n.d.), B.L., Shelfmark 1876.l.41. There is a Catnach version, 1813–38.

'The Farmer's Daughter', *A Garland of New Songs* (Newcastle-upon-Tyne: J. Marshall, n.d.), B.L., Shelfmark 11621.a.2. J. Marshall was in operation 1801–24.

'The Farmers Ingle' (n.p., 1825?), B.L., Shelfmark 1078.m.24.

'The Farmer's Song. A New Song Sung at Sadler's Wells' (London: S. Paul, n.d.), B.L., Shelfmark HS.74.11250.

'The Farmer's Treasure', *The Farmer's Treasure* (Greenock, W. Scott, c.1815) B.L., Shelfmark rb.s.1955.

'The Farmer's Wish', *Mad Tom's Garland. Composed of Six Excellent Songs* (Newcastle, 1775?), B.L., Shelfmark 11621.c.4.(18).

'Forestalling Done Over', *A Garland of New Songs* (Newcastle upon Tyne: J. Marshall, n.d.), B.L., Shelfmark 11621.a.2. Marshall's years: 1801–24.

'The Ground Ivy Girl', by Mr Upton, *The British Minstrel* (London: Vernor & Hood, 1820?), B.L., Shelfmark 11622.a.46.

'The Happy Farmer' (Salisbury: Fowler, n.d.), B.L., Shelfmark 11622.c.7.

'The Happy Milk Maid' (n.p., n.d.), B.L., Shelfmark 11622.a.46. There is another version from 1805.

'Harvest Home', *The Lincolnshire Knight; or, the Poor Rich Man* (Glasgow: J. and M. Robertson, 1802).

'Honest Bob of the Mill', *The Ladies' Evening Companion. Being an Entire New and Choice Collection of the Most Admired Songs* (London: T. Evans, 1810?), B.L. 1077.g.47.(13).

'Honest Will, the Farmer' (n.p., n.d.), B.L., Shelfmark 1876.l.41.

'Hoppicker's Song' (n.p., n.d.), B.L., Shelfmark 1876.d.41.

'The Husbandman and Servant Man' (n.p., n.d.), B.L., Shelfmark 1876.l.41. There is a Catnach version, 1813–38.

'If so Happy a Miller, then Who'd be King' (n.p.: Dodsley, n.d.), B.L., Shelfmark 11661. eee.22. Another version of 'The King and the Miller' (London: J. Huggonson, 1741), Bodleian Library.

'The Jolly Farmer; or, All Trades Beholden to the Plow', *The Jolly Farmer's Garland Containing Five Excellent New Songs* (1750) B.L., Shelfmark c. 116.bb.11.

'The Jolly Thrasherman' (n.p., n.d.), B.L., Shelfmark HS.74.11250.

'The Labouring Man' (n.p.: Ryle, n.d.), B.L., Shelfmark HS. 74.11250.

'The Land' (n.p., n.d.), B.L., Shelfmark HS. 74 11250. Catnach version: 1813–38.

'The Last Shilling', *The Last Shilling* (Stirling, 1806?), B.L., Shelfmark 11606.aa.23.

'Little Bess the Ballad-Singer', *A Garland of New Songs* (Newcastle: J. Marshall, n.d.) B.L., Shelfmark 11621.c.4. John Marshall was in business 1801–c.1824.

'Love in a Barn, or the Country Courtship' (Newcastle, 1780?), B.L., Shelfmark 111621.c.4.

'A Man's a Man for A'That' (n.p.: E. Hodges, n.d.), B.L., Shelfmark HS 74 1250.The *Bibliotheka Lindesiana* (the catalogue for the Lauriston Castle collecton) lists E. Hodges as c.1840. But this song is much older, because it was reworked by Robert Burns.

'The Merry Reaper of the Moor' (n.p., n.d.), B.L., Shelfmark 1077.g.47.

The Milking Pail. To Which are Added The North Country Lass. Oxter My Laddie. Old King Goul. The Humble Beggar (Glasgow, 1801), B.L., Shelfmark HS 74 1250.

'The Miller's Song', *The Wood-lark; a Choice Collection of New Songs* (Tewkesbury, 1790).

'The Muirland Farmer' (Stirling: J. Fraser & Co., c.1820), B.L., Shelfmark 11621.c.10. (20).

'The Muirland Farmer', *The Muirland Farmer, O Lassie Art Thout Sleeping Yet. With her Answer. The Turnimspilu, and the Smiling Morn* (Stirling, 1820?), B.L., Shelfmark 11621.c.10.(20).

'The New-Fashioned Farmer' (J. Catnach, n.d.), B.L., Shelfmark 1876.l.41. J Catnach was in business from 1803 to 1838.

'Painful Plough' (Manchester: Bebbington, n.d.), B.L., Shelfmark 1876.l.41. There is a Catnach version, 1803–38.

'Pedlar's Song', *The Delight of the Muses. Being a Choice Collection of Dibdin's Favorite Songs* (London: J. Evans, 1794) B.L., Shelfmark 1077.g.47.

'The Pleasures of a Country Life' (Glasgow, 1802), B.L., Shelfmark 11621.b.9.

'The Plough Boy', *Three Celebrated Songs* (Newcastle: J. Smith, 1800?), B.L., Shelfmark 11621.b.9.

'The Ploughboy Turned Soldier' (n.p., 1801?), B.L., Shelfmark 11606.aa.23.

'The Ploughman' (n.p., n.d.), B.L., Shelfmark 1876.d.41.

'Poor Fanny', *The New Myrtle and Vine; Or, Complete Vocal Library* (London: Thomas Tegg, 1806), B.L. Shelfmark AB.1.80.117.

'Poor Kate, the Lavender Girl', by R. Morley (n.p., n.d.), B.L., Shelfmark11661. eee.22.

'The Poor Peasant Boy' (Birmingham: Jackson and Son, n.d.), B.L., Shelfmark 1876.l.41.

'The Poor Poet' (n.p.: Fowler, printer, n.d.), B.L., Shelfmark 11622.c.7. This could be the printer Fowler from Salisbury, 1770–1800.

'The Pope's Pedigree: Or, the Twining of the Wheel Band, Shewing the Rise and First Pedigrees of Mortals Inhabiting beneath the Moon' (Northampton: William Dicey, 1719–57), B.L., Johnson Ballads, fol. 342.

'Popular opinions, or a picture of real life, exhibited in a dialogue between a Scotish farmer and a weaver' (Glasgow: J. Hodderwick, 1812), B.L., Shelfmark 11643.d.7.

'Rigs of the Fair' (n.p., n.d.), B.L., Shelfmark HS.74 11250.

'Rural Life' (London: Thomas Evans, c.1805), B.L. Shelfmark 11606.aa.22.

'The Sheep Shearers' (n.p., Toy and Marble, n.d.), B.L., Shelfmark HS 74 1250. Pitts version: 1819–44.

Six Favorite New Songs Called Life's Like a Sea. Davy Jones's Locker. Gorg is the Liquor of Life. The Sea-worn Tar. Green with Moorings. The Milk Maid (n.p., n.d.), B.L., Shelfmark 111606.aa.22.

'Song of the Haymakers' (n.p.: Hodges, n.d.), B.L., Shelfmark 11621.k.4 vol. 2.

'The Song of Phoebe', *Phoebe, the Cottage Maid* (London, 1811), B.L., Shelfmark ch 810.

'A Summer Piece', *The Buxom Dame of Reading or, the Cuckold's Cap* (Glasgow: J. & M. Robertson, 1802), B.L. 11621.c.4.

'The Summer was Over' (Glasgow, 1801), B.L., Shelfmark 11606.aa.23.

'In Tattered Weed', *In Tattered Weed* (Edinburgh, 1819), B.L., Shelfmark 11621.b.12.

'Times Altered or, the Grumbling Farmers', *The Universal Songster; or, Museum of Mirth* (London: Jones and Co., c.1835), vol II. B.L. 11881.eee.22. There is a version by J. Catnach which the Bodleian Library lists as 1813–38.

'A Touch on the Times', *The Bold Sailor* (Glasgow: J. & M. Robertson, 1800), B.L., Shelfmark 11621.b.13.

'The Villager' (Salisbury: Fowler, n.d.), B.L., Shelfmark 11622.c.7.

'The Wand'ring Beggar Boy', by James Lamb, *A Small Collection of Original Pieces in Verse, Consisting of Epistles, Songs, Rural Ballads, and Hymns* (London?, 1819). B.L. Shelfmark 11646.ff.24.(1).

'Wandering Mary', *The New Myrtel and Vine; or, complete Vocal library* (London: Thomas Tegg, 1806), B.L., Shelfmark AB.1.80.117.

'Young Ralph the Waggoner' (n.p., n.d.), B.L., Shelfmark 1077.g.47. There is a J. Evans version, 1780–1812.

Edward Hyder Rollins, ed., *The Pepys Ballads*, 8 vols, (Cambridge, MA, 1930).

'The Bountiful Knight of Somersetshire' (1685), *The Pepys Ballads*, vol. 3.

'The Poor Folks Complaint' (registered 1675), *The Pepys Ballads*, vol. 3.

'The Poor Man's Distress & Tryal, Or, Fortune Favours after her Frowns' (1685), *The Pepys Ballads*, vol. 3.

'The Present State of England: Containing the Poor Man's Complaint in a Land of Plenty, Occasioned by the Many Abuses Offer'd by the Ingrossers of Corn, and Likewise Brandy-Stillers, which Makes a Scarcity in a Time of Plenty' (1688) *The Pepys Ballads*, vol. 4.

Houghton Library

Hark Away. The Boys of Kilkenny, the Land of Delight, The Plowman, Love in the Horrors (Glasgow, n.d.) Shelfmark 25276.19, vol 2, Houghton Library.

'John and Nell' (Greenock: W. Scott, c.1815), Houghton Library.

Jubilee for Jubilee; or Fifty Year Shepherd for Fifty a King. To Which Are Added, The Cambridge Tender, With the Answer. The Death of General Wolfe. Smirky Nan the Milk-Maid. The Humble Beggar (Glasgow: J. and M. Robertson, 1809), Houghton Library Collection.

Philander's Garland; Composed of Five Delightful New Songs (n.p., n.d.), Houghton Library.

The Pretty Milkmaid's Garland, Composed of Several Excellent New Songs (n.p., n.d.), Houghton Library.

'Resolute Dick', *Resolute Dick's Garland. Composed of Several Excellent New Songs* (n.p., n.d.), John Bell Ballad Collection, Houghton Library.

Bodleian Library

Francis Douce (1757–1834)

'The Crafty Miller, or, Mistaken Batchelor' (London: W. and C. Dicey, 1736–63), Bodleian Library, Douce Ballads 3(13b).

'The Farmer' (London: W. and C. Dicey, 1736–66), Bodleian Library, Douce Ballads 3(30a).

'The Northern Ditty: or, the Scotsman Outwitted by the Country Damsel', by Thomas d'Urfey (Newcastle, n.d.), Bodleian Library, Douce Ballads 3(70a).

Charles Harding Firth, seventeenth to nineteenth century

'The Disobedient Daughter' (Berkeley: Lewis Povey, 18–), Bodleian Library, Firth b. 26(6).

'The Merchant's Daughter and the Constant Farmer's Son' (n.p., n.d), Bodleian Library, Firth c.12(438).

Harding Ballads, seventeenth to nineteenth century

'Bill Brown' (Coppergate, York: C. Croshaw, 1814–50), Bodleian Library, Harding B28(286).

'The Bloody Gardener's Cruelty, Or the Shepherd's Daughter Betrayed' (London: J. Jenning,1790–1840), Bodleian Library, Harding B1(101).

'Down by the Dark Arches Near the Adelphi' (n.p., n.d.), Bodleian Library, Harding B11(1645).

'The Dustman's Brother' (London: J. Pitts, 1819–44), Bodleian Library, Harding B11(1264).

'The Farmer's Lamentation' (Newcastle: Angus, 1774–1825), Bodleian Library, Harding B 25(629).

'The Gipsy Queen' (London: J. Pitts, 1819–844), Bodleian Library, Harding B11(3990).

'The Gipsy's Tent' (Durham: G. Walker, 1797–1834), Bodleian Library, Harding B 11(175).

'Helen the Fair' (London: J. Pitts, 1819–44), Bodleian Library, Harding B11(237A).

'Lillies and Roses. A favourite Song' (London: J. Jennings, 1790–1840), Bodleian Library, Harding B25(1109).

'The Milkmaid' (Chester: R. Evans), Bodleian Library, Harding B25(397).

'The Milkmaid' (London: J. Pitts, 1802–19), Bodleian Library. Harding B25(1250).

'The Milk Maid' (n.p., n.d), Bodleian Library, Harding B6(8).

'The Miller's Advice to His Three Sons, in Taking of Toll' (London, W. and C. Dicey, 1736–63), Bodleian Library, Harding B 5(7).

'A New Song, Called The Plough Boy' (n.p., n.d.), Bodleian Library, Harding B 25(1507).

'The Poacher' (London, J. Evans, 1780–1812), Bodleian Library, Harding B25(1508)

'The Request of the Poor' (London: J. Pitts, n.d.), Bodleian Library. Harding B11(3263) Pitts' years: 1819–44.

'The Wandering Bard' (Liverpool: W. Armstrong, 1820–24), Bodleian Library, Harding B28(82).

John Johnson Ballads, 1503–1939

'The Village-Born Beauty' (n.p., n.d), Bodleian Library, Johnson Ballads, 2955.

Miscellaneous

'The Merry Milkmaids: Or, The Country Damosels Pleasure in their Rural Labours. To the Tune of: The Milking-Pail' (London: J. Deacon, 1671–1704). Bodleian Library Don.b.13(63).

'The Milkmaid' (Liverpool: G. Thompson, n.d.), Bodleian Library, 2806 c.17(281). G. Thompson's years: 1789–1828.

'The Milkmaid' (Norwich: R. Walker), Bodleian Library, 2806 c. 18(203). R. Walker's years: 1780–1830.

'Milkmen' (London: J. Pitts, 1802–19), Bodleian Library, 2806 c. 18(205).

St Bride Printing Library
'Melancholy Death of Five Poor Distressed Hay-Makers' (London: J. Catnach, 1803–38), St Bride Printing Library Broadside Collection.

Robarts Microfilm Collection
'The Bonny Milkmaid', *A Collection of New Songs Call'd the Milk-maids Garland* (London, 1705). Robarts Library Microfilm Collection. ESTC 10776.
'A Dialogue between Will and Jack', *The Jolly Tar's Garland, Furnished with Two Comical New Songs* (Newcastle, 1780). ESTC 872.
'The Merchant's Son, and the Beggar-wench of Hull' (Northampton: William Dicey, 1730?), Robarts Library Microfilm Collection. ESTC 1491.

The Roxburghe Ballads
'Come, Buy this New Ballad, before You Doe Goe: If You Raile at the Author, I Know what I Know. To the Tune of Ile Tell You but So', *Roxburghe Ballads*.
'The Milke-maid's Life', Introduction, *Roxburghe Ballads*.

Miscellaneous
'A New Song on the Times' (London: J. Pitts) in Roy Palmer, *A Ballad History of England from 1588 to the Present Day* (London, 1979).
'Sudborough Heroes', in Roy Palmer, *A Ballad History of England from 1588 to the Present Day* (London, 1979).

List of printers with known dates

Angus (Newcastle), 1774–1825
Armstrong, W. (Liverpool), 1820–24
Batchelar, T. (London), 1813–15
Catnach, J. (London), 1803–38
Corshaw, C. (York), 1814–50
Davenport, J. (London), 1799–1807
Dean and Munday (London), 1811–41
Dicey, William (Northampton), 1719–57
Dicey, W. and C. (London), 1736–63
Evans, J. (London), 1780–1812
Evans, J. & Son (London), 1813–20
Fowler (?Salisbury), 1770–1800
Fraser, J. & Co. (Stirling), c.1798–1827
Hawke (Dublin), 1820?
Herrop, J. (Alston), 1820?
Hodges, E. (London), c.1840
Hutchinson, Robert (Glasgow), 1815–30
Jenning, J. (London), 1790–1840
Johnston, T. (Falkirk), c.1801
Jones and Co. (London), c.1835

Marshall, J. (Newcastle), 1801–c.1824
Morren, J. (Edinburgh), 1800–20
Pitts, John (London), 1819–44
Robertson, J. and M. (Glasgow), c.1800
Scott, W. (Greenock), c.1815
Smith, J. (Newcastle), c.1800
Swindells, G. (Manchester), d.1796
Tegg, Thomas (London), 1806
Thompson, G. (Liverpool), 1789–c.1828
Walker, G. (Durham), 1797–1834

Other primary sources

Anon. *An Address to the Good Sense and Candour of the People, in Behalf of The Dealers in Corn: With Some Few Observations on a Late Trial for Regrating. By a Country Gentleman*. London, 1800.

Anon. *Aristotle's Compleat Masterpiece in Three Parts*, 23rd edition. London, 1749.

Anon. *The Aviary: Or, Magazine of British Melody Consisting of a Collection of One Thousand Four Hundred and Forty-Three Songs*. London, 1745.

Anon. *The Beggar's Complaint, Against Rack-rent Landlords, Corn Factors, Great Farmers, Monopolizers, Paper Money Makers, and War, and Many Other Oppressions, by One who Pities the Oppressed*. Sheffield, 1812.

Anon. *A Defence of the Land-Owners and Farmers of Great Britain; And an Exposition of the Heavy Parliamentary and Parochial Taxation under Which they Labour*. London, 1814.

Anon. *The Happy Shepherd: Or, Rural Retirement: A Moral Tale*. Gainsborough, 1806.

Anon. *Pursuits of Agriculture: A Satirical Poem, in Three Cantos*. London, 1808.

A. F. 'Tale LXV', *The General Entertainer*. London, 1746.

Adcock, Anna. *Cottage Poems*. London, 1808.

Allen, Rose. *The Autobiography of Rose Allen*. London, 1847.

Anderson, R. *Ballads in the Cumberland Dialect*. Carlisle, 1805.

Bamford, Samuel. *Early Days*. London, 1849.

Barre, William. *The Months: A Rural Poem; And Other Pieces*. London, 1813.

Bingley, Rev. W. A. M. *North Wales; Including the Scenery, Antiquities, Customs, and Some Sketches of Natural History*. London, 1804.

Blackner, John. *The History of Nottingham, Embracing its Antiquities, Trade and Manufactures, from the Earliest Authentic Records, to the Present Period*. Nottingham, 1815.

Bloomfield, Nathaniel. *Elegy on the Enclosure of Honington Green and other Poems*. London, 1798.

Bloomfield, Robert. 'The Farmer's Boy', in *Poems*. London: John Van Voorst, 1845.

Brougham, Henry Esq., M.P. *Speech to the House of Commons, Tuesday, 9th of April, 1816; in Committee of the Whole House, upon the State of Agricultural Distress*. London, 1816.

Burke, Edmund. *Thoughts and Details on Scarcity*. London, 1800.

Burns, Robert. *The Complete Poetical Works*, ed. James A. Mackay. Darvel, Ayrshire, 1993.

Carew, Bamphylde-Moore. *The Life and Adventures of Bamphylde-Moore Carew, the Noted Devonshire Stroler and Dog-Stealer*. Exon: The Farleys, 1745, edited by C. H. Wilkinson and reprinted Oxford: Clarendon Press, 1931.

Carey, David. *The Pleasures of Nature; Or, the Charms of Rural Life. With other poems*. London, 1803.

Catton, Samuel. *A Short Sketch of a Long Life of Samuel Catton, Once a Suffolk Ploughboy*. London and Ipswich, 1863.

Clare, John. 'Journey out of Essex', in Eric Robinson and David Powell, eds, *John Clare By Himself*. Manchester: Carcanet Press, 1996.

Clarkson, William. *An Inquiry into the Cause of the Increase of Pauperism and Poor Rates; With a Remedy for the Same*. London, 1815.

Cleland, John. *Fanny Hill, or Memoirs of a Woman of Pleasure*, ed. Peter Wagner. London: Penguin Books, 1985, First Published 1748–49.

Colquhoun, Patrick. *A Treatise on Indigence*. 1806.

Crabbe, George, 'The Parish Register', in *The Complete Poetical Works*. Vol. I, ed. Norma Dalrymple-Champneys and Arthur Pollard. Oxford: Clarendon Press, 1988.

Curwen, Mr. *Thoughts on the Present Depressed State of the Agricultural Interest of this Kingdom; And on the Rapid Increase of the Poor Rates*. London, 1817.

Dale, Nathaniel. *The Eventful Life of Nathaniel Dale, with Recollections & Anecdotes Containing a Great Variety of Business Matters, &c., as Occurred in the Life of the Author*. Printed for the author.

Darby, Thomas, Jn. *Poems Descriptive of Rural Scenery*. Birmingham, 1815.

Davies, David. *The Case of Labourers in Husbandry*. 1795, Reprinted Fairfield: Augustus M. Kelly, 1977.

Duck, Steven, 'On Poverty', in *Poems on Several Occasions*. First printed 1736, Menston Scolar Press, 1973.

Dunin, John. *Outlines of the History and Antiquities of Bromley, in Kent*. Bromley, 1815.

Dyer, George. *The Complaints of the Poor People of England*. London, 1793. Reprinted Oxford and New York: Woodstock Books, 1990.

Eden, Frederic Morton. *The State of the Poor*. London, 1797. Reprinted by George Routledge & Sons, Ltd, 1928.

Estcourt, Thomas. *An Account of the Result of an Effort to Better the Condition of the Poor in a Country Village and Some Regulations Suggested by Which the Same Might be Extended to Other Parishes of a Similar Description*. London, 1804.

Evans., Rev. J. *Letters Written during a Tour Through South Wales, In the year 1803, and at Other Times, Containing Views of the History, Antiquities, and Customs of that Part of the Principality*. London, 1804.

Farmer, John S., ed. *Merry Songs and Ballads, Prior to the Year A.D. 1800*. New York, 1964.

Fielding, Henry. *A Proposal for Making an Effectual Provision for the Poor, for Amending their Morals, and for Rendering them Useful Members of Society*. Dublin, 1753.

Gay, John. *The Shepherd's Week*. London, 1714.

Graham, James. *A Lecture on the Generation Increase and Improvement of the Human Species*. London, 1780.

Hanway, Jonas. *Virtue in Humble Life*. London, 1774.

Harris, William. *On the Present Distress of the Country and Suitable Remedies.* London, 1816.

Herron, Bonnie Lorraine, ed. 'An Old Ballad Monger': Hannah More's Unpublished Letters, 1798–1827. Unpublished dissertation. University of Alberta, 1999.

Hollway, William. *The Peasant's Fate: A Rural Poem, With Miscellaneous Poems.* London, 1802.

Howlett, John. *An Examination of Dr. Price's Essay on the Population of England and Wales and the Doctrine of an Increased Population in This Kingdom Established by Facts.* 1781, Reprinted New York, 1968.

Howlett, John. *An Essay on the Population of Ireland.* London, 1786.

Howlett, John. Appendix to *Dispersion of the Gloomy Apprehensions, of Late Repeatedly Suggested from the Decline of our Corn-Trade, &c.* London, 1797.

Humphries, R. *The Amusing Instructor, Or, Tales and Pables in Prose and Verse, for the Intertainmnet and Improvement of Youth: With Useful and Pleasing Remarks.* Dublin, 1769.

Huntington, Rev. W. *The Sinner Jaded; or Memoirs of the Life of the Rev. W. Huntington, The Coal Heaver, Late Minister of Providence Chapel.* London, n.d.

Hurn, D. *Rural Rhymes; Or, a Collection of Epistolary, Humorous, and Descriptive Pieces.* Spalding, 1813.

Johnston, William. *The Life and Times of William Johnston, Horticultural Chemist, Gardener, and Cartwright,* ed. Reginal Alenarly, Esq. Petershead, 1859.

Jones, William. *Liberty and Property Preserved against Republicans and Levellers.* London, 1792.

Lamb, James. 'The Pious Cottager', in *A Small Collection of Original Pieces in Verse, Consisting of Epistles, Songs, Rural Ballads, and Hymns.* 1819.

Lawrence, William. *The Autobiography of Sergeant William Lawrence, A Hero of the Peninsular and Waterloo Campaigns.* London, 1886.

Malcolm, Jacob. *General View of the Agriculture of the County of Buckingham.* London, 1794.

Malkin, Ben Heath. *The Scenery, Antiquities, and Biography of South Wales, from Material Collected during two Excursions in the Year 1803.* London, 1804.

Malthus, T. R. *An Essay on the Principle of Population,* 1798. Edited by Anthony Flew, Penguin Books, 1970.

Masters, Thomas. *A View of Agricultural Oppressions: And of their Effects upon Society.* 2nd edition, Regist, 1798.

Maude, Thomas. *Wensley-Dale, or, Rural Contemplations: A Poem.* London, 1780.

Mayett, Joseph. *The Autobiography of Joseph Mayett of Quainton 1783–1839,* ed. Ann Kussmaul. Buckinghamshire Record Society, 1986.

More, Hannah. *The History of Mary Wood, the House-Maid; or, The Danger of False Excuses.* Dublin: Sold by William Watson, and Son, 1797.

More, Hannah. *Cheap Repository Shorter Tracts.* London, 1798.

More, Hannah. *The Roguish Miller; or, nothing got by cheating: A True Ballad.* Bath, 1800?

More, Hannah. *The Works,* 5 vols. London: Henry G. Bohn, 1853.

More, Hannah. *Tales for the Common People and other Cheap Repository Tracts.* Selected, with an introduction and notes by Clare MacDonal Shaw. Nottingham: Trent Editions, 2002.

More, Martha. *Mendip Annals: or, A Narrative of the Charitable Labours of Hannah and Martha More in their Neighbourhood,* ed. Arthur Roberts. London: James Nisbet and Co., 1859.

Newenham, Thomas. *A Statistical and Historical Enquiry into the Progress and Magnitude of the Population of Ireland.* London, 1805.

Nicholson, William. *Tales in Verse, and Miscellaneous Poems: Descriptive of Rural Life and Manners.* Edinburgh, 1814.

North, Roger. *A Discourse of the Poor. Shewing the Pernicious Tendency of the Laws Now in Force for their Maintenance and Settlement.* London, 1753.

Paterson, James. *Autobiographical Reminiscences: Including Recollections of the Radical Years, 1819–1820 in Kilmarnock.* Glasgow, 1871.

The Penny Magazine (1832)

Pratt, Samuel Jackson. *Cottage-Pictures; Or, the Poor: A Poem, With Notes and Illustrations.* London, 1803.

Pringle, Andrew. *General View of the Agriculture of the County of Westmoreland.* Edinburgh, 1794.

Quick, Henry. *The Life and Progress of Henry Quick, of Zennor, Written by Himself,* ed. P.A.S. Pool. 1844.

Rennie, George, Brown, Robert & Shirreff, John. *General View of the Agriculture of the West Riding of Yorkshire.* Edinburgh, 1799.

Roberts, William. *Memoirs of the Life and Correspondence of Mrs. Hannah More.* Vol. 2, London: R.B. Seeley and W. Burnside, 1834.

Service, David. *The Caledonian Herd-Boy; A Rural Poem.* Yarmouth: J.D. Downes, 1802.

Sherston, Peter Esq. *The Months, Commencing with Early Spring; A Poem Descriptive of Rural Scenes and Village Characters.* Bath, 1809.

Smith, George. 'Pastorella', in *Pastorals,* 2nd edn. London: Whittingham and Rowland, 1811.

Templeman, James. 'Farmer Hobson, a Rural Poem', in *Poems and Tales,* Vol. 1. London, 1809.

Tilke, Samuel Westcott. *An Autobiographical Memoir.* London, Printed for and sold by the author, 1840.

Townsend, Joseph. *A Dissertation on the Poor Laws.* 1786, reprinted Berkeley, Los Angeles and London: University of California Press, 1971.

Trimmer, Sarah. *The Servant's Friend, An Exemplary Tale; Designed to Enforce the Religious Instruction Given at Sunday and Other Charity Schools, by Pointing out the Practical Application of them in a State of Service.* London, 1787.

Venette, Nicholas. *Conjugal Love Revealed.* 7th edition, London, 1720.

Wedgwood, Josiah. *An Address to the Young Inhabitants of the Pottery.* Newcastle, 1783.

Whitby, Thomas. *Retrospection: A Rural Poem.* London, 1820.

Wight, William. *Cottage Poems.* Edinburgh, 1820.

Wollstonecraft, Mary. *Original Stories from Real Life.* London, 1791. Reprinted Otley and Washington, DC: Woodstock Books, 2001.

Wordsworth, William. 'Goody Blake and Harry Gill', in *Complete Poetical Works,* ed. Ernest De Selincourt. Oxford and New York: Oxford University Press, 1936.

Secondary sources

Allen, Robert C. *Enclosure and the Yeoman*. Oxford: Clarendon Press, 1992.

Altick, Richard D. *The English Common Reader: A Social History of the Mass Reading Public, 1800–1900*. 2nd edn, Columbus: Ohio State University Press, 1998 (1st edn, University of Chicago Press, 1957).

Anderson, Michael. 'Population Change in North-Western Europe, 1750–1850', in Michael Anderson, ed., *British Population History from the Black Death to the Present Day*. Cambridge: Cambridge University Press, 1996, 191–281.

Appleby, Joyce Oldham. *Economic Thought and Ideology in Seventeenth-Century England*. Princeton: Princeton University Press, 1978.

Archer, John. *By a Flash and a Scare: Incendiarism, Animal Maiming, and Poaching in East Anglia, 1815–1870*. Oxford: Clarendon Press, 1990.

Archer, John. *Social Unrest and Popular Protest in England, 1780–1840*. Cambridge: Cambridge University Press, 2000.

Atkinson, David. *The English Traditional Ballad: Theory, Method, and Practice*. Aldershot: Ashgate, 2002.

Barker-Benfield, C. J. *The Culture of Sensibility: Sex and Society in Eighteenth-Century Britain*. Chicago: University of Chicago Press, 1992.

Barrell, John. *The Idea of Landscape and the Sense of Place 1730–1840: An Approach to the Poetry of John Clare*. Cambridge: Cambridge University Press, 1972.

Barrell, John. *The Dark Side of the Landscape: The Rural Poor in English Painting, 1730–1840*. Cambridge and New York: Cambridge University Press, 1980.

Bate, Jonathan. *John Clare: A Biography*. New York: Farrar, Straus and Giroux, 2003.

Beier, A. L. *Masterless Men: The Vagrancy Problem in England, 1560–1640*. London and New York: Methuen, 1985.

Bermingham, Ann. *Landscape and Ideology: The English Rustic Tradition 1740–1860*. Berkeley, Los Angeles and London: University of California Press, 1986.

Brewer, John. *The Pleasures of the Imagination. English Culture in the Eighteenth Century*. Chicago: University of Chicago Press, 1997.

Brooks, Emily. 'The Milkmaid's Tale', *The National Trust Magazine*, 93(3) (2001): 40–8.

Carter, Ian. *Farm Life in Northeast Scotland 1840–1914. The Poor Man's Country*. Edinburgh: John Donald Publishers, 1979.

Charlesworth, Andrew and Adrian Randall, eds. *Markets, Market Culture and Popular Protest in Eighteenth-Century Britain and Ireland*. Liverpool: Liverpool University Press, 1996.

Charlesworth, Andrew and Adrian Randall, eds. *Moral Economy and Popular Protest*. Hampshire and London: Macmillan Press, 2000.

Clare, Johanne. *John Clare and the Bounds of Circumstance*. Kingston and Montreal: McGill-Queen's University Press, 1987.

Clark, Anna. *The Struggle for the Breeches: Gender and the Making of the British Working Class*. Berkeley, Los Angeles and London: University of California Press, 1995.

Collingwood, Jeremy and Margaret. *Hannah More*. Oxford: Lion Publishing, 1990.

Collinson, Robert. *The Story of Street Literature, Forerunner of the Popular Press*. London: Dent, 1973.

Craig, David. *Scottish Literature and the Scottish People 1680–1830*. London: Chatto and Windus, 1961.

Crawford, Thomas. *Society and the Lyric: As Study of the Song Culture of Eighteenth-Century Scotland.* Edinburgh: Scottish Academic Press, 1979.

Deacon, George. *John Clare and the Folk Tradition.* London: Sinclair Browne, 1983.

Demers, Patricia. '"For Mine's a stubborn and a savage will". "Lactilla" (Ann Yearsley) and "Stella" (Hannah More) Reconsidered', *Huntington Library Quarterly*, 56(2) (1993): 135–50.

Devine, T. M. *The Transformation of Rural Scotland: Social Change and the Agrarian Economy, 1660–1815.* Edinburgh: Edinburgh University Press, 1994.

Dyck, Ian. *William Cobbett and Rural Popular Culture.* Cambridge: Cambridge University Press, 1992.

Easly, Alexis. 'Wandering Women: Dorothy Wordsworth's Grasmere Journals and the Discourse on Female Vagrancy', *Women's Writing*, 3(1) (1996): 63–77.

Feather, John. 'The Country Trade in Books', in *Spreading the Word: The Distribution Networks of Print.* Detroit, MI: St Paul's Bibliographies, 1990, 165–72.

Ferguson, Moira. *Eighteenth-Century Women Poets: Nation, Class, and Gender.* New York: State University of New York Press, 1995.

Fletcher, Anthony. *Gender, Sex and Subordination in England 1500–1800.* New Haven, CT, and London: Yale University Press, 1995.

Ford, Charles Howard. Hannah More: A Critical Biography. Unpublished dissertation, Vanderbilt University, Nashville, TN, May 1992.

Foucault, Michel. *The History of Sexuality: An Introduction*, Vol. 1, New York: Random House, 1978. Reprinted, Vintage Books, 1990.

Fox, Adam. *Oral and Literate Culture in England.* Oxford: Clarendon Press, 2000.

Foxon, David. *Libertine Literature in England, 1660–1745.* New York: University Books, 1965.

Gammon, Vic. 'Song, Sex, and Society in England, 1600–1850', *Folk Music Journal*, 4(3) (1982): 208–46.

Gammon, Vic. *Desire, Drink and Death in English Folk and Vernacular Song.* Aldershot: Ashgate, 2008.

Gatrell, V. A. C. *The Hanging Tree: Execution and the English People 1770–1868.* Oxford: Oxford University Press, 1994.

Gillis, John. *For Better for Worse: British Marriages, 1600 to the Present.* New York: Oxford University Press, 1988.

Ginsburg, Carlo. *The Cheese and the Worms: The Cosmos of a Sixteenth-Century Miller,* trans. John and Anne Tedeschi. Harmondsworth: Penguin, 1982.

Gray, B. Kirkman. *A History of English Philanthropy from the Dissolution of the Monasteries to the Taking of the First Census.* London: P.S. King & Son, 1905.

Gregory, E. David. *Victorian Songhunters: The Recovery and Editing of English Vernacular Ballads and Folk Lyrics, 1820–1883.* Lanham, MA: The Scarecrow Press, Inc., 2006.

Hammond, J. L. and Barbara Hammond. *The Village Labourer, 1760–1832: A Study in the Government of England before the Reform Bill.* London: Longman's, Green, 1980.

Harris, Michael. 'A Few Shillings for Small Books: The Experience of a Flying Stationer In the Eighteenth Century', in Robin Myers and Michael Harris, eds, *Spreading the Word: The Distribution Networks of Print 1550–1850.* Detroit, MI: St Paul's Bibliographies, 1990.

Harris, Tim. 'Problematising Popular Culture', in Tim Harris, ed., *Popular Culture in England, c. 1500–1850*. New York: St Martin's Press, 1995, 1–28.

Harrison, Gary. *Wordsworth's Vagrant Muse: Poetry, Poverty and Power*. Detroit, MI: Wayne State University Press, 1994.

Hay, D. 'Poaching and the Game Laws on Cannock Chase', in *Albion's Fatal Tree: Crime and Society in Eighteenth-Century England*. New York: Pantheon Books, 1975.

Hess, Marlene Alice. The Didactic Art of Hannah More. Unpublished dissertation, Michigan State University, 1984.

Hilton, Boyd. *The Age of Atonement: The Influence of Evangelicalism on Social and Economic Thought, 1795–1865*. Oxford: Clarendon Press, 1988.

Himmelfarb, Gertrude. *The Idea of Poverty: England in the Early Industrial Age*. New York: Alfred A. Knoph, 1984.

Hindley, Charles. *The Life and Times of James Catnach, Ballad Monger*. London: Reeves and Turner, 1878.

Hindley, Charles. *The History of the Catnach Press*. London, 1887.

Hitchcock, Tim. 'Paupers and Preacher: The SPCK and the Parochial Workhouse Movement', in Lee Davison, Tim Hitchcock, Tim Keirn and Robert B. Shoemaker, eds, *Stilling the Grumbling Hive: The Response to Social and Economic Problems in England, 1689–1750*. New York: St Martin's Press, 1992.

Hitchcock, Tim. 'Redefining Sex in Eighteenth-Century England', *History Workshop Journal*, 41 (Spring 1996): 73–93.

Hitchcock, Tim. *English Sexualities 1700–1800*. New York: Macmillan, 1997.

Holderness, B. A. and Michael Turner, eds. *Land, Labour and Agriculture, 1700–1920*. London: The Humbledon Press, 1991.

Hole, Robert. 'Hannah More on Literature and Propaganda, 1788–1799', *History*, 85(280) (2000): 613–33.

Howkins, Alun and Ian Dyck. '"The Time's Alteration": Popular Ballads, Rural Radicalism, and William Cobbett', *History Workshop Journal*, 23(2) (1987): 20–39.

Humphries, Jane. 'Enclosures, Common Rights, And Women: the Proletarianization of Families in the Late Eighteenth and Early Nineteenth Centuries', *Journal of Economic History*, 50(1) (1990): 17–42.

Humphries, Jane and Sara Horrell. 'Old Question, New Data, and Alternative Perspectives: Families' Living Standards in the Industrial Revolution', *Journal of Economic History*, 52(4) (1992): 849–80.

Humphries, Robert. *No Fixed Abode: A History of Responses to the Roofless and the Rootless in Britain*. Hampshire and New York: Palgrave, 1999.

Innes, Joanna. 'Parliament and the Shaping of Eighteenth-century English Social Policy', *Transactions of the Royal Historical Society*, 40 (1990) :63–92.

Jones, M. G. *Hannah More*. Cambridge: Greenwood Press, 1952.

Kahn, Madeline. 'Hannah More and Ann Yearsly: A Collaboration Across the Class Divide', *Studies in Eighteenth-Century Culture*, 25 (1996): 203–23.

King, Peter. 'The Origins of the Gleaning Judgement of 1788: A Case Study of Legal Change, Customary Right and Social Conflict in Late Eighteenth-Century England', *Law and History Review*, 10(1) (Spring, 1992): 1–33.

Kussmaul, Ann. *Servants in Husbandry in Early Modern England*. Cambridge: Cambridge University Press, 1981.

Kussmaul, Ann. *A General View of the Rural Economy of England 1638–1840.* Cambridge: Cambridge University Press, 1990.

Landry, Donna. *The Muses of Resistance: Labouring-Class Women's Poetry in Britain, 1739–1796.* Cambridge: Cambridge University Press, 1990.

Laqueur, Thomas. *Religion and Respectability: Sunday Schools and Working-Class Culture, 1780–1850.* New Haven, CT: Yale University Press, 1976.

Leavis, Q. D. *Fiction and the Reading Public.* New York: Chatto and Windus, 1965. First published 1932.

Legman, G. *The Horn Book: Studies in Erotic Folklore and Bibliography.* New York: J. Cape, 1964.

Lucas, John. *England and Englishness: Ideas of Nationhood in English Poetry, 1688–1900.* Iowa City: University of iowa Press, 1990.

Macaulay, T. B. *History of England*, Vol. 1. London: Longman, Green and Co., 1906.

MacKay, Lynn. 'The Mendicity Society and Its Clients: A Cautionary Tale', *Left History*, 5(1) (1997): 39–64.

Maxted, Ian. 'Single Sheets from a Country Town: The Example of Exeter', in *Spreading the Word: The Distribution Networks of Print 1550–1850.* Detroit, MI: St Paul's Bibliographies, 1990, 109–29.

Mingay, G. E. *Land and Society in England 1750–1980.* London and New York: Longman, 1994.

Morgan, David H. *Harvesters and Harvesting 1840–1900. A Study of the Rural Proletariat.* London and Canberra: Croom Helm, 1982.

Nardin, Jane. 'Hannah More and the Rhetoric of Educational Reform', *Women's History Review*, 10(2) (2001): 210–27.

Neeson, J. M. *Commoners: Common Right, Enclosure and Social Change in England, 1700–1820.* Cambridge: Cambridge University Press, 1993.

Neeson, J. M. 'English Enclosures and British Peasants: Current Debates about Rural Social Structure in Britain c.1750–1870', *Jahrbuch fur Wirtschafts Geschichte*, 2000/2: 22.

Neuburg, Victor E. *Popular Education in Eighteenth-Century England.* London: Woburn Press, 1971.

Olejniczak, William. 'English Rituals of Subordination: Vagrancy in Late Eighteenth-Century East Anglia', *Consortium on Revolutionary Europe 1750–1850: Selected Papers*, 1994: 628–37.

Ong, Walter. *Orality and Literacy: The Technologizing of the Word.* London and New York: Methuen, 1982.

Palmer, Roy, ed. *A Touch on the Times: Songs of Social Change, 1770–1914.* Harmondsworth: Penguin Education, 1974.

Palmer, Roy. *The Folklore of Warwickshire.* London: Batsford, 1976.

Palmer, Roy. *A Ballad History of England from 1588 to the Present Day.* London: B. T. Batsford, 1979.

Palmer, Roy. *The Sound of History: Songs and Social Comment.* Oxford and New York: Oxford University Press, 1988.

Palmer, Roy. *The Folklore of Hereford and Worcester.* Herefordshire: Logaston, 1992.

Payne, Christiana. *Toil and Plenty: Images of the Agricultural Landscape in England, 1780–1890.* New Haven, CT: Yale Centre for British Art and Yale University Press,

1993.

Pedersen, Susan. 'Hannah More Meets Simple Simon: Tracts, Chapbooks, and Popular Culture in Late Eighteenth-Century England', *Journal of British Studies*, 25(1) (1986): 84–113.

Pickering, Michael and Tony Green, eds. *Everyday Culture: Popular Songs and the Vernacular Milieu*. Milton Keynes, Philadelphia: Open University Press, 1987.

Pittock, Murray G. H. *Poetry and Jacobite Politics in Eighteenth-Century Britain and Ireland*. Cambridge: Cambridge University Press, 1994.

Porter, Roy and Leslie Hall. *The Facts of Life: The Creation of Sexual Knowledge in Britain*. New Haven, CT: Yale University Press, 1995.

Preston, Cathy Lynn. '"The Tying of the Garter": Representations of the Female Rural Laborer in 17th, 18th, and 19th Century English Bawdy Songs', *Journal of American Folklore*, 105(417) (1992): 315–41.

Raven, James. *Judging New Wealth: Popular Publishing and Responses to Commerce in England, 1750–1800*. Oxford: Clarendon Press, 1992.

Reay, Barry. *Popular Culture in England 1550–1750*. London and New York: Longman, 1998.

Reed, Mick and Roger Wells, eds. *Class, Conflict and Protest in the English Countryside, 1700–1880*. London: Frank Cass, 1990.

Ribton-Turner, C. J. *A History of Vagrants and Vagrancy and Beggars and Begging*. London: Chapman and Hall, 1887.

Rogers, N. 'Policing the Poor in Eighteenth-Century London: The Vagrancy Laws and their Administration', *Histoire Sociale*, 24(47) (1991): 127–47.

Rogers, N. 'Vagrancy, Impressment and the Regulation of Labour in Eighteenth-century Britain', *Slavery and Abolition*, 15(2) (1994): 102–13.

Rogers, Pat. *Literature and Popular Culture in Eighteenth Century England*. Brighton: The Harvester Press, 1985.

Rose, Lionel. *'Rogues and Vagabonds': Vagrant Underworld in Britain, 1815–1985*. London and New York: Routledge, 1988.

Rude, George. *Hanoverian London 1714–1808*. London: Secker & Warburg, 1971.

Scheurmann, Mona. *In Praise of Poverty: Hannah More Counters Thomas Paine and the Radical Threat*. Lexington: The University Press of Kentucky, 2002.

Searle, C. E. 'Customary Tenants and the Enclosure of the Cumbrian Commons' *Northern History*, 29 (1993): 126–53.

Shaw, Clare Macdonald. Introduction to *Hannah More, Tales for the Common People and other Cheap Repository Tracts*. Nottingham: Trent Editions, 2002.

Shepard, Leslie. *The Broadside Ballad: A Study in Origins and Meaning*. London: H. Jenkins, 1962.

Shepard, Leslie. *John Pitts, Ballad Printer of Seven Dials, London, 1765–1844*. London: Private Libraries Association, 1969.

Shepard, Leslie. *The History of Street Literature: The Story of Broadside Ballads, Chapbooks, Proclamations, Newssheets, Election Bills, Tracts, Pamphlets, Cocks, Catch-pennies, and Other Ephemera*. Detroit, MI: Singing Tree Press, 1973.

Short, Brian, ed. *The English Rural Community: Image and Analysis*. Cambridge: Cambridge University Press, 1992.

Smith, Len. *The Carpet Weaver's Lament: Songs and Ballads of Kidderminster in the*

Industrial Revolution. Kidderminster: Kenneth Tomkinson Ltd., 1979.

Snell, K. D. M. *Annals of the Labouring Poor: Social Change and Agrarian England 1660–1900.* Cambridge: Cambridge University Press, 1985.

Snell, K. D. M. 'Agricultural Seasonal Unemployment, the Standard of Living, and Women's Work, 1690–1860', in Pamela Sharpe, ed. *Women's Work: The English Experience 1650–1914.* London: Arnold, 1998.

Spufford, Margaret. *Small Books and Pleasant Histories: Popular Fiction and its Readership in Seventeenth-century England.* Cambridge and New York: Cambridge University Press, 1985.

Stapleton, Barry, ed. *Conflict and Community in Southern England.* Stroud: Alan Sutton, 1992.

Stone, Lawrence. *The Family, Sex and Marriage in England, 1500–1800.* New York: Harper Row, 1979.

Stott, Ann. *Hannah More: the First Victorian.* Oxford: Oxford University Press, 2003.

Taylor, James Stephen. *Poverty, Migration, and Settlement in the Industrial Revolution: Sojourners' Narratives.* Palo Alto, CA: The Society for the Promotion of Science and Scholarship, 1989.

Thomas, Keith, ed. *The Oxford Book of Work.* Oxford: Oxford University Press, 1999.

Thompson, E. P. *Whigs and Hunters: The Origins of the Black Act.* New York: Pantheon Books, 1975.

Thompson, E. P. *The Making of the English Working Class.* London: Gollancz, 1980.

Thompson, E. P. *Customs in Common.* New York: The New Press, 1993.

Trumbach, Randolph. *Sex and the Gender Revolution, Vol. 1 Heterosexuality and the Third Gender in Enlightenment London.* Chicago and London: University of Chicago Press, 1998.

Turner, Michael. *Enclosures in Britain 1750–1830.* London: Macmillan, 1984.

Valenze, Deborah. 'The Art of Women and the Business of Men: Women's Work and the Dairy Industry c. 1740–1840', *Past & Present*, 230 (1991): 142–69.

Vicinus, Martha. *The Industrial Muse. A study of Nineteenth-Century British Working-Class Literature.* London: Croom Helm, 1974.

Wagner, Peter. *Eros Revived: Erotica of the Enlightenment in England and America.* London: Secker & Warburg, 1988.

Waldron, Mary. *Lactilla, Milkwoman of Clifton: The Life and Writings of Ann Yearsley, 1753–1806.* Athens and London: the University of Georgia Press, 1996.

Watts, Michael R. *The Dissenters*, Vol. II. Oxford: Clarendon Press, 1995.

Weeks, Jeffrey. *Sex, Politics and Society: The Regulation of Sexuality Since 1800.* London and New York: Longman, 1981.

Wells, Roger. 'The Devlopment of the English Rural Proletarian, 1700–1850', in Reed and Wells, eds, *Class, Conflict and Protest in the English Countryside, 1700–1880.* London: Frank Cass, 1990.

Wiles, Roy Mckeen. 'The Relish for Reading in Provincial England Two Centuries Ago', in Paul J. Korshin, ed., *The Widening Circle: Essays on the Circulation of Literature in Eighteenth-Century Europe.* Philadelphia: University of Pennsylvania Press, 1976, 85–117.

Williams, Raymond. *Culture and Society, 1780–1950.* Harmondsworth: Penguin

Books, 1962.

Williams, Raymond. *The Country and the City*. New York: Oxford University Press, 1973.

Wood, Andy. 'The Place of Custom in Plebeian Political Culture: England, 1550–1800', *Social History*, 22(1) (1997): 46–61

Wood, Andy. *The Politics of Social Conflict: The Peak Country, 1520–1770*. Cambridge: Cambridge University Press, 1999.

Wood, Andy. *Riot, Rebellion and Popular Politics in Early Modern England*. Basingstoke and New York: Palgrave, 2002.

Wurzbach, Natasha. *The Rise of the English Street Ballad, 1550–1650*. Cambridge and New York: Cambridge University Press, 1990.

Index